THE ENGLISH NOBILITY
IN THE
LATE MIDDLE AGES

Chris Given-Wilson

THE ENGLISH NOBILITY
IN THE
LATE MIDDLE AGES:

The Fourteenth-Century
Political Community

ROUTLEDGE & KEGAN PAUL
London and New York

First published in 1987 by
Routledge & Kegan Paul Ltd
11 New Fetter Lane, London EC4P 4EE

Published in the USA by
Routledge & Kegan Paul Inc.
in association with Methuen Inc.
29 West 35th Street, New York, NY 10001

Set in Bembo
by Inforum Ltd, Portsmouth
and printed in Great Britain
by Billings, Worcester

Library of Congress Cataloging in Publication Data

Given-Wilson, Chris.
    The English nobility in the late Middle Ages.

    Bibliography: p.
    Includes index.
    1. England—Nobility—History. 2. England—
Gentry—History.   3. Social history—Medieval,
500–1500.   4. England—History—Medieval period,
1066–1485.   I. Title.
HT653.G7G58 1987   305.5′223′0942   86–33862

British Library CIP Data also available

ISBN 0-7102-0491-4

For ALICE, *with love and gratitude*

Contents

Illustrations

Maps

Tables

Preface

> The reason for dissension among the northern lords was this: all were gentlemen and nobles [*generosi et nobiles*], though one might be called an earl [*comes*], another a baron [*baro*], and others lords [*domini*], but when it came to taking money, they claimed to be equal; this being refused to them, they departed to their homes.[1]

I use the word 'nobility' in quite a broad sense in this book, to describe not just those individuals or families, numbering a hundred or less in late medieval England, who were distinguished by their receipt of individual summonses to parliament (that is, the peerage), but also those whom modern and late medieval historians more commonly refer to as the gentry. What made a man or a family 'noble' in fourteenth-century England is difficult to define precisely. Good birth, inherited land and lordship, and membership of the 'officer' ranks in battle were probably the most important determinants of status. Title, legal privilege, a substantial degree of wealth, and the trappings of the noble lifestyle provided the visible evidence of that status. Ultimately, though, what mattered most was the extent to which a man's standing in society was accepted by those whom he regarded as his social equals.

> The essence of social class is the way a man is treated by his fellows (and, reciprocally, the way he treats them), not the qualities or the possessions which cause that treatment. It would be possible, and perhaps useful, to group people simply in terms of their attributes, without asking how those attributes affected their social relations, but the result would be a study of social types, not of social classes.[2]

This is what makes social categorisation so tricky, especially at six hundred years' remove. Seen from this point of view, we are entitled to wonder whether it is at all possible to get to the essence of 'social class' in the Middle Ages, or whether we must simply be content with describing social 'types'. Nevertheless, there are indicators, and the attempt has to be made: not only because it is an interesting subject *per se*, but also because in the Middle Ages social status was closely related to political authority, and it is impossible to understand the English polity without reference to the classes in which society was ordered. That is why much of the first part of this book is devoted to the problem of social stratification.

On the whole, this book is an attempt to synthesise recent research rather than to present a substantial body of new evidence. In the thirty years and more since K.B. McFarlane inspired a new generation of scholars to take a fresh look at the medieval English nobility, there has been a great deal of research on the subject – some on individuals, some on families, some on regional societies, and some on more general problems. In certain important respects, the thrust of this recent research has changed direction. Whereas McFarlane was for the most part concerned with the peerage, and with national politics, the emphasis during the last fifteen or so years has shifted more towards the study of the lesser ranks of the nobility (that is, the gentry, broadly speaking), and of local rather than national politics – or at least the interplay of local and national. This is a shift which I have tried to reflect. I have drawn heavily on this growing body of research (much of it unpublished), and, as is evident from the Bibliography, my first and greatest debt is to those historians upon whose work I have relied.

My second major debt is to my students. This book grew out of a special subject on the English nobility in the reign of Edward III which I taught for several years at the University of St Andrews. It is often said that students little realise how much their lecturers learn from teaching them, but that makes it no less true, and I am grateful to them for their patience, their hard work, and the frequent inspiration which they provided. I am also grateful to Andrew Wheatcroft, who first suggested that I might write this book; to Elaine Donaldson of Routledge & Kegan Paul, for her meticulous and well-informed work on the typescript; to Nick Hooper now of Westminster School, who read parts of the typescript and corrected several errors; and to Bridget Harvey, from whom I have learned much about the Berkeleys in the fourteenth century. My special thanks, as ever, go to Alice, who makes most things possible.

Chris Given-Wilson
St Andrews

Maps

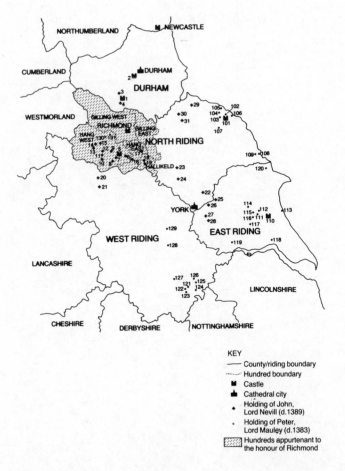

MAP 1 *Yorkshire and Durham, principal holdings of the Nevills and Mauleys*

(a)	Nevill lands	(b)	Mauley lands
1	Raby	101	Mulgrave
2	Brancepeth	102	Lythe
3	Cockfield	103	Mickelby
4	Staindrop	104	Ellerby
5	Middleham	105	Seaton-by-Hinderwell
6	East Witton	106	Sandsend
7	Coverham	107	Egton
8	Carlton	108	Scarborough
9	West Witton	109	Cukewald
10	Newbiggin	110	? Bransholme
11	Thoralby	111	Nessingwike
12	Aysgarth	112	Berg-by-Watton
13	Bainbridge	113	Atwick
14	Askrigg	114	Bainton
15	Nappay	115	Kilnwick
16	Thornton	116	Lockington
17	Crakehall	117	Etton
18	Snape	118	Sutton-in-Holderness
19	Welle	119	Cliff
20	Kettlewell-in-Craven	120	Hunmanby
21	Conistone	121	Doncaster
22	Sheriff Hutton	122	Hexthorpe
23	Sutton-in-Galtres	123	Balby
24	Raskelf	124	Rossington
25	Skirpenbeck	125	Wheteley
26	Stamford Bridge	126	Sandal
27	Elvington	127	Hooton
28	Sutton-on-Derwent	128	Skinthorpe
29	Wilton-in-Cleveland	129	Bramham
30	Hemelyngton	130	Heelaugh
31	Stokesley	131	Reeth

KEY

— County boundary

····· Hundred boundary

▲ Chief religious house

◪ Castle/head of barony

• Holding of Thomas, Lo Berkeley (d.1361)

MAP 2 *The Berkeleys, Courtenays, Montagues, and Beauforts, principal holdings in the south-west*

I   The Berkeleys

1 Berkeley
2 Alkington
3 Appleridge
4 Hinton
5 Hurst
6 Slimbridge
7 Coaley
8 Cam
9 Symondshall
10 Wotton
11 Ham
12 Arlingham
13 Uley
14 Kingscote
15 Frampton-on-Severn
16 Awre
17 Bledisloe
18 Etloe
19 Beachley
20 Upton St Leonards
21 Falfield
22 Iron Acton
23 Portbury
24 Portishead
25 Tickenham
26 Bedminster
27 Redcliffestreet
28 Kingston Seymour
29 Kingsweston
      (granted to John of Beverstone)
30 Long Ashton
31 Edingworth
32 Brigmerston
33 Milston
34 Beverstone
35 Syde
36 Woodmancote
37 Tockington
38 Over
39 Compton Greenfield
40 Barrow Gurney
41 Sock Dennis
42 Down Hatherley
43 Westonbirt
44 Alderton
45 Bradfield
46 Langley Burrell
47 Chippenham
48 Winterbourne
49 ? Shaw
50 Orcheston
51 Elston
52 Maddington

Hundreds
Aa Berkeley, with
      detached portions
B Bledisloe
C Portbury
D Hartcliffe with
      Bedminster

Inherited by Thomas,
3rd Lord Berkeley (d.1361)

Granted to John
of Beverstone

Acquired by Thomas,
3rd Lord Berkeley (d.1361)

Continued on page xvi

II The Courtenays

100 Okehampton
101 Plympton
102 Tiverton
103 Dolton
104 Chulmleigh
105 Chawleigh
106 Sampford Courtenay
107 Topsham
108 Exminster
109 Kenn
110 Budleigh
111 Aylesbeare
112 Whimple
113 Colyford
114 Colyton
115 Musbury

Inherited by Hugh, earl of Devon (d.1377)

116 Cadeleigh
117 Newnham
118 Honiton

Entailed on younger sons in 1377

119 Crewkerne
120 Hemington
121 Iwerne Courtenay
122 Ibberton
123 Townstall
124 Holbeton
125 ? Northpool
126 Norton by Stoke Fleming
127 Whitford

Acquired by Hugh, earl of Devon (d.1377)

128 Milton Damerel
129 ? Morton
130 West Coker
131 East Coker
132 Torweston
133 Sampford Brett
134 Broadwindsor
135 Hill by Iwerne Minster

Entailed on younger sons in 1377

Hundreds (held by Hugh, earl of Devon, d.1377)
E Plympton
F South Tawton (part of Wonford)
G Wonford
H Exminster
J Budleigh
K Colyton
L Hayridge
M Tiverton
N Crewkerne
P Coker

III The Montagues

(manors and hundreds held by John Montague, earl of Salisbury, at his death in January 1400)

200 Knowle
201 Shepton Montague
202 Yarlington
203 Charlton Horethorne
204 Henstridge
205 Goathill
206 Chedzoy
207 Donyatt
208 Canford Magna
209 Poole
210 West Lulworth
211 Puddletown
212 Amesbury
213 Winterbourne Earls
214 ? Winterbourne Stoke
215 Pyworthy
216 Oakford
217 Clyst St Mary
218 Stokenham
219 Chillington
220 Noss Mayo
221 Yealmpton

Hundreds
Q Coleridge
R Cogdean
S Amesbury
T ? Alderbury

IV The Beauforts

(Principal acquisitions in Somerset *ca* 1390–1450)
300 Langport
301 Curry Rival
302 Martock
303 Curry Mallet
304 Stoke-sub-Hampden
305 Queen Camel
306 Whitcomb
307 Kingsbury Regis
308 Ryme (Dorset)
309 West Harptree
310 Farrington Gurney
311 Welton
312 Midsomer Norton
313 Stratton-on-the-Fosse
314 Shepton Mallet
315 Laverton
316 Englishcombe
317 Bruton

Hundreds
U Abdick and Bulstone
V ? Somerton
X Martock
Y Horethorne

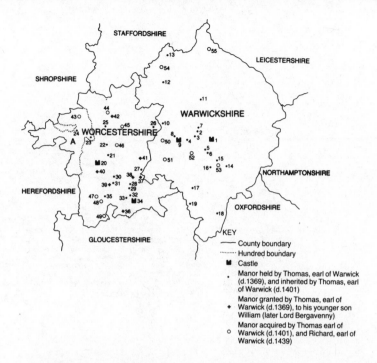

A. **Doddingtree Hundred (held by the Beauchamp earls as hereditary sheriffs of Worcestershire)**

(N.B. Thomas, earl of Warwick (d.1369), was also sheriff of Warwickshire and Leicestershire for life from 1344 to 1369.)

1	Warwick castle and manor	19	Ilmington	38	Naunton Beauchamp
2	Haseley	20	Worcester castle	39	Pirton
3	Budbrooke	21	Hindlip	40	Powick
4	Claverdon	22	Salwarpe	41	Little Intebergh
5	Sherbourne	23	Shrawley	42	Chaddesley Corbett
6	Barford	24	Abberley	43	Ribbesford
7	Beausale	25	Elmley Lovett	44	Harvington
8	Henley-in-Arden	26	Beoley	45	? Hull's Place (in Grafton)
9	Beaudesert castle and manor	27	Grafton Flyford	46	Hadzor
10	Tanworth	28	Wyre Piddle	47	Hanley castle and manor
11	Berkswell	29	Wick by Pershore	48	Upton-on-Severn
12	Yardley	30	Stoulton	49	Bushley
13	Sutton Coldfield	31	Wadborough	50	Oldberrow
14	Lighthorne	32	Little Comberton	51	Haselor
15	Ashorne	33	Great Comberton	52	Snitterfield
16	Wellesbourne	34	Elmley castle and manor	53	Moreton Morrell
17	Whitchurch	35	Earls Croome	54	Erdington
18	Brailes	36	Kemerton	55	Baxterley
		37	Sheriffs Lench		

MAP 3 *The Beauchamp earls of Warwick,*
manors in Warwickshire and Worcestershire

[xvii]

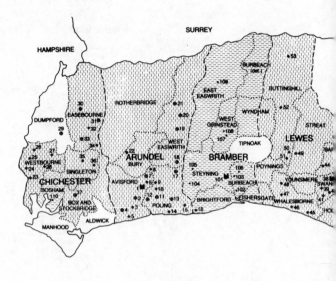

MAP 4   *Principal holdings of the Fitzalans and Mowbrays in Sussex*

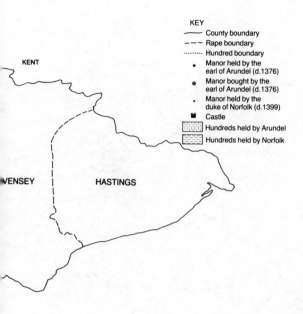

KENT

KEY
—— County boundary
– – – Rape boundary
········· Hundred boundary
♦ Manor held by the earl of Arundel (d.1376)
◉ Manor bought by the earl of Arundel (d.1376)
• Manor held by the duke of Norfolk (d.1399)
🏰 Castle
▦ Hundreds held by Arundel
▤ Hundreds held by Norfolk

PEVENSEY   HASTINGS

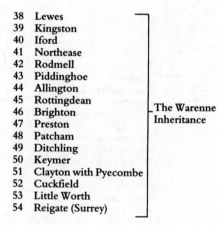

38	Lewes	
39	Kingston	
40	Iford	
41	Northease	
42	Rodmell	
43	Piddinghoe	
44	Allington	
45	Rottingdean	
46	Brighton	The Warenne Inheritance
47	Preston	
48	Patcham	
49	Ditchling	
50	Keymer	
51	Clayton with Pyecombe	
52	Cuckfield	
53	Little Worth	
54	Reigate (Surrey)	

(b) Mowbray holdings

101	Bramber
102	Shoreham
103	Beeding
104	Findon
105	Washington
106	Beaubusson
107	West Grinstead
108	Knappe
109	Horsham
110	Bosham

N.B. The hundreds of Manhood and Tipnoak were held by the bishop of Chichester. The hundred of Aldwick was held by the archbishop of Canterbury.

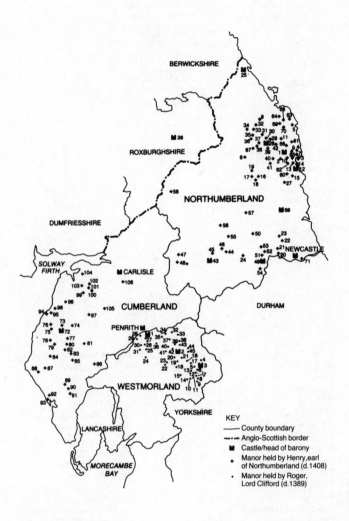

MAP 5 *Manors of the Percys and the Cliffords in Northumberland, Cumberland, and Westmorland*

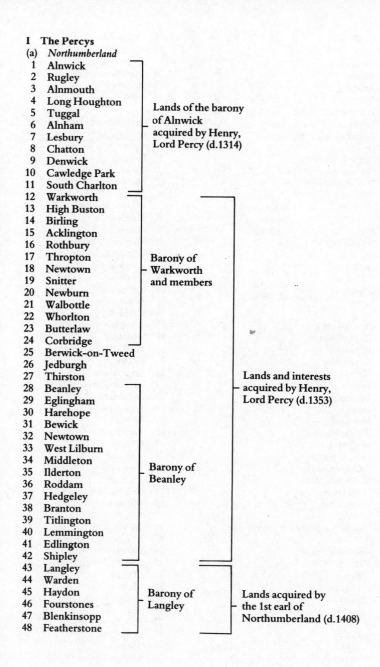

I The Percys

(a) *Northumberland*

1   Alnwick
2   Rugley
3   Alnmouth
4   Long Houghton
5   Tuggal
6   Alnham
7   Lesbury
8   Chatton
9   Denwick
10 Cawledge Park
11 South Charlton

Lands of the barony of Alnwick acquired by Henry, Lord Percy (d.1314)

12 Warkworth
13 High Buston
14 Birling
15 Acklington
16 Rothbury
17 Thropton
18 Newtown
19 Snitter
20 Newburn
21 Walbottle
22 Whorlton
23 Butterlaw
24 Corbridge
25 Berwick-on-Tweed
26 Jedburgh
27 Thirston

Barony of Warkworth and members

28 Beanley
29 Eglingham
30 Harehope
31 Bewick
32 Newtown
33 West Lilburn
34 Middleton
35 Ilderton
36 Roddam
37 Hedgeley
38 Branton
39 Titlington
40 Lemmington
41 Edlington
42 Shipley

Barony of Beanley

Lands and interests acquired by Henry, Lord Percy (d.1353)

43 Langley
44 Warden
45 Haydon
46 Fourstones
47 Blenkinsopp
48 Featherstone

Barony of Langley

Lands acquired by the 1st earl of Northumberland (d.1408)

[xxi]

49	Prudhoe	
50	Ingoe	
51	Ovingham	
52	Horsley	
53	Harlow	Barony of Prudhoe
54	Hedley	
55	Barrasford	
56	Birtley	
57	Kirkwhelpington	
58	Kielder	
59	Mitford	
60	Guyzance	
61	Rennington	
62	Shilbottle	Detached manors of barony of Alnwick
63	Swinhoe	
64	Lucker	
65	Bilton	
66	Broxfield	
67	Fawdon	
68	Newham	
69	Newstead	Lands of Hotspur (d.1403)
70	Ellingham	
71	Byker	

Lands acquired by the 1st earl of Northumberland (d.1408)

(b) Cumberland

72	Cockermouth
73	Papcastle
74	Setmurthy
75	Great Broughton
76	Little Broughton
77	Lorton
78	Dean
79	Mockerkin
80	Thackthwaite
81	Braithwaite
82	Lowesewater
83	Brackenthwaite
84	Kirkland
85	Buttermere
86	? Rosewain
87	Wilton
88	Egremont (⅓ of barony)
89	Wasdale
90	? Whinfell
91	Eskdale
92	Drigg
93	Carleton
94	Birkby
95	Crosby
96	? Allerby
97	Uldale
98	Aspatria
99	Waverton
100	Wigton

101	Aikhead
102	Oulton
103	Dundraw
104	Kirkbride
105	Caldbeck
106	Woodside

II The Cliffords in Westmorland

1	Brougham
2	Appleby
3	Brough
4	Helbeck
5	Musgrave
6	Kaber
7	Kirkby Stephen
8	Hartley
9	Nateby
10	Waitby (½ of manor)
11	Crosby Garrett
12	Winton
13	Soulby
14	Smardale
15	Little Asby
16	Great Asby
17	Warcop
18	Sandford
19	Hoff
20	Colby
21	Ormside
22	Crosby Ravensworth
23	Maulds Meaburn
24	Bampton
25	Whale
26	Lowther
27	Clifton
28	Yanwath
29	Barton
30	Askham
31	Helton Fletham
32	Milburn
33	Knock
34	Newbiggin
35	Temple Sowerby
36	Cliburn
37	Kirkby Thore
38	Dufton
39	Marton
40	Bolton
41	King's Meaburn
42	Crackenthorpe
43	Brampton
44	Murton
45	Helton Bacon

Introduction

By the second half of the fourteenth century the English peerage, those sixty to seventy lords each of whom was entitled to an individual summons to parliament, had emerged as a distinct and privileged group at the top of English lay society. Their social and political pre-eminence stemmed firstly from their role as the chief military commanders and advisers of the king, and secondly from the lordship of land and men which they exercised in their localities – or, as they sometimes described them, their 'countries'. In a sense, England was a federation of lordly spheres of influence. It was largely for their local authority that the king valued his peers. It was for the same local authority that the gentry, without whose consent and co-operation it could hardly be exercised, valued them.

A picture of England as a jigsaw of lordly spheres of influence is, however, prone to oversimplification, and it is advisable to begin with some caveats. What the peers enjoyed in their 'countries' was leadership and influence, it was not 'control'. Dependent as it was on the consent of both the king and the local gentry, it could never be that. Nor were their spheres of influence clearly demarcated. Sometimes peers were entrusted with specific rights within quite clearly defined areas (a county, for example), but for the most part lordship was not so much a consolidated territorial power-block as a bundle of rights and a series of connections, overlapping and intermingling with a number of other sources of authority. Moreover, there was nothing immutable about them. They were continually expanding and contracting, and frequently changing hands. Local leadership was a question of degree, of individual ability, often of luck.

Lords and their 'countries' are discussed more fully in the later stages of this book. First, however, it is important to understand the social and political hierarchy which underlay the exercise of power. It is thus with the question of social stratification, and its implications for political society, that the first part of this book is concerned. Before even that process can be attempted, however, something needs to be said of the origins of the fourteenth-century English nobility, and of the ethos, lifestyle, and common assumptions which underlay their behaviour.

The noble ethos was essentially chivalric – which is as much as to say that it was militaristic, elitist, and ostentatious. To the theorists, the defence of the community was the *raison d'être* of the nobility. Through his participation in warfare, the noble justified his privileged position in society – and in the great majority of cases the theorists were right. It is rare to find a member of the nobility who did not take up arms at some time in his life. Although good birth was always important, for the cult of chivalry placed a strong emphasis on hereditary nobility, the elitism of the nobility was 'a matter of worth as much as . . . lineage'.[1] In other words, while a man might be born into noble society, he must continue to justify his place within it by leading a lifestyle worthy of his station. Yet the nobility was not just a fighting class, it was also a ruling class. Participation in warfare and in government (whether local or national) were duties, and it was the performance of these duties which justified nobility itself.

Almost from birth, the child who was born into the nobility was prepared for his eventual fulfilment of the noble's traditional role. According to contemporaries, 'the care of boys from their earliest years should be arranged with warlike ends in mind'.[2] Formal, 'bookish' education was by no means neglected, but it was given a much less prominent place than it is nowadays. Two points about the education and upbringing of medieval nobles need especial emphasis. Firstly, it was done almost as much subconsciously as consciously. Education was not regarded as a separate element in a child's upbringing, divorced, through the medium of professional schoolmasters, formal classes, and so forth, from the other growing-up processes. It was an integral part of life, a process which flowed imperceptibly into adulthood rather than a demarcated stage in a child's development. Secondly, and this is particularly true of the nobility, education was not normally acquired in formal institutions such as grammar schools, universities, or (for lawyers) the Inns of Court. All these existed in fourteenth-century England, but – apart from those sons of the nobility intended by their parents for the church, who would often be sent to university – the nobility hardly used them. The educational forum of the noble child was the noble household, and the noble household was of course much more than an educational institution.

While there were no rules governing the upbringing of noble children, there were nevertheless conventions. For the first five or six years of their lives children were normally kept at home, often in a largely female environment. After this it was common either to send them away to other (preferably greater) households, or to introduce male tutors to the familial home. These men were not professional schoolmasters, even though in the later Middle Ages it did become increasingly frequent to hire professionals in noble households.[3] In fact the 'tutors' who had charge of boys in noble households were frequently knights, or sometimes clerks, and their job was not bookish education but the inculcation of noble qualities and accomplishments.[4] Naturally, there was considerable emphasis on physical training. This might include athletics and ball-games, but much more important was training in horsemanship, the wielding of arms, hunting and archery. Archery was more of a sport than a training for war, since it was the ranks, not the officer class, who used the bow in battle, but hunting was regarded as much more than a sport. It taught courage, the use of weapons, orientation, and above all horsemanship. Good horsemanship took a great deal of practice, and the nobility, who fought as cavalry, had to learn not only how to ride a horse well, but to do so in formation, while encased in armour, while using heavy and unwieldy weapons (as well as shields), and while keeping a constant eye out for potential assailants. A strong emphasis on horsemanship was thus not misplaced.

In addition to their military training, boys were also brought up to indulge in the traditional noble pastimes. Music, for example, was 'a courtly activity *par excellence*'. In an age which distinguished much less between the professional and the amateur musician, to be skilled in singing and/or playing was widely regarded as characteristic of the nobility. Dancing was a common skill, and frequently taught in noble households.[5] Chess, which was regarded as educational as well as enjoyable, was also a common pastime, and much time and money were spent on dicing and other forms of gambling such as backgammon – though to be excessively fond of 'gaming' was not to be encouraged. Of the gentler outdoor pursuits, the most popular was falconry, less physically demanding and less closely related to warfare than hunting. It was generally a winter sport, the summers being reserved for the chase. Unlike hunting, it was also a sport in which women participated fully. Nor, of course, were reading and grammar neglected. Despite Professor Galbraith's much-quoted verdict on the medieval English nobility as consisting mainly of men of 'arrested intellectual development', it is now widely accepted that by the middle of the thirteenth century, at the latest, the ability to read was pretty general among lay as well as clerical nobles, and by the fourteenth century it is far from uncommon to find noble authors. In the mid-twelfth century, it is doubtful whether this had been the case, but the increasing use of the written word as a means of government and communication had by now made it a necessary skill.[6]

Sir John Fortescue (later fifteenth century) described the royal household as 'the supreme academy for the nobles of the realm, and a school of physical activity [*strenuitas*], behaviour [*probitas*], and manners [*mores*], by which the realm gains honour, flourishes, and is secured against invaders'. And it was said of Henry of Grosmont, duke of Lancaster (d. 1361), that he took young knights into his household 'to be doctrined, learned and brought up in his noble court in school of arms and for to see noblesse, courtesy and worship'.[7] The emphasis on military training is unsurprising, but what is also important to note is that in each case it was not academic but social skills which were regarded as the natural accompaniments of the born soldier. Manners, behaviour and courtesy were the desiderata, in other words, the noble way of life. Formal education could be gained in many places. From the fourteenth century onwards, there is increasing evidence that some members of the gentry were turning to the schools and the Inns of Court in an attempt to improve their children's career prospects, but the reason why the greater nobility continued (until the sixteenth century, for the most part) to shun them was that the upbringing which could be had in the noble household was something that could not be had anywhere else. It was here, surrounded by servants and the trappings of wealth, mixing with other young men of their own status, accustoming themselves to the constant passage of the great, that they learned what it was to be a noble. What the twentieth century defines as 'education' would have seemed to them little more than a narrow clerkish respectability.

It was usually during his late teens that the young noble began to slip the reins of tutelage and strike out on his own. In few cases did this actually involve the choice of a career. For the most part, nobles' careers were mapped out for them from an early age, either by their parents or simply by custom. Those who were intended for the church (usually younger sons) would generally have been set on this path by about the age of twelve, probably by being given a benefice in the family's gift, and might well proceed to university. The same is true for those among the lesser nobility who had been marked out for some specific form of service such as the law, and who would have been sent to one of the Inns of Court. For the rest, youthful service in a noble household would probably just evolve into a more permanent sort of attachment until the time came to take up their inheritances. And even then, there was often no real break with the past. Although there is plenty of evidence to show that nobles cared greatly about the profitability of their estates and the general management of their business concerns, there were few who wished to confine themselves wholly, or even principally, to these tasks. Service to one's betters remained the norm throughout the ranks of the nobility, partly for the financial benefits it conferred, and partly for the opportunities for advancement and involvement in high matters which it opened up. Some retained their positions as knights or esquires in the households of the baronage or the king; others took posts as estate administrators or councillors to the great, or involved themselves in politics at either the local or the national level. Here, of course, there might well be decisions to be made, but even so they were often quite limited in scope. Patterns of service were quite well established by custom in late medieval England. The traditions of family and locality were both strong. Again and again, generations of fathers and sons, cousins and nephews, are found in the service of the same great family, usually one of the dominant landholding families of their neighbourhood. It was through such ties, reinforced just as much by tradition as by tenurial or other such formal ties, that the affinities of the great, the most powerful components of the political nation, were built up and maintained.

But service of this sort was not, of course, at the expense of a young noble's military career. The first sign that he had come through his period of training would probably have been his participation in a tournament, perhaps around the age of sixteen. Tournaments were great social and ceremonial occasions. Men went to them to acquire fame, to mingle with the elite, and to impress women.[8] But they were also vital military training, and there was nothing soft about them. Even if by the fourteenth century they were less violent affairs than they had been in the twelfth, there were still plenty of fatalities as well as lesser accidents. The extinction of the Hastings earls of Pembroke, for example, was brought about by the death in a tournament of John, the seventeen-year-old heir to the earldom, in 1389. For many a young noble, a tournament must have provided a nerve-tingling initiation into the world of the warrior. But inevitably, perhaps, once he had a few tournaments behind him, his thoughts would begin to turn more to the real thing.

Crusading was one alternative: despite the decline of the crusade in the later Middle Ages, a surprisingly large number of fourteenth-century English nobles still joined the war against the Infidel at some time during their lives, be it in the Levant, in southern Spain, or in Prussia and Poland, the fringes of the Christian world.[9] Mercenary activity was another, thought not usually for those who had inherited any substantial amount of land. Nevertheless there were plenty of young English bloods among the gangs of *routiers*, or 'Free Companies', which terrorised France during the middle decades of the fourteenth century, and the bands of *condottieri* employed to fight their wars for them by the Italian communes – most notable of which was the infamous 'Company of St George' commanded by Sir John Hawkwood. For most young nobles bent on a military career, however, opportunities were closer at hand. It was in the near-continuous French and Scottish wars of the fourteenth century that they could normally expect to play out their military careers, in the paid service of either the king himself or one of his high-born deputies.

As the greatest of the nobility, it was the king above all upon whom fell the duty to uphold the honour of the warrior nobility through the prosecution of war. It was through his initiative, and under his leadership, that the nobility looked for the opportunities to fulfil their own (as they saw them) God-ordained role in society – and, of course, to enrich themselves into the bargain. And by his success or failure they judged him. The often-quoted remark of the duke of Gloucester in 1391, that he opposed Richard II's projected peace with France because the livelihood of the 'poor knights and esquires of England' depended upon the continuation of the war, is a reminder that military service was a career in more ways than one for the nobility.[10] Naturally, the royal success-rate varied. Of the fourteenth-century English kings, Edward II and Richard II won little credit on the battlefield, while Edward III was, for most of his reign at any rate, a conspicuously successful war-captain. But of all the kings of medieval England, none provided opportunities for the advancement and enrichment of his nobles on a scale even remotely comparable with William the Conqueror. The Norman Conquest of 1066 heralded many changes in English society, but the principal and most enduring one was the establishment in England of an alien and almost entirely new ruling class. As the companions of William, and as his comrades in arms and conquest, the barons and knights of eleventh-century Normandy (who themselves were descended from the Viking 'Northmen' who had wrested what came to be known as the duchy of Normandy from the French kings in the early tenth century) implanted their families and followers on English soil on a scale that amounted, within a few years, to the almost complete transference of landlordship in England. It was from these men, almost to a man, that the nobility of medieval England descended. It is from them, therefore, that the origins of the late medieval English nobility are to be traced.

William the Conqueror did not, as a policy, simply dispossess the Anglo-Saxon nobility wholesale. Yet within twenty years of the battle of Hastings, Domesday Book shows that what may not have been intended as a policy had become reality. From the information given in Domesday Book, it has proved possible to compile figures which show clearly the distribution of English land during the twenty years following the Conquest. By 1086, there were, at the top of English lay society, about 170 great tenants-in-chief – those who held land directly from the king, and who held sufficient land from him to justify the description of barons. Just two of these were Englishmen, the rest Normans.[11] As far as the landholding class was concerned, therefore, the Conquest had drawn a line beneath what had gone before. Between them, these 170 were enjoying almost exactly 50 per cent of the land of England. A further 17 per cent was kept by the Conqueror as his own demesne land, a quarter was granted to the church, and the remaining 8 per cent was divided between minor royal officials and lesser tenants-in-chief. To say, however, that 170 tenants-in-chief shared out half of England is to gloss over the immense differences in wealth and status between different members of this group. At the top of the scale, for example, came Robert, count of Mortain and earl of Cornwall, the new king's half-brother, with a total of 797 manors said to be worth £2,500 a year. At the bottom end came men like Robert of Aumâle, with fifteen manors in Devon worth just £26.[12] Tenurially, Robert of Mortain and Robert of Aumâle may have been on an equal footing, but when the landed income of the former exceeded that of the latter by a factor of a hundred, the gulf between them, in some senses at least, must have been enormous. In fact about a quarter of England was concentrated in the hands of a small group of only ten very great barons: Robert of Mortain and Odo of Bayeux (also the king's half-brother), William FitzOsbern, Roger of Montgomery, William of Warenne, Hugh of Avranches, Eustace of Boulogne, Richard of Clare, Geoffrey of Coutances, and Geoffrey of Mandeville.[13] The other 160 split the remaining quarter in varying proportions.

The continental origins of these men are readily apparent from most of their names. Indeed, for the first 150 or so years after the Conquest it is more appropriate to talk of an Anglo-Norman nobility than of an English one, for the fact that they had been granted lands in England (and frequently married English heiresses) did not of course mean that they relinquished the lands which they held on the other side of the Channel. Like the Norman and Angevin kings of England, they divided their time between England and the continent, and were involved as much in French politics and warfare as in English.[14] Between 1202 and 1224, however, Kings John and Henry III lost most of their continental empire to Philip Augustus and Louis VIII of France, and from this time onwards a more truly English nobility developed. Even so, the process of anglicisation took a long time. A recent study of the 300 or so leading families among the thirteenth-century English nobility shows that even by this time only about a third of them had adopted the names of their

English rather than their continental lordships.[15] The language they employed also marked them off from the great mass of the people whom they ruled. For about three hundred years after the Conquest, French (or, more correctly, Anglo-Norman, a language which despite its name owed much more to French than to English) was the language of the nobility, while English was the language of the peasantry. Not until 1362 was English declared in parliament to be the proper language for legal proceedings, and it is only in the early fifteenth century that it is at last clear that English is once again the normal spoken and written language of the nobility. The survival over three centuries of two languages side by side is remarkable testimony to the exclusivity of England's ruling class.

The English nobility, then, was truly a class apart. Yet one of the surprising features of the Anglo-Norman aristocracy of the twelfth century is the failure of any really great families to emerge, families that might vie in wealth and status with, for example, the great peers of France, or the dukes and margraves of Germany. 'On a European scale,' as Professor Barlow has pointed out, 'the social position of the Anglo-Norman nobility would seem to be among the lowest.'[16] There were probably two main reasons for this. The first is that English royal cadets failed to found dynasties which endured. Not until the middle of the thirteenth century did the younger son of an English king receive a landed endowment which was to remain out of the king's hands for more than two generations. This was Edmund 'Crouchback', second son of Henry III and younger brother to Edward I, who became earl of Lancaster, Leicester and Derby, thus laying the foundations for the great Lancastrian duchy of the later fourteenth century, the most significant territorial agglomeration on the English map since the break-up of the Anglo-Saxon earldoms. The earls, and later dukes, of Lancaster could certainly compare with the great peers of France, as was recognised by the pope in 1254 when he offered the crown of Sicily to Edmund, even though the scheme never came to anything. Richard of Cornwall, Henry III's younger brother, was equally eminent in his day, and was even elected to the German imperial throne in 1257 (though his election was disputed by King Alfonso of Castile), but his lands reverted to the crown at the death without issue of his son, another Edmund, in 1300.

The second reason for the English nobility's failure to throw up any enduringly outstanding families for two centuries after the Conquest was the geographical distribution of land at that time. Even the greatest Anglo-Norman landholders found that the fiefs which they received from William were spread over a number of counties, thus reducing their ability to establish the sort of consolidated territorial power-block which was more typical of the great French peers and German princes. This may have been deliberate policy on the Conqueror's part, though since he had not effected a wholesale dispossession of the Anglo-Saxon nobility, and since therefore much of the land which passed into Norman hands came in bits and pieces (as men died or rebelled), the process of redistribution was necessarily somewhat piecemeal. Even so, there were significant exceptions to the rule: in Cornwall, for example, where he gave 'nearly the whole of the county' to Robert of Mortain, in Sussex, along the March of Wales, and in many parts of the north.[17] In general, though, a patchwork of often widely scattered holdings remained the norm for the English aristocracy of the twelfth and thirteenth centuries. Once established, moreover, the pattern was virtually impossible to alter. Inheritance customs tended to encourage it, for although primogeniture meant inheritance by the eldest son should there be one, it also meant partibility among daughters in the absence of any sons, and since over the course of the centuries the great majority of families failed on at least one occasion to continue the male line, this process of division and subdivision was continually being repeated. At the same time, there was naturally a constant process of acquisition and unification. This might be by purchase, or it might be by forfeiture or escheat to the king and consequent re-grant by him to another lord, but the most common way in which substantial areas of land changed hands in the Middle Ages was through marriage, in the form either of dowries or the inheritances of heiresses, and naturally there was an element of haphazardness involved in either of these processes. While a landholder might try to arrange his heir's marriage so that the family acquired new property in the vicinity of its existing holdings, and thus consolidated its territorial power, it was just as likely that the bride would bring with her a few scattered manors from some distant part of the country. Moreover, the accidents of birth and death all too often undermined such arrangements. For most medieval English landholders, territorial consolidation was probably to be desired, but was in practice difficult to achieve, and even when it was achieved, it was often only temporary.

It remains true, however, that every great landholder in medieval England had his *caput honoris*, and the inalienability of the *caput*, together with the lands and rights which surrounded it and which constituted the 'barony', was almost a cardinal rule of the nobility. The *caput honoris* – literally, the head of the honour – was the lord's principal residence and administrative centre. Here he would build his castle, the symbol of his lordship (and initially, after the Conquest, of occupation), and nearby would be the chief religious house patronised by the family, often indeed founded by it, where successive generations of lords and their families would be buried. Around these twin symbols of authority was usually a group of 'home manors' whose produce was used to supply the lord's household. Assuming the family survived in the male line, then as the years passed, the tombs multiplied, the original wooden motte and bailey gave way to something grander and more permanent in stone, and the home farms were augmented, the sense of local identification can only have grown stronger. Traditions of service and loyalty were at the heart of medieval lordship. They both enhanced and justified authority. What is more difficult to be sure of, however, is the levels at which such authority was exercised.

Social stratification is a hazardous business, but also an important one. It is important for two reasons: firstly because it helps to explain what medieval people meant when they used the word 'nobility', and secondly because in the Middle Ages social strata were closely linked to layers of political authority and thus help to analyse the workings of political society. So who, in medieval England, was considered to be noble? And by what criteria were some considered to be more 'noble' than others?

It is abundantly clear that the number of persons considered to be of the nobility in twelfth- and thirteenth-century England should be numbered in thousands rather than in hundreds, but it is easier to start by looking at the top end of the scale. As already seen, Domesday Book reveals the existence of about 170 great tenants-in-chief in 1086, roughly corresponding to what contemporaries described as the 'baronage'. To hold one's lands 'by barony' from the king did to a certain extent put one in a class apart from those who held by knight service. In clause 2 of Magna Carta (1215), for example, it was said that heirs of earls or barons should pay a relief of £100 to enter into their inheritances, whereas those who held by knight service should pay £5 'at most'. These sums were said to correspond in each case to 'the ancient relief', and while there had often been disagreement over the size of reliefs demanded by the king, they do at least indicate a substantial gulf between earls or barons and knights. These reliefs, however, were for 'a whole barony' or 'a whole knight's fee'.[18] In fact, of the 210 English baronies recorded between 1086 and 1327, less than forty remained in the same male line for more than two centuries.[19] Of the remainder, some were transferred wholesale to other families, but most were divided into fractions of varying size (usually as a result of partible inheritance by heiresses), and redistributed accordingly. There are frequent references in the exchequer rolls of the twelfth and thirteenth centuries to reliefs payable on halves, quarters, and sometimes even thirty-sixths of baronies.

A simple list of tenants by barony (which could include the holder of one thirty-sixth of a barony) is thus clearly inadequate for any serious attempt at social stratification. Yet the idea of the 'baronage' as a recognisable group in English society persists, reinforced from time to time by references to the 'greater barons'. In clause 14 of Magna Carta, for example, King John declared that for the purpose of granting an aid 'we will have archbishops, bishops, abbots, earls and greater barons [*maiores barones*] summoned individually by our letters' to a council. The *Dialogus de Scaccario*, a commentary on the operation of the royal exchequer written about 1178, also made the distinction between the holders of 'greater and lesser baronies'. Again it was the payment of reliefs which was under discussion, and the distinction seems to be between the holders of more or less whole 'honours', or baronies (the *maiores* barons), and the holders of lesser estates such as knights' fees.[20] By the 'greater barons', therefore, what is meant appears to be what modern historians more commonly term the 'baronage', while the term 'lesser barons' is closer to what is now frequently referred to as the 'knightly class'. In reality it is, of course, quite impossible to make such clear-cut categorisations, for between the one group and the other there was no neat cut-off point.

By what criteria, then, might it be possible to distinguish an elite group of landholders at the top of English lay society, corresponding roughly to what contemporaries described as the greater baronage? It has recently been said that, around 1200, 'at the top of the heap there were the barons, about 160 of them, who had an average income of around £200'.[21] On the face of it, this compares nicely with the 170 great tenants-in-chief of Domesday Book. For any such figure to be meaningful in social as well as tenurial terms, however, it is clearly necessary to consider further types of evidence. A recent study of the thirteenth-century nobility has concentrated on three main types of evidence: military summonses, conciliar and parliamentary summonses (mainly from the second half of the century), and tenure by barony (in cases where at least half a barony was held). By analysing these sources, Mr Wells concluded that there were about 300 families in thirteenth-century England who at one time or another during the century seem to have been considered to be of the greater baronage. Allowing for the constant process of extinction and recruitment, the number at any one time was more like 200 to 220. Perhaps the most significant aspect of these findings, suggesting that they are meaningful in social and political as well as tenurial terms, is the high degree of overlap between the different types of evidence. 'In other words,' as Mr Wells points out,

> the three main criteria employed do not provide us with three
> separate lists . . . but, in effect, one main list, the names on
> which usually derive from two, and sometimes three, of the
> different types of sources used, with a few additional names
> drawn from only one type of record. This strongly reinforces
> the view that there was in reality an upper stratum to the
> landholding class in thirteenth-century England, numbering in
> the region of 300 families, who may not have been marked off
> from the lesser nobility by clearly definable ranks or privileges,
> but who nevertheless did enjoy higher status and usually greater
> wealth than their fellows.[22]

There is no denying, of course, that the 'baronage' of thirteenth-century England was considerably more fluid than the 'peerage' of late fourteenth-century England was to become. There were no very clear barriers between them and the rest of the landholding class. Social stratification, however, is more a question of contemporary

social perceptions than of legal or tenurial definition, and given this
evidence the conclusion is probably justified that during the twelfth
and thirteenth centuries there was in England a group of between 150
and 250 greater landholders at any one time, who formed a reasonably distinct (to their contemporaries) upper stratum of noble
society, namely the layer that came immediately below the king in
the social and political hierarchy. The actual personnel of the group
was of course constantly changing. As with most nobilities, the
most frequent cause of derogation was a simple failure of male heirs,
while the usual routes to recruitment were through royal service and
marriage. What distinguished these men from the rest of the nobility
was their direct dependence on and access to the king and the size of
their estates, leading to greater wealth, a more extensive type of
lordship, and hence status. In other words, the differences were in
degree rather than in kind: that is why they are, in a technical sense,
undefinable.

Those who came below the 'baronage' and made up the rest of the
English nobility are commonly and conveniently referred to as the
'knightly class' or, among later medieval and modern historians, as
the gentry. The development of this group through the twelfth and
thirteenth centuries is far from clear. It is impossible to say how
many knights there were in twelfth-century England. It is only
possible to say that eleventh-century arrangements seem to envisage
between 4,000 and 5,000 knights, but owing to the common practice
by great landholders of granting less than one 'knight's fee' to many
knights, there may in practice have been rather more than this.
Equally, there is evidence from the reign of Henry II (1154–89) that
there should have been about 6,500 knights in England, but in fact
the number was probably not so great.[23] By the late thirteenth
century we seem to be on firmer ground. There is now fairly general
agreement that around 1300 the 'knightly' or gentry class consisted
of between 2,500 and 3,000 landholders, roughly half of whom were
real (that is, dubbed) knights, while the other half (generally styled
esquires) were men who for various reasons had decided not to
assume actual knighthood, but who were of roughly equivalent
status and wealth to the dubbed knights.[24] Thus what the twelfth
and thirteenth centuries saw was in essence a crystallisation of the
lesser ranks of the nobility. 'In the eleventh century,' according to
Professor Barlow, '*milites* and their servants, *armigeri*, squires, seem

in most literary contexts to be little more than common soldiers; knighthood conferred as yet no social distinction; and the emergence of knights as a distinct and honourable class did not get under way before Henry I's reign.'[25] Many of those described as knights in England at this time seem to have held no more than about one and a half hides of land.[26] On the other hand, it is dangerous to assess social status in terms of wealth alone. While many of them may have held little land, they nevertheless fought as the companions of their lords, may well have received maintenance (and quite possibly expensive military equipment as well) in a lord's household, and engaged in the honourable pursuits of the warrior class. Moreover, some of them clearly held a great deal more than one and a half hides of land.

Even so, there is little doubt that the 3,000 or so of the late thirteenth-century 'knightly class' enjoyed – as a group – considerably higher social status and landed wealth than their eleventh- and twelfth-century namesakes, and this transformation in the fortunes of the lesser nobility was due to a number of factors. One of these was military. It has recently been argued that the late eleventh and twelfth centuries were a key period in the development of 'a new method of cavalry warfare', during which western knights came to perfect the art of the controlled mass cavalry charge as an effective weapon of warfare. But in order to be effective, cavalry warfare of this type required a higher degree of training, as well as a greater investment in equipment: a heavier lance, better armour, and good horses, as well as the servants necessary to care for the mounts and equipment. These developments, Dr Keen argues, did not only 'foster a sense of identity among those who, by one means or another, could manage to fit themselves out as mounted warriors', but also 'strengthened the aristocratic bias of recruitment into knighthood, and sharpened in its ranks the awareness of a common bond, called chivalry, uniting all who could aspire to ride to wars and tournaments'.[27] In other words, for the man who would fulfil his martial role in society *in the way that was expected of him*, both wealth and lineage were becoming increasingly important. The word *miles* (knight) now comes to signify not just any soldier, but a trained mounted warrior, and as such it becomes an increasingly exclusive term. By the thirteenth century, it has come to indicate not just a specific type of martial activity, but also social status. Those who are still knights are more substantial men than their antecedents. And inevitably, therefore, they are fewer.

Economic forces seem, in the long term, to have been working in the same direction. The initial parcelling out of land following the Conquest, during which the barons and other great landholders (such as the great ecclesiastical tenants-in-chief) subinfeudated their land to their followers, gradually underwent a process of rational-isation by which estates became consolidated in fewer hands. As extinction or political misfortune carried off some families, those who were lucky enough to survive picked up the crumbs and built on what they had inherited. Obviously, this was by no means a one-way process. Every new reign or political vicissitude brought its clutch of parvenus. At the same time, though, this process of consolidation may have been encouraged by the so-called 'crisis of the knightly class' of the thirteenth century, a time when, it is argued by some historians, economic circumstances (and more especially the severe inflation which afflicted England in the years *circa* 1180–1220) resulted in substantial numbers of the lesser nobility slipping down the social scale and out of reach of nobility.[28] Over the period 1100–1300 as a whole, there also appears to have been a more widespread shift of land out of the hands of the king and baronage, and into the hands of the church and the knightly class,[29] which, taken together with the corresponding and simultaneous concen-tration of a higher percentage of knightly estates in fewer hands, reinforces the view that the median income of the 3,000 in 1300 must have been substantially higher than that of the twelfth-century knights.

The third factor contributing to the crystallisation of the knightly class through the twelfth and thirteenth centuries is to be found in their developing administrative and political role. The 3,000 or so knights and esquires who, together with the baronage, comprised the nobility of late thirteenth-century England were not just sol-diers, they were also the political communities of their localities, the so-called *busones* of the shires, serving both king and baronage in a variety of offices, and representing the aspirations and grievances of those who lived within their spheres of administration.[30] At the instance of the monarchy, they had come to be regularly involved in the judicial and financial administration of their shires, meeting every forty days in the county court, serving as jurors, tax assessors, military arrayers, escheators, coroners and sheriffs. For the magnates, they served as stewards and councillors. They formed the vital link (in both directions) not only between the king and the shire communities, but also between the great lords and the reeves and bailiffs who ran the manorial administration at grass-roots level. As Mr Denholm-Young once remarked, 'if every baron was a politician, it may be added that most knights were administrators'.[31] And administrative activity led almost inevitably to political activity – most notably, for example, in the demands for reform of local government which characterised the opposition to royal government in the years 1258–9.[32] It was also, of course, during the thirteenth century that representatives from the shires began to be summoned to the king's parliaments, which was both a recognition of their growing importance in local government and an opportunity for them to make their views known on a wider political stage. Initially, it is true, the weight they carried in the king's parliaments was quite limited. By the second half of the fourteenth century, though, it was to be a different story.

It was a common maxim of medieval writers that 'royal service ennobles'. For those further down the social scale, baronial or even knightly service might also ennoble. Service to one's social betters had always been one of the principal paths to advancement for the nobility, but there is no doubt that as the Middle Ages progressed the knights and esquires became ever more involved, not just in politics and justice, but also in the more routine aspects of royal and noble administration – partly, of course, because the spread of lay literacy gradually broke down the barriers demarcating the work of laymen from the work of clerics. Does this mean, then, that the classic function of the nobility, martial activity, was becoming diluted? Although the majority of dubbed knights were still active (i.e. fighting) knights, there seems to have been a growing minority who were not. This was partly because there were some who simply preferred different kinds of service, political or administrative, to the military kind, but it was also because knighthood itself was becoming increasingly a question of lineage. Lineage, of course, had always been an important element of knighthood, but what seems to have happened is that it became even more important just at the time when the escalating cost of knightly equipment and of the ceremony of dubbing (which became ever more lavish and costly) was deterring a greater number of potential knights from assuming the honour. Thus a lesser knightly class, generally known to historians as the squirarchy, rose to take its place alongside the knights. The squirarchy was, in the words of Dr Keen, 'a kind of diminutive of chivalry'.[33] Esquires, or at least some of them, were clearly considered to be of the nobility. They were not, however, of the knighthood. Knighthood, therefore, had lost its role as a binding force for the chivalric class, and came instead to mean one of two things: the dubbed knight was either a man whose ancestors had traditionally taken knighthood, and who could still afford it, or he was a man who had earned the honour by service (preferably to his prince) on the battlefield or in the council chamber, and, again, who could afford it (though in this case it would probably be up to his king or other lord to make available to him the means by which he could afford it).

Yet despite the social cachet attached to late medieval knighthood, the gap in status between the knights and at least some of the esquires was a fairly narrow one. Esquires could go to tournaments or join noble 'Orders', and by the mid-fourteenth century they were permitted to bear coats of arms. The wealthier esquires, therefore, were clearly of the nobility. As a social group, they can be characterised as 'a nobility of blood marked out by the capacity to receive knighthood'.[34] As an economic group, they were roughly those who held between £20 and £40 worth *per annum* of land (though a few certainly held more). They were precisely that group whom successive thirteenth- and fourteenth-century kings of England attempted to 'distrain to knighthood'.[35] As such, though not of the knighthood, they were potential knights, and thus of the 'knightly class'. The knightly class was, therefore, the nobility.

To summarise, the concept of the nobility had undergone a subtle though significant change between the twelfth century and the late thirteenth. At the top of English lay society there was still the baronage, numbering around 200 families at any one time. This much probably had not changed to any significant degree. Below the baronage came the gentry, or knightly class, an economically diverse group of some 3,000 landholders almost all of whom held land worth at least £20 *per annum*, roughly evenly divided between actual knights and potential knights. The hallmark of this group was still its warrior ethos, but an even greater degree of importance than earlier was now placed on two other aspects of nobility: lineage, and service of a non-martial character. The growing importance of lineage was, to some extent, a defensive reaction to the dilution of the nobility's martial role in society. It was also a defence against the growing wealth of the merchant class. The growing importance of non-martial service was a consequence of the spread of lay literacy, of the general growth in the size of royal and noble administrative machines, and of the way in which 'self-government at the king's command', as the Angevin approach to local government has aptly been termed, led to the formation of the *busones* class in the shires. The fall in the number of knights can best be explained in terms of the increasing cost of knighthood, together with the long-term process of rationalisation which is perceptible among the estates of lesser landholders, aggravated perhaps by the thirteenth-century 'crisis of the knightly class'. Together, these factors had combined to produce in England a nobility which effectively dominated the military, economic, political and social life of the country.

It was the land, and the labour of men far humbler than themselves, which provided the nobility with the wealth to maintain that dominance. Lordship of land and men was the birthright of the noble. It was both a system of social control and a means of keeping the nation's wealth in the hands of the elite. It had various aspects, moral and customary as well as judicial and financial. Usually, though, land was at the heart of it. The evolution of feudalism in eighth- and ninth-century France, whence it had spread throughout most of western Europe, including England, had brought with it a fusion of lordship over land and over men, so that in general the latter now followed from, and was a natural concomitant to, the former.[36] To hold land was not merely to enjoy the profits of it, it was also to exercise certain rights over those who worked on it.

In its details, the effect of the Norman Conquest on the extent and quality of the lordship exercised by England's landholders varied from place to place. In general, though, it seems likely both that its extent was widened and its hand strengthened. It is true that slavery, which had not been uncommon in pre-Conquest England, disappeared fairly rapidly after 1066, but in its place there came the reduction of a greater number of men to the state of serfdom. In pre-Conquest England there had been great variation in the status of the peasantry, ranging from the entirely free to the entirely unfree

(the slaves). Anglo-Norman lordship tended to blur these distinctions. Naturally it did not do so entirely: there were still many free
peasants after the Conquest, especially in the north of the country.
Yet a far greater number of men now found themselves subjected to
both the stigma and the unwelcome demands of servility. The
differences between the free man and the unfree man (or serf, or
bondman) were, in theory at least, many. The unfree man had no
standing in law, no access to courts other than his lord's court. He
had to perform unpaid labour services for his lord on a (theoretically)
regular basis, whereas if a lord wished a free man to work for him he
had to pay him wages. The unfree man was also liable to a number of
financial exactions on the part of the lord, some of which could be
heavy. He could not buy or sell land, or leave the manor without the
lord's permission. He had to pay a fine for marrying off his daughter
(*merchet*), or if his daughter was found to be a fornicator (*leyrwite*), or
if he wished to send his son to school, or put him into the church. At
his death, his lord took his best beast as a *heriot*. He was also subject
to tallage, a theoretically arbitrary financial exaction which the lord
could demand at any time from his unfree tenants. In practice, some
of these rights were often waived or ignored by landlords. Nor,
indeed, was the distinction between free and unfree men nearly as
simple as it might sound. Some men were in effect half-free, and in
both theory and practice the demands which lords made upon their
serfs varied considerably from region to region, even from manor to
manor. In a sense, though, these variations may well have increased
the sense of injustice, for it was above all the arbitrariness of the
lord's demands which created resentment. It would be futile not to
recognise the disabilities of serfdom: for most of the peasantry, the
Norman Conquest was a misfortune.[37]

Allied to the widespread imposition of serfdom after the Conquest
was the development of feudal courts. 'Private' courts were not of
course new to post-Conquest England, but they do seem to have
become both more diffuse and more powerful. They were essentially of two types: honorial courts and manorial courts. Honorial
courts were the prerogative of the greater lords, and impinged little
on the peasants' life, but the same was not true of manorial courts.
Each manor had its court, a partly judicial, partly administrative
gathering, where the business of the community was transacted and
transgressors were brought to justice. Naturally, the profits of the

justice meted out in the manorial court went into the lord's pocket. At the same time, many hundreds fell into private hands, so that the local court also became the lord's court, and contributed further to the swelling of his coffers.[38] Technically, a private hundred was a 'franchise' (or 'liberty'), a royal right, according to the king's lawyers, which could only be held by an individual following a specific act of delegation by the king, but in practice it seems that many franchises were more or less assumed by lords over the years.[39] They were undoubtedly sources of considerable profit, as indeed they were intended to be. They included, for example, the right to license (and draw profit from) weekly markets and annual fairs in specified towns, or to exact tolls on bridges, or ferries, or certain sections of road. Some lords also exercised the much-prized franchise of 'return of writs' within given areas, that is, the right to implement royal writs through their own agents rather than allowing them to be implemented by the king's agents. It was, in general, a consequence of the more rigid feudal lordship introduced by the Normans to England that judicial rights became both more fragmented and more privatised, not merely in order to wrest more money from the peasantry but also to ensure that at each level tenurial obligations were accompanied by the means necessary to enforce them. For many peasants, this meant even more direct dependence on their lords. In some areas, notably the March of Wales, the ramifications of lordship spread further than this, amounting to the almost total dependence of the peasantry on the lord.[40] But while Marcher lordship was exceptionally strong, it would be dangerous to think that lordship throughout the rest of the country was weak.

As to the land itself, there was no doubting that it existed primarily in order to provide wealth for the lord – unless, of course, he wished to subinfeudate it in return for service. Given an estate in land, there were essentially two ways in which a landlord could extract money from it: either he could rent it out in return for an annual sum, or he could manage it directly, through his own agents and workforce. The advantages of renting were that the lord received a guaranteed income from his land, and that he didn't have to concern himself with organising its cultivation. On the other hand, there was a strong customary element in rents, which could thus fall far behind, for example, rises in prices. Given the right circumstances, however, direct cultivation (or 'demesne-farming') was potentially more profitable than renting. The balance between renting and demesne-farming is important not only in its economic implications, but also in its social ramifications, for it was largely on the lord's demesne that serfs were required to work, and it follows therefore that significant fluctuations in the amount of land held in demesne led to significant fluctuations in the incidence of serfdom in medieval England. It follows too that a landlord's decision to rent or manage directly was in large part governed by economic circumstances.

In outline, there is a reasonable level of agreement about long-term economic trends in twelfth- and thirteenth-century England.[41] For at least two centuries after the Conquest, the population of England rose steadily and continuously, probably from around two million in 1086 to around five million by 1300. For much of this period the rise in population was accompanied by a continuous process of land reclamation which, in the absence of any serious improvements in agricultural techniques, provided the principal means by which this expanding population could be fed, but by the middle of the thirteenth century the land available for colonisation was beginning to run out, so that the ratio between land and people was becoming unbalanced. Peasant holdings gradually became smaller, and intensive cultivation probably led to soil exhaustion, especially on marginal land. At the same time, England suffered from quite severe inflationary pressures. The sharpest inflation occurred during the years *circa* 1180 to 1220, during which time many prices tripled or at least doubled. After this, inflation slowed down, but even between *circa* 1220 and 1300 there was roughly a doubling of prices. As price inflation tailed off, however, rent inflation accelerated. The most marked rises in rents occurred during the second half of the thirteenth century, as the land-hunger became more intense, and as the customary element in rents, which had helped to protect tenants from at least some of the effects of inflation before about 1250, began to lose its restraining power.

Squeezed between the declining size of their holdings and the need to pay more both for the right to work what land they had and to buy whatever they were unable to produce, many peasants looked to employment to make up the shortfall in their incomes, but here too there was little comfort to be found. The pressure on jobs was just as intense as the pressure on land, and real wages dropped accordingly – possibly by as much as 50 per cent over the century as a whole. The thirteenth century may have been an age of urban expansion, but it is clear that the towns were unable to take up the slack in the agrarian economy. In every way, then, life was becoming harder for much of the peasantry as the thirteenth century progressed, and at the end of the century even worse was to come, for it was from the 1290s that the military activity of the English kings in France and Scotland became near-continuous, bringing with it constant and often heavy demands for monetary taxation, purveyance (supplies in kind for the royal armies), and military service.[42]

For the landlords, however, the thirteenth century was on the whole a time of prosperity. They had what everyone wanted: land. Rising rents brought more into their coffers, price inflation meant that (at least as far as agricultural prices were concerned) they got more for the produce of their estates (and the growth of towns, most marked in the century from 1150 to 1250, also made it easier to dispose of), and low wages meant that they had to pay out less to those who worked for them. In addition, the deprivations of the thirteenth century forced many tenants to take lands which were held by servile tenure, thus providing lords with another source of cheap labour, their serfs. Not surprisingly, with prices high and labour cheap, many landlords turned to large-scale direct cultivation of their estates for the market. During the twelfth century, most of them had preferred either to farm (i.e. lease) out whole manors, usually to lesser landholders such as knights or esquires, or, on those manors which they did not farm out, to rent out substantial portions of the land to tenants. Now, when it was possible, they reclaimed their lands and exploited them for the market; hence the thirteenth century is sometimes described as the era of demesne-farming. Whether the lesser landholding class benefited as much from these developments as the 'baronial' class, or the great ecclesiastical land-lords, is a much-debated point. The so-called 'crisis of the knightly class', it has been suggested, was not merely the consequence of the increasing expense needed to maintain a knightly way of life, but also of the fact that, with their smaller endowments, and the strong restraining force of customary rents, many of them were unable to take advantage of the prevailing economic trends and thus found themselves slipping down the social scale.[43] Yet while there is certainly evidence of some middling landlords being forced to sell out to greater ones, it is by no means clear that the group as a whole was in difficulty, and such examples might just as easily be viewed as part of that constant process by which families rose and fell.

The trend towards demesne-farming continued until roughly the middle of the thirteenth century. It was accompanied by renewed interest in both the theory and practice of estate management, and by a substantial growth in the number of men employed by lords in the administration of their estates.[44] Yet it is a trend which needs to be kept in perspective. Even at the height of the demesne-farming era, which probably coincided with the third quarter of the thirteenth century, the majority of landlords still drew most of their income from rents, and from this time onwards, due principally it seems to the late thirteenth-century explosion in rents and entry fines, it is clear that the trend had reversed itself and that most landlords had begun to rent out demesne land again.[45] This brings us back to an important general truth: throughout the Middle Ages, nearly all landlords were basically *rentiers*. And while the 'demesne-farming era' of the thirteenth century was a significant one, it needs to be seen within this context.

The significance of the move towards larger demesnes was not simply that it provided very substantial profits for many landlords; it also led to much reimposition of servile labour obligations, in order to provide the labour with which demesnes were worked. Equally, one of the major consequences of the renewed process of demesne-leasing was that serfdom during the late thirteenth and fourteenth centuries gradually declined. This too, however, is a trend that must be seen in perspective. The 'decline of serfdom' at this time did not normally entail its abolition but its commutation, and what commutation consisted of was, in effect, the selling back to the serf of his customary obligations, often on an annual basis. It did not mean that the serf ceased to be a serf; there was always the possibility that at some future date his obligations would be reimposed, and in the event, although in much-changed economic circumstances, this may well be what happened during the third quarter of the fourteenth century.[46] Thus while the process of demesne-leasing was to remain a fairly constant one through the fourteenth century, serfdom, as the demands of the rebels of 1381 make clear, was still alive and well in late fourteenth-century England. Not until late in the fifteenth century could it truly be said that serfdom had more or less vanished from the English countryside.[47]

Lordship bore hard on the peasantry of medieval England. Its weight varied from one region to another, from one period to another, and from one landlord to another, but essentially it achieved what it was designed to do: to transfer wealth into the pockets of lords, and to place in their hands effective machinery for the control of the mass of the population. And as society evolved, so did lordship. As towns grew, and the wealth of the country diversified through trade and industry, so lords found ways either of gearing their own economies to participation in such enterprises, or simply of creaming off the merchants' and producers' profits. The attempts by thirteenth- and fourteenth-century monarchs to tax the English wool trade, for example, are merely symptomatic, at the highest level, of what many lords were doing on a lesser scale in towns and industries throughout England, using rights such as tolls, private courts, fairs and markets, and tallage. Lordship in the Middle Ages was much more than landlordship. The yield of the soil and the labour of the peasant combined with the skill and enterprise of the artisan or merchant, just as the theorists said that they should, to provide the noble with the means to sustain his lifestyle. They built his castle, equipped him for war, funded his travels, paid for his leisure and his hospitality, salaried his servants, and underwrote his largesse. There was plenty of idle pleasure in the noble lifestyle: 'they drank their good wines freely, and all the talk was of arms and of love, or hounds and hawks and of tournaments.'[48] In other words, in their everyday lives they behaved much as elites always did. But beyond the idle pleasure and the militaristic ethos, there were three principal preoccupations of the medieval noble: politics (both local and national), the lands, and the family. It is with these themes that this book is concerned.

PART I

THE RANKS OF THE NOBILITY

CHAPTER 1

Kings and the titled nobility

Before 1337, the only heritable title in England apart from the king's was that of earl, and for the most part English kings had been extremely cautious about creating earldoms. At the end of the Conqueror's reign there were probably nine English earls. By 1307, at the death of Edward I, there were eleven. Only once during the intervening centuries had the title been in serious danger of becoming cheapened: this was during Stephen's reign (1135–54), when the king and his rival, the Empress Matilda, both created a number of earldoms in an attempt to outbid each other for the support of the leading barons, so that at various times during the reign there were thirty or more men who could claim the title. By the time Henry II died in 1189 the number had dropped to twelve again.

Thus those men who held earldoms were an extremely select group at the top of English lay society, and their exclusivity was matched by their wealth, status, and political influence. Many of them were closely related to the king. Indeed, some kings seem to have taken the view that new earldoms should normally only be created for members of the royal family. During the fourteenth century, however, the English kings were prepared to be rather more generous than this. Between 1307 and 1397, twenty-four new earldoms were created outside the immediate royal family – three by Edward II, eleven by Edward III, and ten by Richard II. These creations were both personal and political acts on behalf of the king. Frequently, it is clear that those who received titles were personal friends (or 'favourites', to use a more loaded term) of the monarch.

Politically, there were both dangers to be faced and benefits to be gained from new creations. The chief danger was likely to be a feeling that the king was promoting the wrong sort of men, or, among those who already held titles, that their exclusivity was being threatened. The chief benefit was that by his patronage the king created a powerful fund of support among the leading men of his kingdom. Thus kings were well advised to tread warily in this matter. Relations between the king and the titled nobility were a crucial factor in the politics of any reign, and, despite the greater willingness of fourteenth-century kings to bestow titles on their greatest subjects, the earls remained a very select group. At no time during the fourteenth century did their number rise higher than twenty. They were the men with the standing and resources to make life either easy or difficult for the king. When danger threatened the crown, it was usually because one or more of them had been alienated.

In 1307, the year that Edward II came to the throne, there were nine English earls and a further two whose principal lands lay outside England but who also held substantial lands within the kingdom. These latter two were John, duke of Brittany, who held the English earldom of Richmond, and Richard de Burgh, earl of Ulster, neither of whom played any significant part in English affairs.[1] Henry de Lacy, earl of Lincoln, was aged fifty-six, and Robert de Vere, earl of Oxford, was forty-nine, but the remaining seven English earls were all younger men, ranging in age between sixteen and thirty-five, and thus of much the same generation as Edward himself, who was twenty-three when he came to the throne.[2] Moreover, none of them had been an earl for more than nine years. The greatest of them was the king's cousin Thomas, earl of Lancaster, who, as well as that of Lancaster, held the earldoms of Leicester, Derby, and (after Lacy's death in 1311) Lincoln, and whose annual income by the time of his death was around £11,000 gross or £8,700 net.[3] The other outstanding member of the group in terms of wealth was the new earl of Gloucester, Gilbert de Clare, whose gross annual income was in the region of £6,000. None of the other English earls could match these two for wealth, but they came mostly from long-established comital families. Robert de Vere, earl of Oxford, Humphrey de Bohun, earl of Hereford and Essex, and John de Warenne, earl of Surrey, could all trace their earldoms back to the twelfth century or earlier, while the Lacy family had held the earldom of Lincoln since 1232. The relative newcomers to the group – although in each case the earldom had already been in the family for a generation – were Guy Beauchamp, earl of Warwick, Aymer de Valence, earl of Pembroke, and Edmund Fitzalan, earl of Arundel, whose fathers had received their titles in 1268, 1275, and 1291 respectively.

As far as the leading members of the nobility were concerned, therefore, the portents were good. Around the king there gathered a new generation of young men from old families, men with the standing and resources to play their part in the king's designs, and with the natural sympathy and shared expectations which arose from being, like Edward himself, on the threshold of their careers, yet who had not been personally involved in the political opposition to Edward I which had erupted in the 1290s. Unfortunately, Edward II lost no time in antagonising them. Five 'new men' were promoted to earldoms during the reign. Two of these were quite unexceptionable in any terms: Thomas and Edmund, the sons of Edward I by his second wife, Margaret of France, and thus half-brothers to the king, were granted the earldoms of Norfolk and Kent, in 1312 and 1321 respectively. As everyone recognised, they were simply taking their natural place, to which they had been born, among the great men of the kingdom. Edward's remaining three creations were a different matter altogether. It would of course be quite wrong to suggest that the king's favouritism was the sole cause of his eventual downfall. His disastrous dealings with the Scots (and especially the humiliation at Bannockburn in 1314), his woeful inability to handle his magnates in general, and his vindictive treatment during the last four years of his reign of those who had opposed him in 1321–2, all contributed to turn his rule of England into one long crisis from which his deposition in 1326–7 must have seemed a merciful release. Yet it would also be foolish to underestimate the political consequences of his favouritism, and this was never more lamentably apparent than during the first five years of the reign.

Within a month of his accession Edward committed his first major blunder by conferring the earldom of Cornwall on his friend Piers Gaveston. Gaveston was apparently witty, personable, and a creditable soldier, but he was hardly a suitable candidate for an earldom. The son of a Gascon knight, and thus both a commoner and a foreigner, he had become intimate with Edward during the last years of the old king's reign (in fact the relationship between the two men was probably homosexual), and so unsuitable a friend for his son did Edward I consider Gaveston to be that in early 1307 he had exiled him from the kingdom. His immediate recall, in July 1307, was ominous enough. His elevation to an earldom was, as was plain to all, simply a consequence of his personal favour with the king. During the next five years, at the insistence of the magnates, he was twice more exiled, only to return. Eventually, despairing of keeping him away from the king by any other means, the earls of Lancaster, Hereford, Arundel and Warwick kidnapped him from the custody of the earl of Pembroke and had him summarily beheaded on Blacklow Hill, near Warwick, on 19 June 1312.

Edward's remaining two comital creations were the direct result of his victory over Thomas of Lancaster at the battle of Borough-bridge on 16 March 1322. Since 1312, the opposition to Edward had come increasingly to crystallise around Lancaster, and the rise of another favourite, in the person of Hugh Despenser the younger, was to prove the catalyst which turned Lancaster's hatred of the king into armed opposition. The younger Despenser was a much more violent and unpleasant character than Gaveston. His ruthless land-grabbing policy in South Wales, which Edward not only connived at but actively supported, provoked the civil war of 1321–2, which resulted in complete victory for the king and Despenser. Six days after Boroughbridge, Lancaster was condemned as a traitor and beheaded outside his own castle of Pontefract. His ally Humphrey de Bohun, earl of Hereford and Essex, had died in the battle, but he too was convicted posthumously of treason. In their place the king promoted two new earls. Andrew Harcla, the victor of Borough-bridge, was made earl of Carlisle. Within a year, however, he had been executed for complicity with the Scots on the northern border, and his earldom was suppressed, never to be revived. Edward's second new earldom was longer-lasting, though not by much. The elder Hugh Despenser, father of the king's new favourite, was made earl of Winchester in May 1322. The younger Hugh was not made an earl, but there can be little doubt that it was intended that he should in the course of time succeed to his father's title.

That the younger Hugh's succession never came about was due to the revolution of 1326–7. For four years after Boroughbridge Edward and the Despensers ruled England as they pleased, brooking no opposition, growing fat on the proceeds of confiscated lands and disinherited heirs. The younger Hugh had by 1326 acquired not only enormous sums in cash, but also a landed estate worth over £7,000 *per annum*, while his father's was worth nearly £4,000.[4] But in September 1326 an invading army led by Edward's own queen, Isabella of France, and her lover Roger Mortimer, lord of Wigmore in Hereford, captured the king and rid the country of his cronies. Both the Despensers were executed, as was Edmund, earl of Arundel, by now a thoroughgoing royalist and the only earl apart from the elder Despenser who stuck with the king to the last. In January 1327 the queen and her supporters completed their task by deposing her husband and choosing his son Edward as king. By the end of September Edward II was dead, murdered at Berkeley castle.

Unfortunately the blood-letting was to continue for a while yet. Edward III was only fourteen in January 1327, and for the first few years of his reign the country was effectively governed by Roger Mortimer, under whose sway Isabella seems to have acted. Mortimer proved to be little better than the men he had supplanted. Certainly he did not lack for personal ambition, even prevailing upon the king to confer the title of earl of March on him in 1328 – a title derived from the siting of his chief seat of power at Wigmore in the Welsh March. Gradually, opposition to the new regime built up. In January 1329 Mortimer had to put down a rebellion led by Henry of Lancaster (the brother of Thomas, he had been allowed to inherit the Lancastrian lands in 1327), and in March 1330 the unfortunate Edmund, earl of Kent, the new king's uncle, was caught plotting against the regime and executed at Winchester. This was done at the behest of Mortimer, apparently without the king's knowledge, and for Edward it seems to have been the last straw. He now determined to rid himself of Mortimer, and in a carefully planned and daring coup at Nottingham castle in October 1330 he managed to effect the arrest of both his mother and her lover. Mortimer was taken to London, tried, and executed for treason on 29 November. Isabella, although forced to give up much of the wealth she had acquired over the previous four years, was granted a generous allowance of £3,000 a year and spent the remaining twenty-eight years of her life in comfortable retirement at her favourite residence of Castle Rising in Norfolk.

Thus at the end of the year 1330, having just turned eighteen,

Edward III entered upon his personal rule, at the outset of a reign which was to see English armies achieve undreamed-of feats abroad, and a lasting period of political harmony at home. To have foreseen such achievements at the time, however, would have demanded powers bordering on the supernatural. Between 1322 and 1330 no less than seven English earls had lost their lives as a result of either rebellion or conspiracy: Lancaster and Hereford in 1322, Carlisle in 1323, Arundel and Winchester in 1326, Kent and March in 1330. Not one of the newly-created earls outside the royal family between 1307 and 1330 had clung to his title for more than five years: all four of them had ended by being beheaded for treason. Partly as a result of these misfortunes, the number of English earls had fallen to eight.[5] What is more, few of them were men after the young Edward's own heart. Oxford was seventy-two and had been retired from public life for many years. Henry of Lancaster, although only restored to his inheritance in 1327, was already forty-nine and going blind. John de Warenne, earl of Surrey, was forty-four and not much of a force to be reckoned with in the new reign,[6] while Thomas of Brotherton, earl of Norfolk, although active militarily during the early years of the reign, was apparently an unpopular figure and there is nothing to suggest that Edward greatly lamented his death in 1338.[7]

The remaining four were younger men, of much the same generation as the king. Edward's younger brother, John of Eltham, aged only twelve when granted the earldom of Cornwall in 1328, was apparently a noted soldier, but unfortunately he was to die during the siege of Perth in 1336. John de Bohun, earl of Hereford and Essex, who like Henry of Lancaster had been restored to his inheritance following the revolution of 1326, was also to die in 1336, aged thirty, though in his case death was probably brought on by some lingering incapacity which had in any case prevented him from playing much of a role in public life. The exceptions in this somewhat unpromising scenario were Warwick and Arundel. Thomas Beauchamp, who had come into his father's inheritance as earl of Warwick in 1329, and Richard Fitzalan, who was restored to his father's earldom of Arundel in the same parliament which condemned Mortimer, were both exactly the same age as Edward, and both were to become firm friends and supporters of the king until their deaths in 1369 and 1376 respectively. They were joined in 1331 by John de Vere, the new earl of Oxford, when his aged uncle eventually died. He too was exactly the same age as Edward, and was to be one of the king's supporters until his death in 1360. But otherwise the early and mid-1330s saw a reduction rather than an increase in the already depleted ranks of the active magnates. Humphrey de Bohun succeeded his brother as earl of Hereford and Essex in 1336, but although aged only twenty-seven at the time he too seems to have been afflicted with some chronic illness which largely incapacitated him and left him, like his brother, childless. By 1337 the situation was becoming critical. England was at war with Scotland, and it was clear that the outbreak of hostilities with France could not be delayed much longer. Edward needed young, energetic and like-minded men around him, imbued with the authority to lend weight to his cause both at home and abroad. Yet the only two new earldoms since 1330 had gone to his eldest son, the Black Prince, who was made earl of Chester in 1333 at the age of three, and to Hugh Courtenay, the sexagenarian earl of Devon who had been deprived of his earldom by a piece of sharp practice on the part of Edward I in 1293, but restored to his rightful title by a more sympathetic monarch in 1335.[8] As it turned out Courtenay died five years later, but even at the time of his restoration the king can hardly have expected much active support from him.

It was in these circumstances that Edward III took the remarkable step of creating six new earls in the parliament of March 1337. William de Montague became earl of Salisbury, William de Clinton became earl of Huntingdon, Robert de Ufford became earl of Suffolk, William de Bohun became earl of Northampton, Henry of Grosmont became earl of Derby, and Hugh Audley became earl of Gloucester. In thus seizing the initiative, the king made his reasoning perfectly clear:

Among the marks of royalty we consider it to be the chief that, through a due distribution of positions, dignities and offices, it is buttressed by wise counsels and fortified by mighty powers. Yet because many hereditary ranks have come into the hands of the king, partly by hereditary descent to co-heirs and co-parceners according to our laws, and partly through failure of issues and other events, this realm has long suffered a serious decline in names, honours and ranks of dignity.[9]

To rectify this situation, Edward not surprisingly chose men who were his friends. Four of them – Northampton, Salisbury, Huntingdon and Suffolk – were knights or officers of the king's household and had been involved with the king in the 1330 coup against Mortimer. Indeed, Montague had been responsible for organising the coup, and although ten years older than Edward he was probably the king's closest personal friend.[10] Suffolk was thirty-nine at the time of his creation, Huntingdon thirty-three, and Northampton twenty-five. The greatest of the six by his birth was Henry of Grosmont, the eldest son of Henry, earl of Lancaster, and thus heir to the greatest comital inheritance in England. What the king was doing was in effect hiving off one of the house of Lancaster's hereditary titles in order to demonstrate his confidence in Grosmont by promoting him before his time. Grosmont was twenty-seven in 1337, and already well on the road to becoming one of the greatest of all fourteenth-century English magnates.[11] The last of the six creations of 1337 was in many ways the odd one out. Hugh Audley was an older man who had been much involved in the politics of the previous reign, and his elevation to an earldom was probably not so much a mark of the king's special favour as recognition of the fact that he had sufficient wealth to support the title – most of which had come to him as the husband of one of the sisters and co-heiresses of Gilbert de Clare, the last of the Clare earls of Gloucester, who had been killed at Bannockburn in 1314.

Thus Edward III had, at a stroke, created a new English higher nobility. Naturally, these men were royal 'favourites' just as much as Gaveston and Despenser had been, but whereas Edward II's promotions had proved politically disastrous, those of his son were to prove an undoubted success. The difference was in the type of men that Edward III chose as his friends. The comments of contemporary chroniclers on men such as William Montague, William de Bohun and Henry of Grosmont were as favourable as those on Gaveston and Despenser had been damning. Even more importantly, Edward managed to create a new higher nobility without alienating the old. His new men blended easily with the more active of the hereditary earls, notably Warwick, Arundel and Oxford, to form a solid group of great men firmly committed to the king's cause for the next thirty years or so, and it was this above all which explains the remarkably harmonious atmosphere of English domestic politics during the central period of Edward's reign.[12]

Earldoms, however, could not be created out of thin air. Men whom the king chose to dignify with great titles had also to be endowed with sufficient resources, preferably landed, to support that dignity, and it was here that more serious problems might arise. The minimum annual income compatible with the title of earl seems to have been reckoned at £1,000 – though this was very much a minimum. There was no way in which chunks of land of this size could be purchased by Edward for his new earls, for great estates hardly ever came on to the market, and even if they had, the price would have been prohibitive. Nor could the new earls be granted crown lands on any scale, for these were regarded as existing for the support of the king and his immediate family.[13] This left three options: forfeiture and re-grant, marriage, or the grant of estates in expectancy backed by a cash annuity until the expectation was fulfilled. Edward used a combination of these methods, with a little help from the crown lands. His methods were somewhat hand-to-mouth, however, and were to create long-term problems which, under a lesser monarch, might have proved much more serious than they did.

Hugh Audley and Henry of Grosmont presented few real problems. Audley's share of the Clare inheritance, together with what he had received from his father, gave him a gross income of well over £2,000 and he seems to have received nothing more in 1337. Grosmont was given a cash annuity of 1,000 marks (£666) out of the royal customs, to last until his father's death.[14] He also had certain lands traditionally attached to the earldom of Derby, and of course the prospect of becoming the greatest landholder in England apart from the king. The other four, however, were more problematical. Within a week of their creations, Huntingdon, Salisbury and Suffolk were each promised 1,000 marks' worth *per annum* of lands or rents, and Northampton was promised £1,000 worth – not because he was especially favoured by the king, but because he was the poorest of the four. But promises were one thing, fulfilling them was another. In fact Huntingdon was already quite well provided for, through his marriage in 1328 to Juliana de Leybourne, the grand-daughter and sole heiress of William Leybourne, who held some forty manors, mostly in Kent.[15] Half of his further 1,000 marks was now given to him in the form of the manor of Kirkton

(Lincolnshire), which was said to be worth 500 marks *per annum*, and which had escheated to the crown following John of Eltham's death in 1336. For the rest, he was granted the reversion (the future expectation) of £100 worth of land presently held by the king's mother, Isabella, but for the moment this and the remaining £230 of his grant could only be made up by the grant of the profits of various town and county farms which would normally have been paid into the royal exchequer. Suffolk was dealt with very similarly. His own inheritance was far from negligible, and in 1331 he had been granted land worth £200 by the king for his part in the arrest of Mortimer. He was now granted land to the value of £410 in Suffolk and Norfolk which had been held by John of Eltham (including the honour of Eye), and a promise of £250 a year from the exchequer to make up the residue. Northampton, the fifth and youngest son of the earl of Hereford who had died at Boroughbridge, had a meagre inheritance but had partly compensated by marrying, in 1335, Elizabeth, one of the four daughters and co-heiresses of Giles, 'the rich' Lord Badlesmere. Nevertheless, he was far from well endowed, and the promise of £1,000 worth of land or rent to him proved very difficult to fulfil. He was granted few lands for the moment, because little could be found to give him, but he was granted the reversion of various lands held by the earl of Surrey, the widow of the earl of Pembroke, and even the new earl of Gloucester. For the moment, his £1,000 was to be taken in cash, partly from customs revenues, and partly from the farms of various shires. He is unlikely to have found this arrangement satisfactory, for revenues of this sort were often slow to mature and difficult to secure. On the other hand he was unlikely to complain at the king's generosity. Moreover, Edward agreed that when Northampton's brother, the earl of Hereford and Essex, died, he would be allowed to inherit his brother's lands and titles. As a result of this, Northampton's son was to become, in 1363 (if only for a decade), a very substantially endowed earl.[16]

The endowment of William Montague, the new earl of Salisbury, raises a different problem. In 1330, as a reward for organising the coup against Mortimer, the king had granted Montague the great Welsh Marcher lordship of Denbigh, worth over £1,000 a year gross. The grant followed directly from Mortimer's downfall for, having been convicted of treason, he forfeited all his lands to the king, Denbigh included.[17] Forfeitures and re-grants, however, were seldom as simple as they might seem. Legally, forfeiture was final, but in practice it was frequently reversed, though usually only after a decent interval or a change of political fortunes. This is what happened in the case of Denbigh. Mortimer's grandson, another Roger, became a friend and servant to Edward III, so much so that in 1354 the king restored him to the earldom of which his grandfather had been deprived in 1330. And in order to do so, he felt compelled to annul the sentence passed on Roger's grandfather in 1330, so that the stain of treason should be removed from the family name and the young earl should be entitled to his ancestral lands. By this time Montague had died (in 1344), to be succeeded by his son, another William, in 1349. There was thus a direct clash over the ownership of Denbigh between the second earl of Salisbury and the second earl of March, which was decided in the court of King's Bench. The decision was given to March. It has often been seen as somewhat arbitrary,[18] but it is difficult to see how a different decision could have been reached. Once he decided to restore Roger Mortimer to his earldom, the king really had no option but to annul the sentence on his grandfather; and once he had annulled the sentence on his grandfather, he was more or less obliged to restore Denbigh to the Mortimers. It is very doubtful, though, whether Edward would ever have treated the first earl of Salisbury in this way. The son, however, was not as close personally to the king as the father had been, and Edward was prepared to deprive him in order to reward a young man who had evidently impressed him. Nor was this the only such case to go against the younger Montague, for when the first earl had been promised a further 1,000 marks' worth of land in 1337, it had proved impossible to find any for him, and instead he had been granted the reversion of various lands in the West Country held by John de Warenne, earl of Surrey, backed for the moment with an annuity of 1,000 marks to be taken from the profits of the Cornish stannaries. The problem was that Warenne's title to these lands was not as secure as it might have been. They had come to him as the result of a complicated series of exchanges with Thomas of Lancaster in the years immediately preceding the battle of Boroughbridge, and had then been confirmed to him following Lancaster's forfeiture in 1322. The heirs to Thomas of Lancaster thus also had a claim to them. When John of Gaunt, Edward III's third son, acquired the Lancastrian inheritance in 1361, he began to press his claim, and within a few years had won some of the lands back. Once again, therefore, Montague was deprived of an estate, and it was from the Cornish tin-mines that he continued to draw a substantial part of his income.[19]

Thus the endowment of Edward III's six new earls in 1337 was both a costly and a potentially divisive business. As his reign progressed, however, the king found himself increasingly able to use marriage as a means of providing for those whom he wished to elevate or reward, and as a consequence future creations were to prove much less of a drain on royal resources than those of 1337. For the great, of course, marriage was hardly ever an affair of the heart at this time. Political alliance, and an orderly and accepted structure for the transfer of property, were its principal functions. That is why it was so important for kings to manipulate the marriage market to their own advantage, in order to make sure that the hands of great heiresses went to those whom they wished to reward. The enormous estates of Gilbert de Clare, earl of Gloucester, provide a good example (see Table 1). At his death in 1314 Gilbert left no children, so that his co-heiresses were his three sisters, Eleanor, Margaret and Elizabeth, who split the lands, worth some £6,000 gross, between them. Eleanor was already married to the younger Despenser, and the other two were soon married off to another two of the rising stars of Edward II's court, Margaret to Hugh Audley, and Elizabeth to Roger Damory. Thus three very substantial inheritances had been created, each of adequate comital size, and over the next eighty years, largely through a series of judicious marriages, they were to be used to endow a number of earls, despite the fact that each third was subjected to forfeiture on at least one occasion. The Despenser third was increased enormously by violence in 1321–6, forfeited in 1326, partially restored in 1328, and eventually descended to the younger Hugh's great-grandson Thomas, who was created earl of Gloucester in 1397.[20] Audley's third was forfeited following his rebellion in 1322 but restored in 1326–7, and was sufficient to elevate him to the earldom of Gloucester in 1337. He died in 1347 leaving only one child, a daughter, Margaret, who in 1336 had been married to Ralph, Lord Stafford. Naturally, Stafford was now a much greater man than he had been before, and he was also a noted soldier and a friend of the king's. Thus when, in 1351, Edward promoted Ralph to the earldom of Stafford it cost him virtually nothing to do

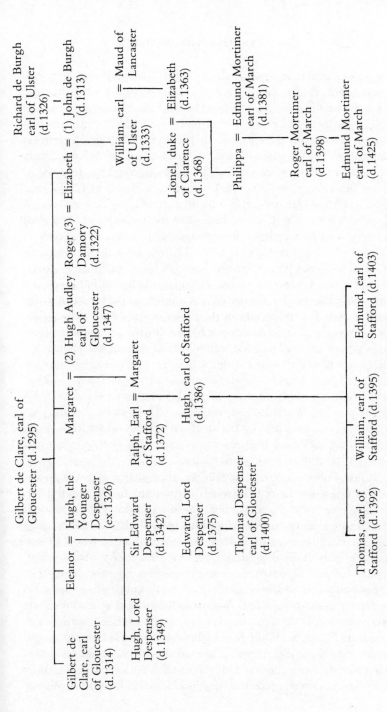

Table 1 Partition and descent of the Clare inheritance in the fourteenth century

so – once again, it was his share of the Clare inheritance which provided the chief element of his endowment.[21] Elizabeth's third did little for her husband, for Roger Damory joined the opposition in 1321 in order to fight for his inheritance and was killed at Borough-bridge. Her lands thus passed to her son by her first marriage, William de Burgh, earl of Ulster. When he died in 1333, aged only twenty-one, the reversion of all his lands (not only a third of the Clare inheritance, but also the lands of the earldom of Ulster) was vested in his only daughter, Elizabeth, born in 1332. Edward III now saw his chance. In 1342 he betrothed his second son, Lionel of Clarence, to Elizabeth; they were aged four and ten respectively. From 1347 Lionel was styled earl of Ulster, and in 1362 he became duke of Clarence, a title derived from his Clare inheritance. Provision for his second son thus cost the king virtually nothing. Nor was this quite the end of the story, for Lionel himself died in 1368, leaving only a daughter, Philippa. Philippa was promptly married, by the king's arrangement, to Edmund Mortimer, the son of the man whom Edward had restored to the earldom of March in 1354, the result of which was to transform the earls of March into the greatest landholders in England outside the royal family.[22] Thus from one earl of Gloucester at the beginning of the fourteenth century to another at its end, the great Clare inheritance had provided a major (and usually the chief) element in no less than seven comital families' landed endowments, largely as a consequence of a series of carefully arranged marriages.

Control of the marriage market was thus vital, and it was principally by this means that Edward III provided for his family. His children excepted, the remaining creations of Edward's reign, apart from those already discussed (Stafford and March), were of no great significance. They included three foreigners, none of whom played any real part in English affairs, and two successive earls of Kent neither of whom outlived their promotions by more than four years.[23] This is hardly surprising, for the king had strained his resources to the limit in 1337, and from this time onwards his efforts were necessarily concentrated on his rapidly growing family. Edward and his queen, Philippa of Hainault, had five sons who grew to manhood. Naturally, it was expected that they would take their places in the very highest rank of English society, and that they would be endowed accordingly. The eldest was Edward of Woodstock, the Black Prince, born in 1330 and, as the heir to the throne, in some ways the easiest to deal with. It was common for the king's heir to be granted lands out of the royal demesne, which would then revert to the crown when he succeeded as king. Thus in 1333 the Black Prince was made earl of Chester, in 1337 he was made duke of Cornwall, and in 1343 he was made prince of Wales.[24] Following the cession of Aquitaine by the French king to Edward III at Brétigny in 1360, Edward also made his eldest son prince of Aquitaine in 1362. At its height, therefore, the Black Prince's estate was, in sheer acreage, about a quarter of the size of his father's kingdom, a magnificent endowment and one which easily set him on a par with the great French dukes of the fourteenth century.

The generosity which Edward III showed to his eldest son meant, however, that his remaining sons could hardly be provided for out of the crown lands. Instead, they were mostly provided for by marriage. Lionel of Clarence, born in 1338, received the earldom of Ulster and a third of the Clare inheritance (see above). Edward's third surviving son, John of Gaunt, born in 1340, was married in 1359 to Blanche, the younger of the two daughters who were the only children of Henry of Grosmont, possessor of the great Lancastrian inheritance. Grosmont's estates in England and Wales were worth about £8,500 *per annum* gross,[25] so even if, as originally envisaged, John of Gaunt had had to share his father-in-law's inheritance, he would still have been a wealthy earl, but as it turned out Blanche's sister Maud died in 1362, just a year after their father, so the entire Lancastrian inheritance came to Gaunt.[26] The king's two youngest sons were not provided for on quite the same scale as the other three, though they did very well for themselves by any other standards. Edward's fourth son, Edmund of Langley, was only a year younger than Gaunt, but he lacked his brother's forceful character and did not receive such rapid promotion. Not until 1362 was he made an earl (of Cambridge),[27] while his main endowment was provided by a complicated transaction in which the lands of John de Warenne, earl of Surrey, were, after his death in 1347, divided between the earl of Arundel (who had a claim to them by marriage), the earl of Salisbury, and Edmund.[28] The Warenne lands which came to Edmund were mainly situated in Yorkshire, centred on the great castle of Conisborough and the towns of Dewsbury and Wakefield – hence his eventual elevation to the dukedom of York. It is clear, though, that his landed estate was not considered to be as great as it should have been, and from time to time the king increased it by granting him certain crown lands as they fell in, but even when he received his dukedom in 1385 he had to be granted an additional cash annuity of £1,000 at the exchequer to support his dignity.[29]

Edward and Philippa's youngest son, Thomas of Woodstock, was only born in 1356, and not until 1373 did a suitable opportunity arise to endow him. In this year Humphrey de Bohun, who in 1363 had united in his person the earldoms of Northampton and Hereford and Essex following the death without children of his uncle, died leaving two daughters as his co-heiresses. Edward III promptly married Thomas to Eleanor, the elder of the two, and not surprisingly Thomas did all he could to ensure that Mary, her sister, remained unmarried, even apparently having her instructed in doctrine and placed in a nunnery. John of Gaunt, however, had other ideas, and considered that Mary would make a suitable bride for his own son Henry. When Thomas left England to lead an expedition in France in 1380, Gaunt saw his chance and, with the help of the girls' mother, spirited Mary away from the nunnery and took her to Arundel castle, where she and Henry were promptly married.[30] By a piece of gross opportunism, therefore, Thomas had been deprived of half of his anticipated inheritance, and the result was that he, like Edmund of Langley, remained rather underendowed. When in 1377 he was made earl of Buckingham, he too had to be granted £1,000 annually at the exchequer until landed provision could be made for him.[31]

Accidents of birth and death, and clever or unscrupulous manipulation of the marriage market, played a crucial role in determining both the survival and the fortunes of all the great noble families of medieval England. By the fortuitous death of a sister-in-law, John of Gaunt doubled his inheritance; by the abduction of a prospective daughter-in-law, he halved his brother's. However skilfully a king controlled the transfer of property between his great men – and Edward III certainly did it better than most – there was always a strong element of chance involved. Edward's 'policy' towards his higher nobility, if indeed it deserves that title, seems to have been essentially twofold. Firstly, and quite deliberately, to use whatever reasonable methods and resources were available to him to ensure that those in the kingdom who stood closest to the crown were men in his own image, that they had the necessary authority, status and resources effectively to buttress the monarchy, and that prospective royal servants were aware that he would not be afraid to use his power to reward them as fully as he was able. In doing so, he could be quite harsh at times on those whose resources he could use for his own ends, as witness his treatment of the second earl of Salisbury, or his somewhat arbitrary decision in 1354 to deprive John, Lord Mowbray, of the Marcher lordship of Gower, thereby 'restoring' it to the earl of Warwick.[32] His success, however, can be measured not only by the fact that he maintained domestic peace throughout his long reign, but also by the fact that, in terms of personnel, he effected a rapid but also a lasting change in the face of the English higher nobility. Of the thirteen English earls and dukes in 1362, only three (Arundel, Warwick and Oxford) were primogenitary descendants of men who had held the same titles in Edward II's reign. The rest were new men.

Secondly, and partly as a result of Edward III's willingness to raise new men to earldoms, he created a special place within the ranks of the higher nobility for the royal family, or at least those members of it whom he considered deserving. It was clearly with this in mind that he created, in 1337, the first dukedom in England, that of Cornwall, for the Black Prince. His new title was intended to mark the heir to the throne off from the rest of the titled nobility, and although it did not remain quite as exclusive as that, only three more dukedoms were created by Edward. Henry of Grosmont became duke of Lancaster in 1351, and the king's second and third sons, Lionel of Clarence and John of Gaunt, became dukes of Clarence and Lancaster respectively in 1362. Grosmont was Edward's second cousin, which was extending a little the idea of the 'royal family', but he was not only the greatest landholder in England after the king and the Black Prince, he is also generally recognised as having been the outstanding noble of his generation, and once again Edward was pronouncing his readiness to reward excellence in due measure.[33] By this time, moreover, the Black Prince was not just a duke but a prince (of Wales), and it may be significant that when his younger brothers were made dukes in 1362, he was simultaneously granted not the duchy, but the principality of Aquitaine, thus reinforcing his special position as heir to the throne. In thus distinguishing the four greatest members of his higher nobility, the king was probably motivated by international as much as domestic considerations, for all of them were much involved on the European stage. Grosmont was regularly entrusted with diplomatic missions at the highest level and held a number of lordships in France. Clarence was lieutenant of Ireland in the 1360s, and his second marriage (in 1368, just before his death) was to the daughter of the duke of Milan. Gaunt also held a number of French lordships, and his second marriage (in 1371) was to Constanza, the daughter of the murdered Pedro, king of Castile. As dukes, they had greater standing in their dealings with the kings, princes and dukes of Europe. Nevertheless, Edward was discriminate with his patronage. It is noteworthy that Edmund of Langley, who was only a year younger than Gaunt, was *not* made a duke by his father, probably because he lacked the character to play a leading political role. Thus Edward's policy of an 'elite within an elite' was carefully controlled.

Unlike the children of so many other English kings, Edward III's sons were strikingly loyal to him, and this too was an important factor in the stability of the reign. Towards the end of the reign, however, the political consensus was beginning to dissolve. By 1372, almost all of the king's real friends among the higher nobility were dead, and a new generation of earls was rising. Increasingly, Edward must have seemed like an old man who had outlived his times, but like any king he had to live with the consequences of his creations and to accept that the wealth and authority which went with earldoms were now vested, not in men he had chosen, but in their sons, whom he had not chosen. So, like the 1320s and 1330s, the 1360s and 1370s were an age of transition among the higher nobility, and the 1370s were also years of political and social crisis. Military failure, chronic government insolvency, and political scandal were the characteristics of this miserable decade in English history. Discontent manifested itself in a series of angry parliaments (notably in the Good Parliament of 1376)[34] and in the great rising of 1381. And when Edward III eventually died, at the age of sixty-five in June 1377, he was succeeded not by the Black Prince, who had died in the preceding year, but by his ten-year-old grandson Richard II. Richard's reign was to follow a pattern depressingly similar to that of Edward II. He too engaged in a series of bitter quarrels with some of his leading magnates, culminating in the elimination of his chief enemies in 1397, his 'tyranny' of 1397–9, and his deposition in September 1399. And like Edward II, many of his troubles stemmed from his unfortunate ability to antagonise his leading subjects.

On the day that Edward III died there were ten dukes or earls in England. The oldest of them was the earl of Salisbury, who was almost fifty; the youngest was Edward Courtenay, the new earl of Devon, who was about twenty. The others were all between twenty-five and thirty-eight. They were therefore much of an age, though on the whole of the generation senior to that of the new king. In terms of landed wealth, the greatest of them was undoubtedly John of Gaunt, followed by March and Arundel;[35] in terms of status, Gaunt again, and Edmund of Langley, by virtue of their royal birth. With the exception of Warwick, whose direct line stretched back to the thirteenth century, the remaining six all traced their titles back to Edward III's generosity.

Richard II was to show before long that he shared his grandfather's taste for conferring new titles, but the first major increase in the number of earls during his reign can hardly be credited to him personally. On 16 July 1377, the day of Richard's coronation, five new earls were created. Thomas of Woodstock, the king's uncle, and Henry of Bolingbroke, the son of John of Gaunt, were made earls of Buckingham and Derby respectively, which was really no more than their birthright. Guichard d'Angle, a French lord who had been Richard's tutor, became earl of Huntingdon. He was to play no part in the politics of the reign, however, dying just three years later.[36] The two most significant new earldoms in 1377 were those of Northumberland and Nottingham. The elevation of Henry Percy to the earldom of Northumberland was probably considered by some to be rather overdue, for the Percys were a great northern family who could trace their line back to the Conquest and who were undoubtedly endowed with sufficient land (mainly in Yorkshire and Northumberland) to support the title. At the age of thirty-six, Henry Percy was taking his rightful place among his contemporaries. The earldom of Nottingham, a title never used before, was conferred on the twenty-one-year-old John Mowbray. The Mowbrays were another great northern family who traced their line back to the Conquest. John's lands, which were situated mainly in Lincolnshire and Yorkshire, were worth about £1,400 *per annum*, but he was also the heir to many of the lands of the old earldom of Norfolk, which had become extinct with the death of Thomas of Brotherton in 1338, and these were probably worth about twice as much again.[37] John, however, died childless in 1383, and the man who inherited both his lands and his title was his brother Thomas, one of the strangest characters of Richard's reign, a man who in his own actions and ultimate fate seems almost to epitomise the political cross-currents of the reign. At first a great favourite of the king, he turned against him in the crisis of 1386–8, was restored to favour in the early 1390s, promoted to a dukedom in 1397, then once again cast down in 1398, to die in exile in the following year, just one week before Richard's deposition. And in securing the deposition of 1399, the two prime movers were Henry of Bolingbroke and Henry Percy, earl of Northumberland. Thomas of Woodstock was also to play a major role in the politics of the reign before his murder, probably on the king's orders, or possibly those of Thomas Mowbray, in 1397. In four out of five cases, therefore, the promotions of 16 July 1377 involved men (or their heirs) who were to be instrumental in shaping the fortunes of the new reign.

Not until 1397 did Richard II attempt radically to revise the composition of his higher nobility, but his first twenty years did witness a steady trickle of additions to their ranks. His half-brothers, Thomas and John Holland, became earls of Kent and Huntingdon respectively, in 1380 and 1388.[38] His cousin Edward, the eldest son of Edmund of Langley, became earl of Rutland in 1390, when still only seventeen. He and John Holland were to be noted supporters of Richard during the later years of the reign, but their promotions at this time were not so much evidence of royal favour as recognition of their birth. The real promotions of Richard's early years, much more significant in political terms, were those of Robert de Vere and Michael de la Pole. Both were intimate with the king, and both were thoroughly unpopular. Born in 1362, de Vere was just four years older than the king and had been brought up with him at the court of Edward III. He was also hereditary earl of Oxford, and was duly allowed his title when he came of age in 1383. It was not this, but his further promotion in 1385–6 which angered the king's opponents. In 1385 he was made marquis of Dublin, the first marquis in English history (a marquis was to rank above an earl but below a duke), and in the following year he was elevated further, to be duke of Ireland. Simultaneously, he was granted 'the whole land of Ireland', the intention being that he should conquer it and then hold it as his lordship.[39] Thus at the age of twenty-four he became only the second duke outside the immediate royal family in England, and there can be little doubt that few thought him worthy of the honour. Michael de la Pole was an older man, probably about forty at the start of the reign. He was also of much humbler birth, being the son of the Hull merchant Sir William de la Pole, who had helped Edward III to organise the financing of his armies during the early stages of the Hundred Years' War. However, Michael had been summoned to parliament since 1366, so he was not quite such a parvenu at the time of his elevation to an earldom as is sometimes suggested. That elevation came in 1385, when he was made earl of Suffolk. He had been the king's chancellor since 1383, and was widely blamed for the government's financial problems. At his trial in 1386, he was also accused of abusing his position to his own advantage.[40] The king probably planned a third new earldom in 1385. One chronicler even stated that on the Scottish campaign of that year he conferred the earldom of Huntingdon on his chamberlain Sir Simon Burley, another highly unpopular royal intimate, but the grant was never ratified – possibly because there was too much opposition to it.[41]

Resentment towards Richard's new creations in 1385–6 stemmed not only from personal considerations but also from anger at the way in which he tried to endow his protégés. The resources available to Richard were very few at this time, and there was strong pressure from parliament to keep what he had in his own hands, and thus to reduce the burden of taxation.[42] Michael de la Pole was provided for by the large-scale transfer of the lands of the old earldom of Suffolk, which had become extinct in 1382 on the death of William Ufford. De Vere and Burley, however, both required substantial new endowments, and in order to provide these the king resorted to the extremely dubious device of trying to seize back lands which had been purchased by Edward III and granted by him to trustees for the performance of various religious benefactions under the terms of his will.[43] Both the trustees and the king's opponents resisted strongly, and in the end Richard's designs were largely frustrated. At any rate, the question of their endowment was soon to become somewhat irrelevant, for in 1386 a full-scale political crisis erupted, with the king and his favourites violently opposed by a group of magnates known to history as the Lords Appellant. The Appellants were Thomas of Woodstock, Henry of Bolingbroke, Thomas Mowbray (all recently created earls), Richard Fitzalan, earl of Arundel, and

Thomas Beauchamp, earl of Warwick. In the Merciless Parliament of 1388 they secured the conviction for treason of de Vere and de la Pole (both of whom fled abroad, never to return to England), and the execution, for treason, of eight of the king's lesser followers, including Simon Burley. Thus rapidly were Richard's promotions of 1385–6 undone.

Richard's patronage in 1385 had also extended to the conferment of dukedoms (of Gloucester and York respectively) on his two youngest uncles, Thomas of Woodstock and Edmund of Langley, which they probably considered no more than their due, and which he no doubt hoped would make de Vere's marquisate more acceptable. His promotions of 1397 were to be much more wide-ranging. Having recovered power from the Appellants in 1389, the king seemed for a while to have learned from his mistakes, but in July 1397 he evidently decided that the time was right to strike back at those who had humiliated him in 1386–9. Woodstock, Arundel and Warwick, the three leading Appellants, were arrested and tried in parliament for treason. Arundel was beheaded, Warwick exiled to the Isle of Man, and Woodstock convicted posthumously following his murder at Calais. Then, having destroyed his enemies, Richard rewarded his friends. Richard's generosity in 1397 makes even the events of 1337 pale by comparison. Before the parliament was over he had created five new dukes, one duchess, one marquis, and four new earls. Four of his new dukes were closely related to him: his half-brother John Holland, already earl of Huntingdon, became duke of Exeter; his nephew Thomas Holland, already earl of Kent, became duke of Surrey;[44] and his cousins Edward, earl of Rutland, and Henry of Bolingbroke became dukes of Aumâle and Hereford respectively. The fifth was Thomas Mowbray, earl of Nottingham, who became duke of Norfolk, largely by virtue of the fact that he was the heir to his grandmother, Margaret Marshal, the possessor of the great Norfolk inheritance. At the same time, Margaret became duchess of Norfolk, the first English duchess in her own right.

The only marquisate created in 1397 also went to a close relative of the king's, John Beaufort, the son of John of Gaunt by his mistress Katharine Swynford. Following Gaunt's marriage (his third) to Katharine in 1396, the Beauforts had been formally legitimated in the parliament of February 1397, at which time John was made earl of Somerset. He was now created marquis of Dorset. The four new earldoms of 1397, however, went to lesser men, and were clearly the reward for political support rather than birth. Thomas Percy, younger brother of the earl of Northumberland, and steward of the royal household since 1393, became earl of Worcester. William le Scrope, chamberlain of the royal household since 1393, and undoubtedly one of the king's closest advisers in the 1390s, was made earl of Wiltshire. Thomas Despenser, the great-grandson of Edward II's favourite Hugh the younger, became earl of Gloucester, and Ralph Nevill, the head of another great northern family with its *caput* at Raby castle in Durham, became earl of Westmorland.

Richard's new magnates were endowed principally out of the lands forfeited by Woodstock, Arundel and Warwick, together with some grants of crown lands. Naturally, the five new dukes already had substantial lands of their own, but they were still given far from negligible additional Appellant estates to support their newly-enhanced dignity. Nevill presented few problems, for the family lands in Yorkshire and Durham were very extensive and in 1396 he had been granted the royal honour of Penrith (hence, apparently, his title).[45] Despenser, too, was far from poor, for the family had continued throughout the fourteenth century to hold much of its original share of the Clare inheritance.[46] William le Scrope was the son of the great Yorkshire baron Richard le Scrope of Bolton-in-Wensleydale, whose lands were worth about £600 *per annum*, and in February 1397 the king had granted him 'the whole county and lordship of Anglesey in North Wales', which until then had been part of the crown patrimony.[47] Yet despite the wealth of the forfeited Appellant estates, the king must have found it difficult to reward his new dukes and earls on the scale which he considered to be commensurate with their dignity. Thomas Percy, for example, held little land of his own, but when, in 1399, he was made to restore to their rightful owners the lands which Richard had granted him from the Appellants' estates in 1397, it was apparently thought that they were only worth 500 marks (£333) a year.[48] John Beaufort's title arose from the fact that his father, John of Gaunt, had purchased a number of Somerset manors for him from the earl of Salisbury, but they were not worth more than £300 *per annum*. He too was granted various lands forfeited by Warwick, as well as a number of lucrative offices, and he had also recently been married, probably by arrangement of the king, to Margaret, daughter and eventual co-heiress of the earl of Kent, but nevertheless his landed estate remained well short of what a marquis's should have been, and in 1404 Henry IV had to grant him an annuity of £1,000 to maintain his rank. The result of this was that until the mid-fifteenth century the Beauforts remained short on land and thus heavily dependent on crown favour, in the form of annuities, wardships and so forth.[49]During the eighteen months following the September 1397 parliament, three more great estates (those of Lancaster, March, and Norfolk) were to fall into Richard's hands, and in each case the profits from them were to be employed either to bolster the crown itself or the king's newly-promoted magnates. One of the reasons for Richard's fatally cavalier attitude to the property rights of his greatest subjects at this time was his feeling that his supporters had not been properly rewarded in 1397.

The chronicler Thomas Walsingham said that Richard II's new magnates in 1397 were commonly referred to as the *duketti* – the little dukes.[50] In most cases, however, those who received dukedoms from Richard were very closely related to him – four out of his five new dukes in 1397, for example, were more closely related to him than Henry of Grosmont had been to Edward III – and close relatives of the king had long been acknowledged as deserving special treatment. Even Edward I, who is not usually renowned for his generosity, promised to endow his two sons by his *second* marriage with lands worth 10,000 marks *per annum*, which would have put them above all their contemporaries bar the earl of Lancaster.[51] The exceptions, in Richard's case, were de Vere in 1385–6, and Mowbray in 1397. With these creations, as with some of his new earldoms both in 1385 and 1397, Richard can with justification be accused of having cheapened the great titles at the crown's disposal, but given the success of Edward III's promotions, and given that there is an inevitable tendency for most titles to become cheapened with time, he can hardly be blamed for thinking that the reaction to his new creations was somewhat excessive. In fact the reaction was probably not so much at Richard's cheapening of titles as at the characters of the people that he promoted, and at the arbitrary methods which he employed in order to try to endow them with sufficient lands. In his search for lands and revenues for his new men, he went much further than Edward III had done, thereby reviving memories of Edward II's enrichment of the Despensers. It was to lead not only to his downfall, but to most of theirs as well. In September 1398, following a quarrel between Thomas Mowbray and Henry of Bolingbroke which involved accusations of treason, Richard exiled both men. It is quite probable that already he had foreseen the possibility of seizing to his own use the great Norfolk and Lancastrian inheritances, to which they were respectively the heirs. At any rate, once the holders of the estates, Margaret Marshal and John of Gaunt, died within a few weeks of each other in February–March 1399, he acted with considerable speed. The Lancastrian inheritance was parcelled out to Aumâle, Exeter, Surrey, and Wiltshire.[52] The Norfolk lands were seized for the crown.[53] It was this action which precipitated Henry of Bolingbroke's invasion and Richard's deposition on 30 September 1399.

For the king's chief supporters, the deposition also proved a chastening experience. Ralph Nevill and Thomas Percy were allowed to keep their earldoms (no doubt because of the support which they gave Bolingbroke in 1399), but all the rest of the men promoted in September 1397 were stripped of their new titles[54] – apart, of course, from Henry himself, who now promoted himself still further, and became King Henry IV. The dismal culmination to this period of turmoil among the higher nobility came in January 1400, when the earls of Kent, Huntingdon and Salisbury, with the newly-demoted earl of Gloucester, plotted to overthrow Henry and all lost their lives. And when Thomas Percy lost his life, again rebelling against Henry, after the battle of Shrewsbury in 1403, it meant that the only one of Richard's creations of September 1397 to last more than six years was Ralph Nevill's earldom of Westmorland. John Beaufort, of course, also kept the earldom of Somerset, but that had been granted to him at the time of his legitimation, in February 1397. Moreover, Henry allowed Michael de la Pole, son of Richard's convicted favourite, to reassume his earldom of Suffolk in 1399. So in these three cases, at least, Richard's promotions bore long-term fruit. Indeed, the Nevills, the Beauforts and the de la Poles were to be three of the very greatest families of fifteenth-century England. On the whole, though, Richard's attempt to create a new higher nobility had been as resounding a failure as Edward III's had been a success.

To summarise, promotions to the highest ranks of the nobility in the fourteenth century took on more blatantly political overtones than they had at any time since Stephen's reign. Most new earldoms were now the result of royal favour rather than of inheritance. This was partly due to the new-found willingness of kings from Edward II onwards to create new earls (to 'buttress' the crown, as Edward III put it), and partly because changes in property law widened the scope of the king's patronage.[55] But whatever the reasons, it meant that as political acts they were judged. The figures speak for themselves: of the sixteen new earls, marquises and dukes outside the immediate royal family created in the years 1307–30 and 1385–97, no less than fourteen were demoted, exiled, or executed within five years of their creation. Of the thirteen created between 1335 and 1377, not one suffered that fate. Much of this had to do with personalities, but the difficulties involved in the endowment of the king's protégés were also severe, leading not only to crown indebtedness to the magnates, but also a degree of unscrupulousness in the manipulation of property rights. Edward III was by no means innocent in this matter, but both his father and his grandson were guilty of it to a far greater degree. In each case, it was one of the chief causes of their ruin.

CHAPTER 2

The peerage

It was not only in its topmost ranks that society was becoming more rigidly stratified in the later Middle Ages. This period also saw the emergence of the parliamentary peerage in England. Dukes, marquises and earls were naturally members of this group, but they were not the only members of it. By the fifteenth century, the peerage consisted of about sixty to seventy families distinguished from the rest of the landholding class by their more or less hereditary right to receive individual summonses to parliament. They were the peers of parliament, the progenitors of the later House of Lords.

Any discussion of the parliamentary peerage of late medieval England should rightly begin with an examination of the views put forward by K.B. McFarlane, whose brilliant studies laid the foundation for most modern research on this topic. In 1965, a year before his death, McFarlane summarised his views when he described the fourteenth and fifteenth centuries as a period when

> a nobility of a type peculiar to England, having little in common with the French *noblesse* and German *Adel*, first came into existence and established itself in that position of dominance in English society which it was to retain and exploit for several centuries to come. The essential changes had already occurred by 1485; they had hardly begun in 1300. In the reign of Edward I a dozen earls, the dwindling survivors of a seemingly obsolescent baronage, shared their nobility with an undifferentiated mass of some three thousand landowners, each of whose holdings were said to be worth £20 a year or over. By the beginning of the sixteenth century a small and graded upper

class of 'lords' numbering between fifty and sixty had emerged
in possession of rank and privileges which marked them off
from lesser men. The interval had been occupied by the gradual
processes of exclusion, definition, and stratification.[1]

In fact, as McFarlane pointed out elsewhere, the processes were
largely complete by 1400.[2] It is to the fourteenth century, therefore,
that we must look for an explanation of this development.

McFarlane's criterion for 'nobility' in the fourteenth and fifteenth
centuries was a simple one: if a man was summoned to parliament,
he was noble. Thus the parliamentary peerage was the nobility, and
anyone who was not summoned to parliament was not noble. By the
late fourteenth century, therefore, perhaps even earlier, an individual summons to parliament had come to assume in certain
respects the same significance, at a lower level, as the bestowal of an
earldom – in other words, it was a conscious, and often politically
inspired, act of promotion. And what McFarlane noted – and it is
undeniable – is that gradually during the course of the fourteenth
century the lists of men summoned to parliament developed their
own internal consistency, so that by 1400 it was unusual for a man to
be summoned unless his ancestor(s) had been summoned, and it was
equally likely that, should he leave an heir, that heir would be
summoned. In other words, the right to a parliamentary summons –
and hence the right to be considered 'noble' – was becoming both
increasingly hereditary and increasingly restricted.

The increasing exclusivity, and hence the more rigid definition, of
the fourteenth-century nobility is surely indisputable, but it is by no
means clear that the 3,000 or so twenty-librate landholders of
thirteenth-century England were quite as 'undifferentiated' as
McFarlane suggested. The problem lies with the sources. Parliaments, so called, did not start meeting until close to the middle of the
thirteenth century, and it is not until the 1290s that we begin to get
reliable and fairly continuous lists of those who were summoned to
them.[3] Now it may be that the development of parliament itself was
one of the most important factors contributing to the emergence of
the English peerage; in other words, that as parliament developed
from an occasion into an institution, this necessitated the standardisation of lists of summonses, and that inevitably, given time,
inclusion on or exclusion from the list would come to be regarded as

determining a landholder's status. But it is worth remembering that what McFarlane was really trying to understand was *not* a legal definition of nobility, but contemporary perception of social status, even though statistically his argument is based on the closest thing we have to a legal definition of nobility in late medieval England – that is, the right to a parliamentary summons.

In fact, as already seen, while there may not be any *simple* criterion for defining nobility in thirteenth-century England, there are nevertheless significant indicators, and these indicators point to the likelihood that there was in reality an upper stratum to the thirteenth-century landholding class, numbering about 200 at any one time, and corresponding roughly to what contemporaries referred to as the 'greater baronage'.[4] This is not to deny McFarlane's view that this group became more exclusive during the fourteenth century. The 'baronage' of the thirteenth century was undoubtedly more fluid than the 'peerage' of the fifteenth century; there is no doubt that it depended less on heredity, that men therefore found it easier both to enter and to drop out, and that some time towards the end of the fourteenth century the barriers more or less came down and left those in possession at the time with both status and privileges to which new men would in future find it much more difficult to aspire. What it does suggest, however, is that the real change which occurred during the fourteenth century was one of legal and social definition rather than of contemporary social perception (though naturally any such definition helped to sharpen social perception). In other words, social distinctions which had in practice been a part of the English scene for a long time became more rigidly defined, more blatantly advertised, and more jealously guarded. There is certainly much evidence to substantiate the view that the later fourteenth- and fifteenth-century peerage was more aware of its exclusivity than had been the case in the thirteenth century. Peers claimed the right, for example, in certain specified matters, to be tried and judged by their own peers in parliament, a right which was even enshrined in statute form in 1341.[5] The development of ranks within the peerage, the popularity of books of courtesy (which, *inter alia*, clarified rules of social precedence), and the blatant social overtones of, for example, the livery laws, or sumptuary legislation, all point to the fact that status was becoming ever more defined.[6] Yet the extent to which all this reflected a real change in the structure of society, as opposed to attempts to define that structure more closely, is open to doubt.

This argument is supported by the careful analysis of the parliamentary lists of summonses undertaken by J.E. Powell and K. Wallis,[7] for, as they demonstrate clearly, the process by which the list became more or less standardised during the fourteenth century was a gradual one, with tendencies towards standardisation already apparent early in the fourteenth century, but only really hardening into consistency during the last quarter of the century. To summarise their evidence, there were a number of changes in the lists between 1309 and 1314, but then from 1314 to 1321 the list was 'absolutely standard until 1321, altered only for deaths and successions'. In 1321–2 there was another series of changes, after which the 1322 list was used for all four parliaments between 1322 and 1325. For the January 1327 parliament – the first following Edward II's deposition – a very different list was drawn up, which was then used as the basis for all the parliaments of the next four years. The same pattern is observable throughout Edward III's reign: the years 1332–6, 1341–8, 1351–68, and 1372–7 were ones during which more or less the same list (allowing, of course, for deaths and successions) was used from parliament to parliament, while in 1331–2, 1336–41, 1348–51, and 1371 a number of additions or deletions were made. The first parliament of Richard II's reign, that of October 1377, also saw a number of additions, but during the next eleven years, according to Powell and Wallis, 'apart from the strange and unique patent to John Beauchamp of Holt, only four men were summoned to parliament without holding the estates of persons who featured in the lists in or before the first half of the fourteenth century. . . . After [Philip] Despenser [first summoned in 1388], no "new man" was summoned for a space of nearly forty years.'[8] Thus the ultimate standardisation of the list was the culmination of a process by which, over the course of a hundred years, a number of different lists had achieved a sort of temporary permanence, making it increasingly likely that in the end a more lasting stability would ensue.

One should not therefore overexaggerate the fluidity of the early fourteenth-century lists of summonses. Extensive changes in the list were usually made only in the wake of major political upheavals (Bannockburn, the Despenser war of 1321–2, Edward II's deposition, the overthrow of Mortimer, and so on). The stability of the intervening periods suggests that even at this time there was a fairly clear idea as to which families constituted the upper stratum of the nobility – though naturally it was always within the king's power to promote new men. On what grounds, then, were men included on or excluded from the list? It is here that Powell and Wallis disagree fundamentally with McFarlane. It is immediately apparent that the criteria by which Powell and Wallis judge a man to have been 'new' are quite different from those by which McFarlane did so. Between 1388 and 1425, according to Powell and Wallis, no new men were summoned to parliament; between 1400 and 1424, according to McFarlane, there were eleven 'new creations'.[9] The difference is explained by the different rules adopted by the authors to define extinction and recruitment. McFarlane regarded extinction as having taken place

> when the head of a family died either (i) leaving no known heirs – this was very rare – or (ii) leaving, according to the common law rules of inheritance for fee simple, only a female heir or heirs, or a male heir or heirs whose claim came through a woman. That is to say extinction is held to have taken place at the point at which, according to modern peerage law, a peerage held in fee simple becomes extinct, passes to a woman or to an heir whose claim comes through a woman, or falls into abeyance between female coheirs or their descendants.[10]

Although simple-sounding, these rules could lead in practice to what can only be regarded as 'theoretical' rather than 'real' extinctions. For example, McFarlane treated the earldom of Warwick as having become extinct in 1369. The position was as shown in Table 2.

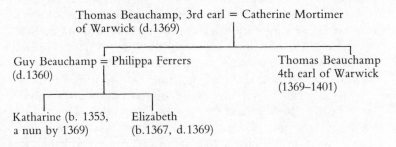

Table 2 *The earldom of Warwick, 1369*

Although the earldom and lands passed from father to son in 1369, the existence of the third earl's two grand-daughters, who could have been considered as his heirs general at his death, meant that by modern peerage law the title technically became extinct in 1369 and was created anew for the fourth earl.[11] In practice, however, it is quite clear that the younger Thomas was simply treated as his father's heir, and to think of his summons to parliament from 1369 onwards as a 'new creation' in no way reflects contemporary thinking.[12]

Thus although it is understandable why McFarlane adopted modern peerage law for his tables on extinction and recruitment to the nobility, there is no doubt that they exaggerate both sets of figures beyond what contemporaries would have thought of as realistic. At the same time, however, Powell and Wallis go to the opposite extreme. Their definition of a 'new man' is implicit in the comment quoted above, that between 1377 and 1388, excepting Beauchamp of Holt, 'only four men were summoned to parliament without holding the estates of persons who featured in the lists in or before the first half of the fourteenth century'. Indeed, it is one of the crucial points of their argument that, from quite early in the fourteenth century, ' "precedent" and "the record" were combining with the shadowy notion of "barony" to produce a limited number of estates whose possessors . . . would be "the baronage in parliament", or "the peers of the realm" ', and by the 1390s they considered this method of 'recruitment' to be almost exclusive.[13] In other words, one of the principal criteria by which a man's eligibility for selection was judged was tenure by barony.

McFarlane considered that attempts to associate selection for the peerage with tenure by barony had 'bedevilled the study of origins'. 'Landed wealth,' he declared, 'however acquired and of whomsoever held, and a capacity to serve provided the main grounds for selection.'[14] The careful researches of Powell and Wallis have surely provided a partial corrective to this assertion, though even in some of those cases which they cite in which new recruitment can be shown fairly conclusively to have followed from the acquisition of lands held by barony (and there are certainly a good number of them), it is not always clear whether the crucial point was that the man in question was now a 'tenurial baron', or simply that he was now a major landholder. There is, however, a further important element in their argument, namely the distinction drawn between the 'barons' of parliament, and the 'bannerets' of parliament. While emphasising the importance attached to tenure by barony, at no point do they deny that the king always had the right to promote to the peerage those who were not tenurial barons: those, for example, who had served him well, or who had acquired sufficient landed wealth held in some other way. Rather, their argument was that a distinction (though not an absolute one) was drawn between different types of recruits. Those who were promoted because of their acquisition of lands held by barony were the 'barons' of parliament, those recruited for some other reason were the 'bannerets' – and they were regarded as slightly inferior to the barons. The term 'banneret' was initially used to designate military rank,[15] but it was not long before it began to acquire social overtones as well, with the status implied falling somewhere between full baronial rank (indicating membership of the peerage) and knightly rank. The factor which served to bring the demarcation lines between the bannerets and, on the one hand, the knights below them, and, on the other hand, the barons above them, more sharply into focus was the number of bannerets summoned to parliament by that martial king *par excellence*, Edward III. For example, all four of the new men summoned to the parliament of January 1348 – Reginald Cobham of Sterborough, Thomas Bradeston, Thomas Dagworth, and Walter Manny – were summoned because they were soldiers who had distinguished themselves in the campaigns of 1345–7, rather than because of any estates which they had inherited, and all were styled bannerets.[16] Naturally, the older-established baronial families feared that their dignity might be diluted by the addition of too many new, and not so well-landed, men – hence the distinction between the two groups.

By the 1370s, there is fairly clear evidence that the bannerets were seen as a distinct group within the peerage.[17] Their position, however, remained equivocal. In 1383 it was specifically stated that Thomas Camoys, who had been elected as knight of the shire for Surrey in the October parliament, could not take his seat because he was 'a banneret as were most of his ancestors', and 'bannerets used not to be elected knights of the shire'.[18] To prove the point, Richard II (who regarded Camoys as a supporter) promptly summoned him as a lord instead, and he continued to be summoned for the rest of his life, even though his father had never been summoned.[19] In fact those who opposed Camoys's election as a knight of the shire in 1383 were making a complex situation sound deceptively simple, for even if *some* bannerets were by now being regularly summoned, there was certainly no established right to be summoned on the part of the group as a whole. Richard II's great wardrobe account for the years 1385–7, for example, lists ten bannerets attached to the royal court, of whom three were never summoned to parliament, and a further three were not summoned until several years later, by which time they had either inherited much greater estates or been promoted to earldoms.[20] Thus while they were assured of their rank on the battlefield, bannerets could not feel sure of converting that rank into durable evidence of status at home unless the king chose to promote them. Not surprisingly, it was at this bottom end of the peerage scale that the king had the most latitude in the matter of promotions to the peerage, but as with most promotions there were disadvantages as well as advantages involved. Those who had little land had to be provided with some, as for example with Reginald Cobham of Sterborough, to whom Edward III granted 400 marks (£266) a year in 1335, 'for his better maintenance in the estate of banneret . . . until the king provide for him four hundred marks yearly in land and rent for life'.[21] The main advantage of promoting men was naturally that the king was thereby encouraging loyal service to himself, though it may also have been in the back of his mind that the addition of more of his supporters to the ranks of the peerage might strengthen his position in negotiating with the commons over matters such as taxation. By the 1390s, however, some of the king's latitude even at this level seems to have been dissipating. The comment by Powell and Wallis that after 1388 no 'new men' were summoned for nearly forty years means essentially that during this period no new bannerets were summoned. Yet what this also meant was that for those who had already made the leap upwards by this date, the signs were good. As their heirs succeeded them, and as their summonses hardened into custom, so gradually the distinction between barons and bannerets evaporated. By about 1425, they were all just 'peers'.[22]

In summary, recruitment to the peerage in the fourteenth century was almost invariably for one of two reasons: either because the man in question had (whether by marriage, or by collateral inheritance) recently become the holder of all or a substantial portion of the lands of a man who had formerly been summoned (and if the lands were held by barony there was an even more compelling reason to summon him), or because the king was exercising his right to promote a loyal servant or prominent political supporter. Those men who were summoned for the first reason joined the older-established barons of parliament, while the latter group were the bannerets of parliament. By the second quarter of the fifteenth century the distinction between the two groups had become virtually meaningless, but in the 1380s it was still very much alive. This is why Richard II's elevation of his household steward, John Beauchamp of Holt, to a 'barony by patent' in 1387 was so perverse. It was the first time that the status of *baron*, rather than banneret, was treated as something which did not arise from the holding of lands by barony.[23] And when, in the Merciless Parliament of the following year, Beauchamp was convicted of treason and executed without being allowed his right to a trial by his peers, the king's opponents were demonstrating not only their dislike of Beauchamp, but also their disapproval of Richard's novel methods of peerage creation.

In part, it was this growing status-consciousness which accounted for the increasingly hereditary and restricted peerage of the later fourteenth and fifteenth centuries. From about the middle of the fourteenth century, it becomes increasingly obvious that a new summons to parliament is coming to be regarded as a deliberate, and often politically inspired, act of promotion, and it was from this time, as McFarlane has shown, that recruitments ceased to keep pace with extinctions.[24] Yet this was not the only factor involved in the emergence of a distinctive peerage at this time. As already noted, the formalisation of parliament, leading to the standardisation of lists of summonses, also played its part. The fact that the fourteenth century saw prolonged periods of warfare, in which the fighting was done by contract armies within which there was an established system of ranks and wage-rates, also helped. In the case of the bannerets, for example, it is clear that something of this more rigid ordering of military ranks carried over into more general social distinctions. And finally, legal and economic changes played their part. By employing the newly-popular devices of the entail and the enfeoff-ment to use, many landholders now had a greater chance of keeping their estates intact *post mortem*, thus reducing the number of estates which were fragmented for lack of male heirs and helping families which had got to the top to stay there.[25] Equally, economic circumstances in post-Black Death England do not seem to have greatly reduced the landed incomes of the greater landholders, but may have had a more severe effect on the lesser ones – the knights and esquires – and this was possibly a situation from which those such as peers could benefit. By buying up the estates of lesser men who had fallen on hard times, or simply by continuing to prosper as others fell away, they were in a position to buttress their hard-won social superiority with a more tangible economic superiority as well, and thus to open up a wider gulf between themselves and the gentry.[26]

Yet however 'closed' one considers the late fourteenth-century English peerage to have been, it was nevertheless, in terms both of individuals and of families, constantly changing. The definition of a 'new man' adopted by Powell and Wallis, which is based on ownership of a specified group of estates rather than the rise or fall of the families which held them, is of little relevance here. McFarlane, who concerned himself with families, calculated the extinction rate among peerage families to average 27 per cent during each twenty-five-year period of the fourteenth and fifteenth centuries, and while his adoption of modern peerage law undoubtedly exaggerated his figures by including 'theoretical' extinctions,[27] his conclusions concerning the *reasons* for extinction are surely indisputable. Forfeiture and bankruptcy played a relatively small part in thinning the ranks of the peerage; the great majority of extinctions occurred simply for lack of male heirs. And in this context it is worth noting that while nearly 300 families were summoned to parliament at one time or another during the fourteenth century, only about thirty of them continued to be summoned from the beginning of the century to its end. Naturally, they included some of the greatest families in the land. Three of them, the Beauchamps, Fitzalans, and de Veres, both entered and left the century as earls, while another nine were granted earldoms at some point during the century.[28] Of the remainder, the greatest never to receive an earldom were probably the Berkeleys of Berkeley, the Rooses of Helmsley, the Cliffords of Skipton-in-Craven and Westmorland, the la Zouches of Harringworth, the Greys of Codnor, and the le Stranges of Knockyn. The greatest of the 'new' families thrown up by the fourteenth century (apart from those who received earldoms or better, such as the Beauforts, de la Poles, and Hollands), were probably the Scropes of Bolton, the Greys of Ruthin and Bedfordshire, the Beauchamps of Abergavenny, the Beaumonts of Beaumanoir, and the Cromwells of Tattershall.

Meanwhile, of course, many of the great families of thirteenth-century England died out. Apart from those who had held earldoms, such as the Bohuns, the Bigods, the Lacys, and the Warennes, the most notable losses in the fourteenth century were the Wakes of Liddell, the Bassetts of Drayton, the Latimers of Corby and Danby, and the Mohuns of Dunster. Yet although it is for obvious reasons tempting, it would be unwise to concentrate too much on families at the expense of individuals. There are numerous examples of men who, despite not coming from peerage families, and despite their failure to leave sons to follow them into parliament, nevertheless while they lived carried far greater influence in the affairs of the kingdom than a dozen of their contemporaries from longer-lasting families put together. Among such in the fourteenth century were Oliver Ingham, who was summoned to only one parliament, that of 1328; Walter Manny and Reginald Cobham of Sterborough (both summoned from 1348 to 1371); Guy Brian (summoned 1351–90), and Roger Beauchamp of Bletsoe (summoned 1363–80). Men like these, who usually fell into the 'banneret' rather than the 'baron' category of the peerage, were probably, to contemporaries, the most significant creations of the kings they served.

By the late fourteenth century, therefore, the English parliamentary peerage was clearly a class apart, a group of about seventy families marked off from their lesser fellows to a greater extent, legally, socially, politically and economically, than they had been a hundred years earlier. As a group, they enjoyed two specific privileges denied to lesser landholders – the right to trial by their own peers in certain cases, and the right to receive individual summonses to parliament. Regular attendance in parliament also gave the group a certain political coherence, a working knowledge of the affairs of the kingdom, a sense of involvement in political decision-making, which in some cases was enhanced by membership of the privy council.[29] This frequent and direct access to the monarch also set them apart from most of the gentry, as did the extent of their landed wealth. 'Averages' for the landed wealth of the peerage can be computed for the early fifteenth century (in 1436, for example, the average for the sixty peerage families assessed for income tax was £768 excluding annuities),[30] but ranges of wealth are probably a more useful guide. The Black Prince and John of Gaunt, the two greatest magnates of late fourteenth-century England, enjoyed landed revenues of about £10,000 gross and £12,000 gross respectively.[31] For an earl, the minimum was £1,000, but most of them enjoyed at least double this; £4,000 or more, however, definitely made one a rich earl. For lesser peers, about £250 *per annum* was probably the minimum compatible with parliamentary status,[32] but most of them (by 1436, at any rate) were in receipt of between £300 and £1,300.[33] It is doubtful, however, whether any of them reached the £2,000 mark. To hold land worth £2,000 a year and not to be an earl would probably have seemed rather strange.

The economic gulf between the peerage and the gentry has been clearly established by T.B. Pugh's analysis of the 1436 income returns.[34] Recent studies of regional landholding groups have tended to confirm his findings, and indeed to amplify them with reference to the judicial and financial rights exercised by the peers. Since these rights were granted individually there are no hard and fast rules, but it does seem clear that there were certain rights which were *normally* granted only to peers. These included the right to license markets and fairs in local towns, rights of free warren in their demesne lands, private hundreds, licences to impark their lands, and honorial courts with view of frankpledge.[35] Although there were exceptions to all these rules, it is probably realistic to draw a distinction not only between the *extent* of the lordship exercised by the peers as compared with the gentry, but also between the *kind* of lordship which the two groups exercised. But the extent of their lordship also set them apart: while every peer had his *caput honoris*, most of them held lands in a number of different areas, which meant that their interests might be less localised than those of the gentry. The geographical diversity of many of the peers' estates was partly due to their marital habits. Since they frequently married within their own social group, and were thus often selecting marriage partners from within a numerically small but geographically widespread group, the territorial acquisitions which resulted from these marriages were also frequently geographically widespread. The more localised marriage patterns of the gentry naturally produced more localised territorial holdings.

In conclusion, some of the characteristics of the fourteenth-century peerage can perhaps be appreciated best by looking in more detail at one particular family. The Mauleys, lords of Mulgrave in Cleveland, were among that small group of families who were summoned to parliament continuously through the fourteenth century, from 1295 until 1414 to be precise. But although they had been tenurial barons since the reign of King John, they never rose above the middling ranks of the peerage. From the outset, their lands were concentrated in three well-defined areas, all in Yorkshire (see Map 1). Around the *caput honoris*, Mulgrave castle, close to Whitby on the Yorkshire coast, was a compact group of at least seven manors and a number of other properties comprising the ancient barony of Mulgrave. In south Yorkshire, the Mauleys held half of the ancient barony of Doncaster, including the town and a number of lesser properties such as Rossington. In the East Riding, mainly in the area to the north of Beverley, lay another group of about nine manors, including Atwick, Lockington, and their favoured manorhouse of Berg-by-Watton. There were also some outlying properties in Swaledale, and at Skinthorpe and Bramham in central Yorkshire. In 1254, Peter, second Lord Mauley, was granted free warren in all his demesne lands, and the right to hold a weekly market and annual fair at his town of Lythe, near Mulgrave – and naturally these rights descended to his successors. They also held various boroughs (such as Doncaster) from which substantial rents and other profits were derived.[36]

The heavy concentration of their lands in Yorkshire meant that the successive Lords Mauley were primarily involved in local affairs within the county, and much of their political and social activity reflects this. From the reign of King John until the extinction of the family in 1414 there were seven Lords Mauley, each one called Peter. They served regularly as commissioners (of array, of oyer and terminer, and so forth) in Yorkshire. Peter, sixth Lord Mauley, was a justice of the peace in the county from 1375 until his death in 1383. The religious houses which they patronised were all Yorkshire ones – St John's at Bridlington, the Friars Minor at Doncaster, and Meaux priory in Holderness. Their marriages were mostly to the daughters or sisters of other Yorkshire peers: Peter III (d. 1309) married the sister of the Yorkshire and Lincolnshire baron Gilbert, Lord Gant; Peter IV (d. 1348) married the daughter of Thomas, Lord Furnivall;

Peter V (d. 1355) married the daughter of Robert, Lord Clifford; Peter VI (d. 1383) married Constanza, daughter of Sir Thomas Sutton of Bransholme castle and Sutton-in-Holderness,[37] and Peter VII (d. 1414) married Maud, daughter of Ralph Nevill, first earl of Westmorland.[38] Many of these marriages brought additional lands to the family, and the wealth of the Mauleys grew accordingly. According to an inquisition taken at the death of Peter II in 1279, all his lands were valued at £321 (though inquisitions *post mortem* are always liable to undervalue lands). By 1414, they were worth about £800 – putting them right in the middle range of the peerage.[39]

But if the concentration of their estates encouraged the Mauleys to involve themselves in Yorkshire affairs, their eminence as lords of parliament thrust more national responsibilities upon them. All of them fought regularly in English armies, primarily on the Scottish border but also in France and Wales. Peter V was at Neville's Cross in 1346. Peter VI was at Poitiers in 1356, and was joint guardian of the Scottish March in 1367 and keeper of the vital border town of Berwick in 1368. Peter IV was apparently an accomplice to the murder of Piers Gaveston in 1312 and an adherent of Thomas, earl of Lancaster, in the years leading up to Boroughbridge – though he seems to have deserted him before the battle. His uncle Edmund, however, a younger son of Peter II, was an associate of Gaveston's and steward of the royal household at the time of Gaveston's death. Peter VII supported Bolingbroke during the invasion of 1399 and was knighted by the new king on the eve of his coronation. Indeed, it was probably from involvement in politics at the highest level that the greatness of the fourteenth-century Mauleys stemmed, for Peter I was originally a humble Poitevin esquire who became intimate with King John, and his marriage to the heiress to the barony of Mulgrave (in 1214) was said to have been the king's reward to him for Peter's part in the murder of John's nephew, Arthur of Brittany. For exactly two centuries, his successors flourished, built upon his legacy to them, and, above all, survived. As with the great majority of their fellow peers, what brought the Mauleys to extinction in 1414 was a simple failure of male heirs.

CHAPTER 3

The gentry

According to T.B. Pugh, the 'gentry' of fifteenth-century England comprised 'all the landowners between the baronage and the yeomanry', whose number 'has been variously estimated at between 6,000 and 9,000 families'.[1] Estimates for later centuries, based naturally on more abundant sources, are rather more precise. In the early eighteenth century, for example, there seem to have been three reasonably clearly defined groups within the English gentry. Firstly, the 'greater gentry', consisting of about 1,000 families each with an income in excess of £1,000 *per annum*, holding between them about 15 per cent of the land of England; secondly, the 'lesser gentry' of about 2,000 families, with incomes ranging between £250 and £1,000, holding in total about 12½ per cent of England; and thirdly, the 'country gentlemen', with incomes around the £250 mark, numbering about 10,000 families, and holding about a quarter of England.[2] By this time, therefore, the whole 'gentry class' included about 13,000 families and held roughly half of the land in England. Comparable 'national' sources are simply not available for the fourteenth century. Any attempt to work out a similar set of figures must be based on a number of separate regional studies, and inevitably therefore they remain somewhat tentative. Nevertheless, regional studies are now beginning to point to the existence of quite clearly defined strata within the fourteenth- and fifteenth-century gentry.

To begin with, there are unmistakable signs of growing status- and rank-consciousness among the fourteenth-century gentry. Around 1300, it is possible to distinguish two 'ranks' within the lesser landholding class: the knights of whom there were about 1,250–1,500, and the esquires. For military purposes, an esquire (designated variously as *vallettus, armiger, scutifer,* or *serviens ad arma*) was paid at half the rate of a knight. In social terms, however, the distinction was much less clear-cut. N. Denholm-Young reckoned that in addition to the knights there were about another 1,500 esquires who were of roughly equivalent wealth and status to the knights but who for various reasons had not assumed knighthood, and that between them they made up a reasonably homogeneous 'knightly class' of around 3,000 families, coming below the baronage but set apart from the rest of the English landholding class.[3] By the end of the fourteenth century, these two ranks had become three. English landholders below the peerage now styled themselves as knights, esquires, or gentlemen, in that order. The use of the term 'gentleman' is attested as early as 1384, when Richard II granted to one of his servants a pension of 7½d. a day 'to enable him to support the estate of a gentleman to which the king has advanced him', though not until the early fifteenth century does the term seem to have come into widespread usage.[4]

For certain purposes, the three groups were quite clearly distinguished. At the beginning of the fourteenth century, for example, knights were allowed coats of arms, but esquires were not. From about 1350, coats of arms were allowed to esquires, but it was another hundred years or so before they were allowed to gentlemen. By 1500, there were said to be 60 peers, 500 knights, 800 esquires, and 5,000 gentlemen entitled to coats of arms.[5] Equally, when they went to battle, the knight received better wages than the esquire, and the esquire received more than the gentleman. As a general rule, too, the three groups enjoyed different levels of wealth.[6] Yet despite these apparently clear differences between the three groups, historians who have tried to make meaningful social distinctions within the gentry as a whole have tended to revert to the idea of a two- rather than a three-rank division. The difficulty comes with trying to view the esquires as a homogeneous group. Some of them are not realistically distinguishable from the gentlemen, while others seem to be of much the same status as the knights. For the Cheshire and Lancashire region around 1400, for example, M.J. Bennett calculated that there were about 600 families of gentleman status or higher, within which there was an elite group of about 100 families composed partly of knights and partly of esquires. N.E. Saul estimated that the real 'gentry' of Gloucestershire 'numbered about fifty families' in the mid-fourteenth century, of whom about thirty were knights (though by 1400 the number of knights within this group had fallen to about fifteen), and P. W. Fleming reckoned that the 'county gentry' of fifteenth-century Kent consisted of about 100 families, 'mainly knights or esquires'. For fourteenth-century Leicestershire, fifteenth-century Warwickshire, and fifteenth-century Derbyshire, studies by G. G. Astill, C. Carpenter, and S. M. Wright respectively have revealed the existence of a 'greater gentry' stratum varying between about fifty and seventy families in each county, comprising both knights and esquires, but clearly marked off from the 'lesser gentry' in each case both by their greater wealth and by their more active role in local politics and administration.[7]

The income tax returns of 1436 point in a similar direction. H. L. Gray's detailed analysis of them revealed the existence of about 950 'knights' (excluding the peerage) with incomes ranging between £40 and £200 (though this included a very small number – ten or less – with incomes substantially in excess of £200), and a further 1,200 or so 'esquires' enjoying incomes between £20 and £40. In addition, there were about 5,000 lesser landholders, some of whom were esquires, but most of whom were 'gentlemen' or merchants, with incomes varying between £5 and £20 *per annum*.[8] It is possible that these different levels of landed wealth correspond to a three-fold social stratification of the gentry similar to that proposed for the early eighteenth century (see above), but the evidence of those regional studies which have been undertaken suggests that it would probably be more correct to consider the two upper groups as in reality forming one reasonably homogeneous stratum within the gentry. In other words, the steady decline in the number of knights (which continued through the fourteenth and fifteenth centuries) led to a corresponding rise in the status of the esquires (or 'potential knights'), so that little distinction was drawn between them in social terms. Most counties seem to have contained between fifty and seventy 'county gentry' families, so that in over-all terms it is probably right to think of the county gentry of England as consisting of between 2,300 and 2,500 families, or about 0.1 per cent of the country's post-plague population.[9]

Below the county gentry came the lesser landholding class, aptly termed by Fleming the 'parish gentry',[10] composed of the poorer esquires, the gentlemen, the lawyers and merchants who had invested in land and acquired 'country seats', and some of the richer yeomen. The size of this group is more difficult to estimate, for there is no very obvious place to draw the line at the bottom end of the scale. It is quite possible that many of those who described themselves as 'gentlemen' in the fifteenth century were not landed at all, but in the service of their betters, or possibly even in trade,[11] but it is by no means clear that contemporaries therefore perceived them as socially inferior to, for example, the merchant who had acquired land to the value of £10 or £15 *per annum*. Gentle birth was every bit as important as a landed income. Gray's figure of 5,000 landholders with incomes of between £5 and £20 provides a starting-point, but Bennett's estimate of 600 gentry families in Cheshire and Lancashire south of the Ribble, in a ratio of 1:5 between 'county' and 'parish' gentry, points to a figure closer to 10,000. As Bennett points out, however, the Lancashire–Chesire area was one in which an abnormally high proportion of the land seems to have been in the hands of the gentry (about 75 per cent with only 25 per cent held by the crown, the peerage, and the church), and it may have been untypical.[12] Wright calculated that the Derbyshire gentry numbered 213, of whom fifty-two were county gentry. In Kent, according to Fleming, the parish gentry 'accounted for over two thirds of the total number of gentry' resident in the county. In Gloucestershire, a commission of 1344 reported that there were 177 landholders in the county with landed incomes of £5 or more *per annum*, including nine peers and the fifty or so members of the county gentry, but this was almost certainly an underestimate since, among other reasons, the commissioners only listed those who had £5 worth of land within the county and there must have been a number of £5 landholders whose estates straddled county boundaries.[13] In general, it seems that the ratio of county to parish gentry varied from one part of the country to another, but that a figure of about 3:1 was probably more common than 5:1. While this presupposes a rather larger number of landholders in the £5 to £20 bracket than the 5,000 counted by Gray in 1436, allowance must obviously be made in any taxation return for evasion and underassessment – especially at the lower end of the scale where men were better able to hide behind their relative obscurity. In summary, it is probably right to think of the 'gentry' of fourteenth-century England as numbering somewhere in the region of 9,000 to 10,000 families in all, of whom about a quarter formed the upper stratum of the county gentry, and the rest were the parish gentry.

What then were the distinguishing characteristics of these two groups? It is the contention of many of those historians who have studied regional gentry societies not only that there was a real gulf between the county and parish gentry in economic and social terms, but also that this gulf has crucial implications for our understanding of the workings of local politics and administration. In other words, it was the county gentry who formed the real 'political community' of the shire. There was, for example, a clear hierarchy in local office-holding. By the second half of the fourteenth century, sheriffs and members of parliament were almost invariably chosen from the county gentry, as were the justices of the peace as, increasingly, their powers developed. The escheatorship seems to have fallen between the two groups, but below this were a number of lesser offices, such as coroner, tax-collector, and juror, which were nearly always held by members of the parish gentry.[14] Such distinctions had not always been so clear: during the thirteenth century it was far from uncommon for quite lowly members of the gentry to act as sheriffs, either on their own account or as deputies for courtiers or magnates.[15] Not surprisingly, the greater local weight which the county gentry carried by the fourteenth and fifteenth centuries is also reflected in their political attachments. C.D. Ross, for example, found that while the greater members of the early fifteenth-century Yorkshire gentry (especially those who were heads of families) usually found service either with the king or with the great local lords such as the earls of Northumberland and Westmorland, younger sons and members of lesser gentry families tended to be attached to the lesser barons. The same seems to have been true of the Bedfordshire and Warwickshire gentry.[16]

In their social and business dealings too, the cleavage seems to have been a clear one. County gentry families tended to marry each other, to conduct their legal and familial transactions with each other, to use each other as witnesses, feoffees, and guarantors. The parish gentry, meanwhile, moved within their own social and business circles.[17] Naturally, kinship ties sometimes cut across these distinctions, but they did not to any meaningful extent undermine the hegemony enjoyed by the county gentry in local political society.[18] The distinction between the two groups also extended to, indeed was underpinned by, economic wealth and patterns of land-holding. The county gentry not only held substantially more land, but they often held land throughout their counties and in other counties as well. Some of them (though a minority) held franchises such as free warren, or occasionally fairs and markets or view of frankpledge. The landed interests of the parish gentry were much more localised, and they virtually never held franchises.[19] In their attitudes and aspirations, it may be that we can also detect significant differences of outlook between the two groups. One of the most important factors contributing to the local dominence of the county gentry was tradition. On the whole, it was the families who had been established in the shire longest who tended to belong to the county gentry. In part, of course (as with the peerage) this was simply a question of the survival of the fittest (and thus the fitness of the survivors), but naturally the county gentry were aware that keeping their estates intact was a way of preserving that dominance, and it is interesting that among the Derbyshire gentry of the fifteenth century, S.M. Wright found that the knights and esquires generally tried to keep their estates intact, while lesser landholders were more likely to adopt some form of partibility. Among the knights of thirteenth- and fourteenth-century Bedfordshire, there was also apparently a 'marked attitude of tenacity towards what they regarded as the patrimony'.[20] Differences of outlook even extended to religious observance and almsgiving. Among the gentry of fifteenth-century Kent, for example, there were 'significant differences' of approach in these matters, with county gentry more likely to hear mass in their private chapels, or to leave bequests to religious houses, and parish gentry more likely to leave bequests for the repair of local roads and bridges, or the upkeep of the parish church – hence reinforcing their links with those parishes by which their horizons were to a large extent bounded.[21]

It seems clear, then, that economic, social and political status went hand in hand: that it was the county gentry – the knights and the richer esquires – who formed the real political communities of their shires. This begs another important question, however. Most of those historians who have undertaken regional studies of the gentry have based their research on the study of one particular county. There are good reasons for this, for the county was a fundamental administrative unit in medieval England. But does this mean that it was also a meaningful political unit? On this question, recent opinion has been much more divided. Moreover, it is not a question which can be considered in relation to the gentry alone, for in some cases it has been argued that the county was also in effect the 'sphere of influence' of a great magnate. M. Cherry, for example, in his study of Devonshire politics and the earl of Devon's affinity in the later fourteenth century, has argued that it was the influence of the earl which welded the county into a 'single lineage' system, and 'dominated the political life of Devonshire to an extraordinary degree', giving direction to the aspirations of the gentry, forming the 'political pivot of the region', and representing 'the single most powerful force there with which governments had no alternative but to deal'.[22] What Cherry is describing is nothing less than a territorial power-block, based partly on a widespread network of estates (see Map 2), and partly on a classic noble affinity which encompassed, in effect, a 'working majority' of the political community of the shire.

Cherry was clearly convinced that in Devonshire the shire was indeed a meaningful political unit, and the same argument has recently been advanced for late fourteenth-century Cheshire. The comparison is instructive, however, for according to Bennett the Cheshire political community was of a rather different nature from that of Devon.[23] 'It was the county', he argues, 'not a particular local magnate, which provided the fundamental source of cohesion,' and, more specifically, he points to three factors which provided the community's cement: marriage and kinship ties, communal involvement in local politics through office-holding, and a common consciousness of 'gentle' status as exemplified by landholding. It seems, then, as if Cheshire and Devon were two very different types of political society. But were they really that different? In fact, much of Bennett's study is devoted to a discussion of the obviously very considerable effect which the patronage of, firstly, Richard II (as both king and earl of Chester), and, secondly, Henry IV and Henry V (as kings and dukes of Lancaster), had on the gentry of the region, and much of the evidence which he cites points surely to the conclusion that each of these kings provided a marked sense of direction to local politics. P.H.W. Booth's study of the Black Prince's administration (as earl of Chester) in the mid-fourteenth century has also made abundantly clear the extent of his power within the county, particularly in relation to financial exploitation. The fifteenth century, moreover, saw the rapid rise to prominence in this area of the Stanleys of Lathom who, according to Bennett, capitalised on the desire for 'good lordship' which had been stimulated by the crown in the late fourteenth and early fifteenth centuries and succeeded in welding the region into a 'single patronage system', revolving around their own pre-eminence, political connections, and ability to act as brokers of royal patronage for the local gentry.[24]

It may equally be wondered whether the hegemony enjoyed by the Courtenay earls was quite as pervasive as has been suggested. For example, Cherry cites numerous examples of members of the earl of Devon's affinity – largely composed of the county's gentry – marrying into each other's families, collaborating on landed and other business transactions, sitting on commissions together, and so forth.[25] But should such evidence necessarily be regarded as symptomatic of the omnipresent power of the affinity, and hence of the guiding hand of the Courtenays, or might it just as easily be a manifestation of that 'natural' community of the gentry which Bennett considered to be the keynote of north-western society? There was nevertheless one major difference between the two counties: the earls of Devon were normally resident in their county, and thus on hand to give a personal lead to local politics. Until the rise of the Stanleys in the fifteenth century, the greatest lords in the north-west (the earls of Chester and the dukes of Lancaster) were to a great extent absentee landlords. This must certainly have had some effect on local political society, but even so it is worth asking whether, while the presence of a great magnate could have a profound effect on the *form* of political relationships among the gentry of his 'country', he would necessarily modify to any great extent the *reality* of those relationships.

To a certain extent, it seems that both types of local society are discernible in fifteenth-century Warwickshire. While the gentry formed their own groups, based, according to C. Carpenter, partly on a natural community of interests and partly on baronial leadership, it was nevertheless possible for a great local magnate, in this case Richard Beauchamp, earl of Warwick (d. 1439), to draw these groups together and create a 'sense of the shire . . . based on an exceptionally wide-ranging affinity'. The Beauchamp affinity, she argues, 'was therefore a source of strength and cohesion for shire society'. More importantly, though, this 'cohesion' was temporary; it collapsed with Beauchamp's death, whereupon local society tended to revert to its previous and more localised groupings. In fact, the whole argument is here taken a stage further: 'the community of the shire,' argues Carpenter, 'as opposed to the sense of unity given by [the Beauchamp] affinity, did not exist.'[26] In other words, only in certain circumstances is it correct to think of the county as meaningful political unit. For the most part, the Warwickshire gentry operated both politically and socially, not as a county-wide grouping, not as the leaders or representatives of 'Warwickshire society', but within smaller and more localised groups, and the fact that, on the collapse of the Beauchamp affinity following Earl Richard's death, they quickly reverted to these more localised associations, suggests that these were really more durable, and in the long term therefore more meaningful, than the sense of county cohesion created by the earl's leadership.[27] This is also the view taken by Astill and Wright in their respective discussions of the fourteenth-century Leicestershire and fifteenth-century Derbyshire gentry. In these cases, though, there was not even a local great magnate to create the (albeit temporary) illusion of a shire community. County and other administrative boundaries were, they argue, largely meaningless in political terms, and what determined local groupings was mainly the pattern of landholding – though kinship also played its part.[28] Indeed, Carpenter, Astill and Wright all attach considerable emphasis to the pattern of landholding within their shires, arguing that it was the geographical distribution of their estates which was the most important determinant of the political and social associations formed by the gentry.

Nevertheless, the concept of the 'political community of the shire', magnate-dominated or otherwise, still commands support. Saul has spoken of the 'growing identity of gentry with shire' in fourteenth-century Gloucestershire, while Maddicott argued that by the late fourteenth century, 'the shire has become a politically-minded community'.[29] In each case, it is clear that this political community was composed essentially of those knights and esquires who formed the 'county gentry'; they were the men who, because of the wider spread of their landed interests and their near-monopoly of the more important administrative and political offices in the shire (sheriff, justices of the peace, and knights of the shire for parliament), could claim to be the true representatives of the shire's landholding class as a whole, and thus naturally took the lead in, for example, trying to secure the alleviation of local grievances in the face of royal or baronial impositions. Moreover, both Maddicott and Saul have argued that the increasing political, judicial and administrative responsibilities thrust upon, or assumed by, these leaders of local society tended to enhance the local particularism of the shire communities during the thirteenth and fourteenth centuries, and thus to promote a sense of regional unity.[30] By the late fourteenth century – and this is a point which is not really in dispute – the local gentry had gained a large measure of control over the institutions of the shire. These institutions were principally three-fold: the county court, the judicial bench, and local crown offices.

County courts were supposed to meet every forty days, and Maddicott, who argues that they formed an important medium through which the community of the shire made its feelings known, estimated that it was far from uncommon for 150 or more people to attend. It was here that local grievances were aired, elections held, directives from Westminster discussed, and a good deal of judicial and administrative work undertaken. Booth has also pointed to the considerable influence of the Cheshire county court, while Saul, although noting that the volume of legal work done in the Gloucestershire county court tended to decline in the fourteenth century, thought that its importance as a 'political assembly' was increasing.[31] In Leicestershire, however, it seems to have been a less dynamic institution; Astill found little evidence to suggest either that it was well attended or that it provided any real focus for the shire's gentry. Much more important, he argued, was the judicial bench, which was 'virtually judicially omnicompetent' in the shire, and Maddicott agreed that by the second half of the fourteenth century the justices' sessions were expanding into more generalised meetings of the shire and thus taking over the role of the county courts.[32] It was from the 1360s, when they finally and irrevocably acquired the power to determine cases of felony and trespass, and when their administration of the labour laws passed in the wake of the Black Death armed them with a powerful weapon of social and economic control, that the justices of the peace really established themselves in the forefront of local affairs. And as their powers grew, so did the stature of those who filled the role: by the fifteenth century, the benches were staffed almost exclusively by the county gentry.[33]

The remaining shire offices were also firmly in the hands of the local gentry by the second half of the fourteenth century. During the thirteenth century it had not been uncommon for offices such as the shrievalty to be granted – as sinecures – to outsiders who took little or no interest in local affairs. For example, Peter de Rivaux, chief minister to Henry III, was at one time in the 1230s sheriff of twenty-one counties simultaneously. From about 1250, however, to the accompaniment of a growing chorus of demands that local offices should go to local men, such practices became rarer, and by the late fourteenth century outsiders were hardly ever appointed to the office. It was as a consequence of this that the 'hierarchy' of local offices established itself among the gentry.[34] In areas where there was a major power other than the crown, a similar process may have been occurring. In the duchy of Lancaster, for example, the dukes enjoyed a considerable degree of independence from the king, and the local authority invested in duchy offices was enhanced accordingly. Interestingly, Bennett found that during the period he studied (1375–1425), it became increasingly common for local duchy offices to go to local men – and the same was apparently true of the earldom of Chester.[35] Local service, both to the crown and to magnates, was of course a traditional part of the gentry's way of life, but there seems little doubt that as the thirteenth and fourteenth centuries progressed, local control of local offices became ever more marked.

It was for precisely this reason that kings and magnates retained or employed members of the gentry, and increasingly so, it seems, as the fourteenth century progressed. By the later years of the century, most peers probably had at least a score of knights and esquires in their full-time retinues, while earls frequently had fifty or more. John of Gaunt had over 200 knights and esquires on his payroll between 1379 and 1383, but he was certainly untypical; his brother the duke of York had only about forty, while the duke of Norfolk retained some seventy men for life between 1389 and 1398.[39] It was also during the last quarter of the fourteenth century that the English kings began to retain the gentry on a regular basis: between 1390 and 1413 the number of knights and esquires retained by the crown was between 250 and 300 at any given time, all of them in receipt of annuities in an attempt to harness their loyalty to the king's cause.[37]

Some retainers, it is true, should be thought of as employees rather than political supporters. Others were probably retained for specific purposes – to provide legal council, for example, or for military service. But above all it was for the local weight that they carried that magnates retained members of the gentry, and not surprisingly, therefore, it was to the county gentry that they looked first. They were the men who had their ears to the ground in the shires, who understood local grievances, influenced and articulated local feeling, and might carry with them the support of the lesser landholders and those beneath them. The county gentry were the natural allies of the peerage. It was to them that the peers looked to consolidate and extend their spheres of influence, to preserve their interests, and to keep them in touch with their 'countries'. Therefore there was a clear territorial logic to the retaining policies of most magnates. Those whose estates were reasonably concentrated, such as the Beauchamps in Warwickshire and Worcestershire, or the Courtenays in Devon, could devote the majority of their resources to one region (see Maps 2 and 3). For those with less compact landed interests, such as the Mowbrays, the jam had to be spread a little more thinly. 'From the 1390s to 1432,' according to R.E. Archer, 'the Mowbrays could count on staunch supporters in Lincolnshire, East Anglia, Sussex and the Midlands.'[38] These were precisely the areas in which their principal holdings were situated. For the king, too, territorial logic played its part: although there were certain areas of the country in which the king held extensive lands, and from which therefore he retained a greater number of men than from other areas (Cheshire, for example, under Richard II; Yorkshire and Lancashire under Henry IV and Henry V),[39] in general his aim seems to have been to retain a fairly even spread of the most influential knights and esquires from the country as a whole, balancing north with south and ensuring that no area was neglected.

The extent to which the kings and magnates of late fourteenth- and fifteenth-century England thought it necessary to retain members of the county gentry is a clear reflection of their enhanced role in local politics in late medieval England. It may be that different local communities were as different as the various regional studies considered here suggest that they were: that in some counties magnates were effectively able to dominate local affairs, that in others a more or less independent gentry operated as a county-wide political community, and that in others more meaningful social and political communities worked at a more localised level. Quite possibly there was an element of each in each region, with the emphasis shifting in response to changing circumstances (external threats, the quality and purpose of magnate leadership, and so forth). Yet there were probably some common factors which affected the balance of political society within any given region. Given that it was often the longer-established families who tended to be the most influential within their localities, the rate of social and regional mobility among the gentry was probably an important factor in determining the extent to which local communities could broaden their associations and encompass the interests of an area such as a shire. Evidence relating to the social mobility of the late medieval English gentry is impressionistic rather than statistical, but it is interesting that it was to the 'Home Counties', to use an anachronism, that those north-westerners who made it in Richard II's and Henry V's service chose to migrate.[40] Here they competed for land with lawyers and courtiers from the capital, and merchants from the East Anglian and south coast continental trading ports. In the remoter northern and western counties, where opportunities for getting rich quick were scarcer, and, perhaps, traditions more tenacious, there is likely to have been rather less·turnover among the landholding class as a whole than in the wealthier and more bustling southern and eastern counties, and possibly therefore more likelihood that political communities would be more broadly based. Although this is only speculation, it is at least given some support by the researches of historians specialising in the sixteenth and seventeenth centuries, some of whom have found a distinction in these terms, between the greater opportunism of the south-east and the more stable base of landed society in the north-west, to be valid for their period.[41]

The balance between magnate- and gentry-held land could also be significant. The presence of a great magnate, with his *caput honoris* and his extensive network of estates, employees, and retainers, could have a marked effect on the political geography of a shire. The knightly families of Bedfordshire, for example, nearly all had their principal residences and estates in the north of the county, whereas the Greys of Ruthin, who were (by the late fourteenth century) the leading peerage family in the shire, were based in the central and southern parts of the county. In Derbyshire, most of the leading gentry families were based in the south, while in the north were situated most of the duchy of Lancaster holdings (the duke was the largest single landholder in the county), together with a host of lesser gentry estates. With regard to Warwickshire, it has even been said that 'the nobility [i.e. the peerage] seem to have had the effect of lowering the status of the gentry' – in other words, that where there were heavy concentrations of magnate lands, there were fewer 'county gentry' families, but where magnate estates were thin on the ground the gentry prospered.[42] It seems likely, therefore, that in those regions where magnate estates were fewer, the gentry were correspondingly both wealthier and more politically assertive. It is in these terms that the apparently high status and independent-mindedness of the Cheshire and Lancashire gentry has been explained, and when, as in this case, the great local magnates were not normally resident in the area, responsibility for leadership of local society was placed even more firmly on the shoulders of the county gentry.[43]

Yet even if it is true that the presence of great magnate estates tended to 'lower the status of the gentry', the effect of any such process must often have been fairly localised. A great landholder like the earl of Devon could certainly act as a focus for the aspirations of the gentry of his 'country'; whether that meant that he could subordinate local politics to his will is quite another matter. The independence of the late medieval English county gentry from royal or baronial domination is well attested. Like most men, they served themselves first, and were quite capable of making up their own minds on the political issues of the day. A classic example is provided by the behaviour of the Mowbray affinity in 1405. From about 1390 until 1432, according to Archer, 'three members of the Mowbray family provided the leadership of an extraordinarily stable and continuous affinity'. The Mowbrays were a great family – Thomas Mowbray was elevated to the dukedom of Norfolk in 1397 – and given the stability of their following might have been expected to command a high degree of loyalty from the men they retained. However, when Thomas, Lord Mowbray, rebelled against Henry IV in 1405, hardly any of his followers rebelled with him. This was not because they rejected the Mowbray allegiance, but because they disagreed with the issue at hand: they 'chose not to become involved in the dubious and ill-considered venture of a witless youth'. Yet once the rebellion was over, they maintained their allegiance to the family and continued to serve Thomas's successor.[44]

There was no question of blind loyalty, therefore, even to the greatest of magnates. Magnates were just as dependent on their followers as their followers were on them. While the gentry were happy to fall in with a pre-eminent local magnate when it suited them to do so, rarely did they regard such alliances as demanding a selfless loyalty. Indeed, many of them, even among the county gentry, seem to have avoided as far as possible involvement in national politics. On the whole, their activities and interests were thoroughly localised. Their lives, according to Saul, were 'bounded by remarkably narrow horizons'. According to Astill, they relied on 'limited family and social contacts', and are 'typified as a social group by their myopic attitudes', while Wright commented that the twin keynotes of the fifteenth-century gentry were their 'independence' and their 'parochialism'.[45] It was precisely this 'parochialism' which made them indispensable to the peerage. The English county gentry of the late fourteenth century, those 2,300 or so knights and esquires who had by this time emerged as the dominant political force in the shires, were, as a group, both more clearly defined and more powerful than had been the case in 1300. Their power stemmed from both their wealth and their control of local institutions, and is reflected not only in the growth of retaining, but also in the striking development in the influence wielded by the knights of the shire in parliament. The enhanced political role of the gentry is one of the key themes of fourteenth-century English history.

PART II

SERVANTS, LANDS, AND THE FAMILY

CHAPTER 4

Households and councils

The great magnate of late medieval England was not just a warrior and a politician, he also stood at the head of a vast business empire. Directly or indirectly, he employed thousands of people, enjoyed the ability to make or break the careers of those who served him, and exercised powers of management over all aspects of his empire. His essential commodity, and chief source of both authority and income, was land. His principal expense was his lifestyle, and at the centre of his lifestyle was his household. The size, splendour and cost of noble households is testimony to one of the most striking differences between medieval and modern society, that is, the extent to which the public and private lives of medieval people were interwoven, and this is especially true of the great. Constantly surrounded by servants and companions, constantly mixing business with pleasure, the medieval noble was hardly ever actually alone, or even alone with his wife and children.

The medieval noble household, great or small, was a collection of servants and other followers, normally living under the same roof as the lord and his immediate family, whose purpose was to cater to his everyday needs, advertise his status, and create the mode of life which he desired. That there was a long-term tendency for households to grow in size during the later Middle Ages is indisputable. To put figures on it is much more difficult. This is partly a matter of definition. Households were run on fairly open lines, with friends, retainers and employees continually coming and going, staying for a few days to do business or keep society with the lord before departing for days or months on end. Even those whom one would normally think of as permanent members of a lord's domestic establishment, such as his chaplains or his steward, can often be shown to have been 'out of court' for lengthy spells. In 1376–7, for example, John of Gaunt made substantial 'out of court' payments of expenses (covering, in each case, several months of the year) to his household steward William Croyser, his household treasurer John Cheyne, and his chancellor John Yerdeburgh, indicating that each of them had spent long periods away from that household of which they were three of the most important officials.[1] The surviving account for the household of Thomas Arundel, bishop of Ely, for the months of November and December 1383, also demonstrates the continually varying size of any great household. Under each day was listed both the number of dishes served (*fercula*), that is, the number of persons eating in the household that day, and the number of guests (*exuli*) visiting the household that day. For the week 6–12 December, when the bishop's household was at Hatfield, the number of mouths to feed varied between forty-five and ninety-six, while the number of guests varied between eleven and twenty-five.[2] Thus only between a quarter and a half of the difference between different days can be explained by the number of guests staying with the bishop; the rest is presumably to be explained by comings and goings among his own household staff. A more accurate indication of the size of his household can be obtained from the list of 'fees of the household for the Christmas term', drawn up on the back of the account. This names ten knights, seven esquires, twenty-two valets, eleven choristers, eighteen grooms, and eight pages, making a total of seventy-six. The knights and esquires, however, or at least some of them, should probably not be thought of as full-time members of the household – they would almost certainly have resided principally on their own estates, perhaps coming in to the bishop's household on a rotational basis – so the number of servants who would normally be attendant on the bishop was probably closer to sixty than to seventy.

Bishop Thomas's establishment can be compared with that revealed by the livery roll of Edward Courtenay, earl of Devon, for the year 1384–5. In this year the earl distributed his livery to seven knights, forty esquires, fifty-two valets, four minstrels, eight chaplains, three ladies-in-waiting, six pages, and fourteen lawyers. As the ladies-in-waiting indicate, the earl's household almost certainly included that of his wife Maud as well, which naturally enlarged it. The fourteen lawyers, however, together with some of the knights and esquires, and perhaps some of the valets too, should probably be thought of as retainers rather than as domestic servants – for liveries, of course, were not just distributed to members of the household – so that the total of 134 should probably be reduced by at least sixty. At the same time there is no mention of grooms (*garçons*), perhaps because they were too lowly to receive liveries. All in all, the livery roll probably points to a permanent domestic staff of about eighty or ninety for the earl and his wife together. These estimates tend to concur fairly well with the impressions of both R.G.K.A. Mertes and K.B. McFarlane, both of whom cautioned against the idea of thinking of noble households as being too big at this time. In the early sixteenth century the third duke of Buckingham had 145 permanent household servants, and the fifth earl of Northumberland had 166, but a century and a half earlier somewhere between fifty and a hundred was probably much more usual for an earl.[3] In his will of 1426, Thomas Beaufort named seventy-three members of his household, and he was duke of Exeter.[4]

Lesser nobles' households were naturally smaller. An indication of the size of household maintained by the various ranks of the nobility is given in the Black Book of Edward IV's household, written around 1480, which suggested ten for an esquire, sixteen for a knight, twenty-four for a banneret, forty for a baron, eighty for a viscount, 140 for an earl, 200 for a marquis, and 240 for a duke.[5] At the top end of the scale, for dukes and marquises, this is probably over-generous, even for the late fifteenth century; at the bottom end it may not be generous enough. According to Astill, a normal 'middling' member of the Leicestershire gentry (i.e. an esquire) in the second half of the fourteenth century probably had between ten and fourteen household servants. Mertes points out that even quite minor noblemen (by which she seems to mean roughly the bannerets) frequently had thirty or more members of their households in the fourteenth century, while esquires often had close to twenty.[6] To attempt to be too precise would be unwise, however. The size of any noble household was determined by a host of factors too numerous to allow of generalisation. The aspirations and inclinations of the lord were crucial: did he wish to emphasise his status by maintaining a splendid entourage, or did he prefer to save his money for other purposes? How did his income match up to his aspirations? How large a family did he have? How thrifty or otherwise was his wife, and how old were his children? And equally importantly, how old was the lord himself? Households were not created at a stroke. They evolved gradually, starting perhaps with a nucleus of men who had been servants of the family before the lord's accession, and growing to include more and different types of men as his interests broadened or his aspirations changed course. In the middle of the fourteenth century, most knights and esquires probably had between ten and thirty full-time household servants at any given time; most bannerets and barons between twenty and fifty; most of the titled nobility between fifty and a hundred. At the beginning of the century the numbers would have been rather lower, at the end a little higher.

As well as growing bigger, later medieval noble households also became more organised. The duties of the servants who worked in them became more specialised and closely defined, and there was a tendency towards standardisation of offices and functions – though it must be said that these developments are much more marked in magnates' households than in those of knights and esquires. Essentially, the members of any lord's household can be divided into two categories: the officers, and the menials (though 'menials' – *meynalx* – did not have the same overtones of disparagement in the Middle Ages as it does today). What this division really corresponds to is the familiar 'upstairs' and 'downstairs' organisation of the eighteenth- and nineteenth-century household. Those who populated the 'upstairs' were drawn, broadly speaking, from a social class not radically different from the lord himself. They were responsible for the general organisation, discipline, and accounting procedures of the household, but they were also there to provide companionship and 'worship' for the lord, to offer their advice to him, and to maintain the links between him and their localities. The task of those who worked 'downstairs' was to make life comfortable for those who lived 'upstairs'.

At the head of the household, acting on directions from the lord himself, there were normally two key officers, the steward and the treasurer.[7] In the household of a peer, the steward would be of at least esquirely status. He had over-all charge of discipline and the day-to-day running of the establishment, and was always a layman. In smaller noble households, the steward might double as treasurer, but in the larger ones there was almost invariably a separate treasurer, responsible for receiving the household's income, disbursing it to the various spending departments, and drawing up final accounts for the lord's scrutiny. Most household treasurers were clerks, though some (and more as time went on) were laymen. In larger households there was often a third chief officer, the chamberlain. Like the steward he was always a layman and usually an esquire or better. He supervised the staff of the chamber, the inner, private enclave of the household. The larger the household, as a general rule, the more prominent the chamberlain, because of the greater need of the lord to be able to escape from the hustle and bustle of the hall (where the menials ate and slept) to the privacy of his chamber, where he could eat, converse, and take his leisure with his chosen companions and advisers. The growing popularity of private chambers has frequently been noted as a feature of castle-building in late medieval England, and was even lamented in verse by William Langland:

> Desolate is the hall each day in the week
> Where neither lord or lady delights to sit.[8]

As supervisors of this household-within-a-household, chamberlains were often on close personal terms with the lords they served. In his will of 1387, William Montague, earl of Salisbury, left 1,000 marks in gold to his chamberlain, the esquire Richard Pavy, and he granted him for life the manor of Hyde (Herts.). John of Gaunt's chamberlain in 1376–7 was Sir Robert Swillington, well known as one of the duke's closest and most trusted supporters.[9]

Beneath this top layer of officers, at least in larger households, came a second layer, of whom the most important were the marshals, the clerk of the kitchen, the butler, and the chief clerk of the chapel (or chief chaplain). There were sometimes servants known as marshals who worked in the hall, the main dining and living area, where they were responsible for seating and discipline at meals, and sleeping arrangements, but the post of marshal was more commonly associated with outdoor activities. He was in charge of the stables (a big job in any medieval household), and organised the lord's hunting and falconry. The butler supplied the household with wine and ale, the clerk of the kitchen had general responsibility for the purchase of food and the accounts concerned with it, and the chief clerk of the

chapel organised the lord's and the household's religious observance. All noble households had private chapels. Even the household
of, say, an esquire who had only ten servants in all, would invariably
include at least one chaplain.[10] The nobility thus largely performed
their religious observance at home – indeed, it was an important part
of the household's communal life. Each day normally began with a
mass, at which the entire household was supposed to be present. The
chaplain(s) would also hear the confessions of both lord and household, and would probably be responsible for the distribution of
alms. Almsgiving was habitual among all ranks of the nobility.[11]
Left-overs would be distributed at the gate, sums of money dis-
bursed on a regular basis, bequests and donations made to favoured
religious houses, and specific paupers frequently maintained for life.
Magnates and peers frequently had separate almoners. Also, the
larger the household, the more likely there was to be a separate
secretariat, with a number of clerks detailed specifically to write the
lord's letters, writs and so forth. In smaller households, however, it
was quite usual for one or more of the chaplains to double as the
lord's secretary as well as his mass-priest, confessor and almoner.
Chaplains and confessors, like chamberlains, often developed close
personal relations with their lords, and were frequently named as
executors of the lord's will, or as trustees in his business affairs. The
moral authority which they exercised also encouraged this.

Below the officer/gentry level, the household was organised
along departmental lines. Valets, grooms and pages, drawn from
much humbler social backgrounds, often from the locality of the
principal residence, were the real work-horses of the household, and
there was generally little social mobility between them and those
who lived 'upstairs'. The main departments of any big household
were the kitchen, pantry, buttery, chamber, hall, and stables,
though they were frequently subdivided. In the bishop of Ely's
household, for example, his grooms and pages were listed under the
bakery, buttery, pantry, chamber, poultery, larder, wash-house,
chapel, hall, and stables.[12] Household organisation by 'offices'
became more marked during the fourteenth century, and is crucial to
an understanding of how noble households functioned. Each of the
offices (often corresponding simply to the rooms in which the
menials worked) was headed by a valet, and probably operated more
or less independently of the others as far as day-to-day tasks were

concerned. What brought them together was their common accountability to the steward and treasurer, communal worship in the chapel, communal eating and sleeping in the hall, and ultimately the knowledge that they existed in order to make life comfortable for the lord, his friends, and his officers.

The household of an esquire would not, of course, be nearly as elaborately organised as this. He might have a steward (in practice, if not in name), who would double as treasurer, much like the nineteenth-century butler, one or two chaplains who would also act as his secretaries, a cook, a valet in charge of the stables, and another half-dozen or a dozen valets and grooms who between them would organise the buying and preparation of food and drink, serving at table, caring for and feeding the horses, cleaning, washing, and all those other tasks which go into the running of a household. According to J.M. Thurgood, the elaboration of ceremony and pro-liferation of offices which was such a marked feature of magnate households in the fourteenth and fifteenth centuries was not nearly so noticeable among the knights and esquires.[13] Among the great, however, rituals and functions became ever more formalised: by the fifteenth century, we frequently find carvers, cupbearers, sewers (waiters), ewerers (who carried round hand-washing bowls after meals), ostlers, and footmen, as well as personal physicians and surgeons, nurses, and the ubiquitous *generosi* (gentlemen) and 'henxtmen' – those well-born young men placed in another household in order to learn the noble way of life.[14] This was not simply ceremony for its own sake: to some extent a lord's 'worship' was judged by the size and stature of his entourage. When he rode to parliament, or to a tournament, he took pride in riding at the head of his household, surrounded and bolstered by his servants and companions, who would usually be dressed in robes of his livery to demonstrate the scope of his largesse. If he went to war, his household – or at least part of it – went with him, both to form the nucleus of his armed retinue and to cater to his domestic needs on campaign. A large household was thus an investment in social standing.

Naturally, though, it all cost a lot of money. For most lords, the maintenance of their households probably took up at least half of their disposable income. John of Gaunt's annual net income in the 1390s was probably around £15,000, and in 1394–5 his expenditure on his household of one year, including his great wardrobe (the department responsible for buying cloth and robes) and his privy purse, but excluding the annuities and fees which he paid to several of his chief officials and retainers, amounted to £7,761.[15] In 1376–7 his disposable income was probably closer to £10,000, while his household expenses came to £5,525.[16] In 1345–6, Thomas, Lord Berkeley, apparently spent £1,309 on his household, but still 'had cleare remaining to his purse in the end of all £1,150. 18s. 8d. of that year's savings'.[17] None of these figures should be taken too precisely, for different lords (or their clerks) would categorise different items under different headings, and the line between 'household' and 'miscellaneous' expenditure was often pretty hazy. Nevertheless, the pattern of roughly 50–60 per cent of disposable income spent on the household seems to hold good for the most part.

Between half and two-thirds of the expenses of most noble households was on food and drink (including provender for the horses). Most of the rest went on wages, fees, liveries, and incidental items such as alms, fuel, medicines, out-of-court expenses, parchment, dishes and storage vessels, hunting and falconry expenses, and gifts.[18] Income was normally received by the treasurer (or steward) from the receiver-general, the official who stood at the head of the lord's estate administration. As far as can be gathered, most noble households did not work off a budget but received money as and when required, though obviously there must have been some idea of how much ought to be spent each year and questions would be asked if expenditure got out of hand. Formal accounts, however, deal mainly with income in cash. There were other, often very important, methods by which households were supported, such as the produce of demesne manors, and rents in kind. The stewards of the Berkeley lords, for example, used to order provisions on a weekly or monthly basis from the reeves of nearby manors (sometimes this was demesne produce, sometimes rents in kind), and in one year the manors of Cam and Coaley, both very close to Berkeley castle, provided the household with 17,000 eggs, 1,008 pigeons, 91 capons, 192 hens, 288 ducks, 388 chickens, 274 pigs, 45 calves, 315 quarters of wheat, and 304 quarters of oats – worth something like £200 in all. In Lent, the Berkeleys frequently used to move with their household to the manor of Arlingham, nestling in a bend of the Severn, for easy access to fish (see Map 2).[19] Elizabeth de Burgh found that her demesne manors were capable of providing about half the basic necessities for her household, though these tended to be the cheaper items and only accounted for about a quarter of the value of the goods consumed. Naturally this demesne produce came almost entirely from her 'home farms', those East Anglian manors which were closest to her principal residence, and she was probably, being an elderly dowager, more sedentary than most fourteenth-century lords.[20] Even so, income in kind was an important source of provisions for any lord. Many households also had their own cottage industries, making items such as bread, cheese, butter, ale and honey. Livestock was often purchased on the hoof and grazed on neighbouring pasture until required; the animals would then be slaughtered in the household, where skins could be turned into parchment or leather, cloth would be spun from the wool, and tallow melted down to make candles or axle grease for the carts. Most residences also had orchards, fish-ponds, deer and rabbit parks and perhaps even a vineyard attached. Interestingly, though, Mertes found that both cottage industries and the conversion of waste or surplus were more common in smaller (e.g. knightly) households than larger ones, indicating a more thrifty approach to household provision among the lesser nobility than among the great.[21] Thurgood also argued that while most knights and esquires continued in the fourteenth and fifteenth centuries to get many of their supplies from demesne produce or rents in kind, among the greater nobles there was a growing tendency to purchase even staple commodities. By the fifteenth century, she discovered, they purchased almost everything that they required.[22] What this suggests is that, although the economy of noble households is very difficult to evaluate in purely monetary terms, if the charge of profligacy is to be levelled against them, it is probably more justified in relation to great lords than lesser ones.

Mertes concluded that a study of nobles' household accounts in late medieval England 'generally gives the lie to accounts of noble profligacy'.[23] Thurgood, while noting that strict control of food allowances and accounting procedures showed much concern for economy, nevertheless pointed to the steady improvement in the quality of life enjoyed by late medieval nobles, especially the peers and magnates: 'by the fifteenth century life for the nobility seems to have become much more elaborate all round and meals had become much more complicated.'[24] This elaboration of ceremonial was also helped by the increasingly sedentary nature of noble households in the fourteenth and fifteenth centuries. Gone were the days when nobles would regularly take their households on extended perambulations of their estates, consuming demesne produce as they did so. Even by the early fourteenth century, most nobles had only one normal residence. Partly as a result of this, and partly because of a generally increasing desire for comfort and luxury, the main residence would now be built and furnished to much higher standards than in the twelfth or thirteenth century. Late medieval English castles, as has often been pointed out, show less emphasis on defensive qualities and more on physical ease. Windows, fireplaces and private apartments become more common, along with luxurious furnishings and wall-hangings.[25] The Black Book of Edward IV's household took as its keynote the twin themes of *magnificencie* and *providencie*: providence downstairs, and magnificence upstairs. The ability to penny-pinch in small matters allowed for a greater degree of splendour when the occasion demanded, and the desire for such splendour was certainly not lacking. There was nothing contradictory, therefore, in the simultaneous desire for both economies and conspicuous consumption.

The role of noble households in local and national economies is not easy to evaluate. However valuable income in kind and domestic industries were, most households relied mainly on purchase – from local farmers, local markets, and sometimes from London or abroad – to provide their needs. The advantage of this, both to farmers and to traders, was that as households became more sedentary, enterprising locals had the chance to secure monopolies on the provision of certain goods. That the presence of a noble household could stimulate local production is surely undeniable.[26] On the other hand, purchase was frequently accompanied by abuse of the lord's rights through purveyance. Purveyance (or *prise*) was the right to pre-empt goods (by compulsory purchase orders, in effect) so that adequate supplies could be maintained for large institutions. It seems to have been consistently abused – indeed, it was one of the chronic evils of medieval society. Non-payment and underpayment were rife, additional demands (such as carriage) were routine, and over-zealous purveyors might create local shortages. Even for the royal household, for which the right to purvey, although in theory carefully regulated, was never actually denied, there were continuous complaints that the purveyors were overstepping their rights.[27] So damaging had the system become to producers and traders that in 1362 the commons succeeded in forcing through a statute which restricted the right of purveyance to the households of the king, the queen, and the heir to the throne, but it is abundantly clear that this failed to stop lords from purveying, and frequent complaints that they did so, often couched in the bitterest terms, continued to be voiced in the parliaments of the later fourteenth century.[28] It was probably the larger noble households which abused the system more. Their demands, and the ability to enforce them, were greater, they relied less on demesne produce, and, according to Mertes, their purchasing systems were more indiscriminate: while small households often had regular patterns of weekly or monthly buying, larger ones often had long-term (e.g. quarterly) patterns for the purchase of non-perishables, but took a more haphazard attitude to short-term purchases.[29]

Nevertheless, even if there is plenty of evidence of extravagance, especially on the part of the magnates, there is little to suggest *over*-extravagance. There are very few examples of great nobles going bankrupt in the fourteenth century. Moreover, as households became more sedentary in the later Middle Ages they presumably established more regular sources of supply, which probably went some of the way towards mitigating the excesses associated with purveyance, even if the problem was far from eradicated. And, on a more positive note, even if it is arguable that the 'nuisance value' of noble households outweighed the advantages to the neighbourhood of having a sizeable local centre of consumption and demand, there is no denying their economic importance in two other respects. Firstly, they played a central role in maintaining England's international trade: in bigger households particularly, luxury items like good wines, fine cloths, spices, fruits, dye-stuffs, jewels and so forth were in continual demand, creating constant opportunities for merchants. Secondly, they were employers of labour on a very substantial scale: even at a fairly conservative estimate, there must have been around 50,000 servants working in the households of the 2,500 or so peers and county gentry of fourteenth-century England at any given time. Many of them must have had wives, children, and other dependants. By 1400, when the population of England was probably about two and a half million, the proportion of that population which was, directly or indirectly, supported through service in the households of the great was unlikely to have been less than 5 per cent. And working in a noble household was undoubtedly regarded as a 'good job'. There were long family traditions of service, and few examples of employees leaving through dissatisfaction. In addition to free board and lodging, a household valet could expect to earn about £2 a year, which was about half as much as a labourer earned at the end of the fourteenth century, but the labourer still had to pay for his food, clothing and shelter.[30]

Noble households thus played an important part in the national economy, and increasingly so as the fourteenth century progressed. From the mid-century, the population declined dramatically. Households continued to grow, however, both in size and in cost. The increasing magnificence of the households of the great in late medieval England is not only a reflection of that growing awareness and propagation of status which is such a feature of contemporary noble society, it is also strongly suggestive of a rise in the nobility's disposable income. As a result of this, they were consuming an evergrowing proportion of the gross national income. It is doubtful whether they saw it in these terms, but their economic role was enhanced accordingly.

By the fourteenth century, the household servants of most lords were quite distinct from the servants who helped them to administer their estates. At the head of a lord's estate administration was his council, not dissimilar to the board of directors of a large modern company. Councillors advised the lord on the general running of his business affairs, on the pursuit of his legal interests, on administrative problems and reforms – indeed, on almost any aspect of his public life and sometimes even on his family and private life. They were also frequently asked, either individually or collectively, to act as his executors, trustees, guarantors, ambassadors and so forth. Councils were composed principally of three types of men: the high-ranking household or estate servants of the lord, landholders of independent political prominence, and lawyers. Whether most lords actually had formally constituted councils, with a defined membership, regular meeting times, and so forth, or whether they preferred to rely on a more fluid body of servants and advisers, is difficult to say. Gilbert de Clare, earl of Gloucester, already had a paid council in the 1270s, and while much depended on the individual lord's inclinations, formal councils probably became more common as time went on.[31] Nevertheless, responsibility for the day-to-day supervision of the estates must often have devolved on a small handful of the lord's closest servants, perhaps even on just one of them.

The council of Edward the Black Prince is a case in point. That the prince had a formal council there is no doubt, and entries in his register make its composition pretty clear. Robert de Ufford, earl of Suffolk, was 'number one' on his council, and John Wingfield 'number two'. The king's justices Sir Henry Green and Sir Robert Thorpe were retained to be of the council with fees of twenty marks *per annum* each, and another seven lesser lawyers were also councillors. The prince's chamberlain (Sir Nigel Loryng), his receiver-general (Peter de Lacy), his household steward (Sir Edmund de Wauncy), and his privy seal keeper (Richard Wolveston) – in other words his most important servants – were also members. Yet the role of some of these men as councillors was probably occasional rather than continual. The real burden of running the administration on a day-to-day basis fell to John Wingfield, who, in addition to being number two on the council, was also appointed to be 'governor of the prince's affairs', for which he received the remarkably generous fee of 10s. a day. After his death in 1361 he was replaced by Sir John Delves, described as 'governor of the prince's business'.[32] The central importance of these two has been demonstrated by P.H.W. Booth. Throughout the 1350s, Wingfield was 'the principal maker of policy for the prince's estate administration . . . acting either alone or in conjunction with two or three of his fellow councillors', and, although he did not exercise quite the same degree of power, Delves performed much the same role after 1361. 'The prince's council, as a body,' says Booth, 'was far less important administratively than the individual councillors. . . . In fact, it seems to be a mistake to think of it as a corporate body exercising a regular administrative role.' Its role was rather to deal with more specific problems (often legal problems) as they arose, while of course the individual servants of the prince, such as his receiver-general and household steward, had their own specific duties within the administrative hierarchy.[33]

The importance of individual councillors rather than the council as a body has also been stressed by R.E. Archer's study of the Mowbrays' estate administration. During the first thirty years of the fifteenth century the men who really dominated the administration of the Mowbray estates were the successive receivers-general, John Lewys and Robert Suthwell, both of whom sometimes made personal perambulations of the manors as well as exercising a close personal supervision of such matters as the raising of revenue for the lord's military retinue and the auditing of local ministers' accounts.[34] It was probably inevitable that the real business of administering the estate would be left to these well-tried professionals. The sort of 'counsel' expected of those independent members of the peerage or gentry who were retained to be of a lord's council was much more occasional and much more varied. Sir Thomas Hungerford of Wiltshire provides a good example. In 1365 he was appointed by the earl of Salisbury to be steward of his lands, but it is probable that the office was more or less a sinecure: 'in case it happen that the said Thomas cannot labour or exercise the office, or he excuse himself for reasonable cause, he shall nevertheless take his fee (twenty marks) yearly, provided that he be with the earl and of his counsel.'[35] Hungerford, an outstanding member of his county gentry who was to be Speaker of the Commons in the parliament of January 1377, was just the sort of man whose influence great lords wanted to have on their side, but he was also too important a man to involve himself in routine administration. That he did not is demonstrable from the number of other, similar, posts which he held: he also acted for the bishop of Salisbury as steward of his cathedral city, and from 1375 until 1393 held the post of steward of all John of Gaunt's lordships south of the Trent, which entitled him to a fee of 100 marks a year and a place on the duke's council. In the words of J.S. Roskell, he was 'a great estate agent and governor of franchises – but he was also a politician: there were strong suspicions that he had used his influence as Speaker to persuade the commons to go along with Gaunt's schemes in 1377.[36] Even more obviously 'political' were councillors like Sir George Felbridge of Norfolk, virtually a professional courtier who was feed as an esquire and then a knight of the royal chamber under both Edward III and Richard II, and was subsequently retained by Henry IV until 1401 (when Felbridge died), so that his career at court spanned over forty years and three reigns. A man with that sort of influence never lacked for patrons: the earl of

March, and the dukes of Norfolk and Gloucester, all retained him for his counsel.[37]

Nevertheless, there is evidence that some men, even among this 'independent' category of councillors, regarded their duties as more full-time, and their attachment to one particular lord as more binding. It is interesting that the beneficed clerk John Redcliffe, who is known to have been a member of the earl of Devon's council, received permission from his bishop to be absent from his parish for three years from 1402 in order 'to attend continually upon the earl'. It may also be instructive that three other esquires who are known to have been members of the earl's council in 1396–7 were all liveried by him thirteen years earlier.[38] What is immediately apparent, of course, is the rather lesser status of these men as compared with Hungerford or Felbridge. They were more likely to make their careers in the service of a single lord, whereas Hungerford and Felbridge could, in effect, sell their connections and influence to a number of different lords. No doubt most lords sought a balance between different types of men on their councils, with lesser figures being retained on a fairly permanent basis and required to involve themselves more in routine business, and greater ones retained on a more casual basis for greater matters. Some lords certainly tried hard to secure the undivided counsel of particular men: in October 1397, for instance, the earl of March appointed Sir Hugh Cheyne to be a life member of his council on the understanding that if the earl predeceased Cheyne, he would continue to advise March's heir and no one else – a precaution which was all too rapidly vindicated when the earl was killed at the battle of Kells in the following year.[39]

Among the lawyers, often the most easily definable category of councillors because of their special skills, a similar distinction seems to have operated. Most lords retained a considerable number of lawyers. The earl of Devon gave liveries to fourteen in 1384–5. There were at least nine on the Black Prince's council in the 1350s, while in November 1389 the earl of Salisbury ordered his treasurer to make annual payments of £2 each to four sergeants-at-law, three apprentices-at-law, an attorney in the Common Bench, and an attorney in the king's exchequer, all of whom were to be 'retained for counsel'. Stipends and 'gifts' to members of the royal administration could be just as rewarding as fees to lawyers. Those who were feed by John of Gaunt in 1376–7 included, besides seven lawyers, four ushers of the king's exchequer of audit, and four ushers of the king's exchequer of receipt. He also made gifts to various members of the staff of the exchequer, and it may not be coincidental that his receipts for the year included £6,255 from the exchequer for arrears of wages of war.[40] In return for their fees, many of these lawyers and other royal servants were probably expected to do little beyond a general safeguarding of the lord's interests in matters with which they were concerned, and the offering of advice on specific matters when asked. But, as Rawcliffe pointed out, there were also a few lawyers who were more closely attached to the full-time service of one lord, advising him on a succession of legal and other business matters, 'known collectively as the council learned . . . a corporate and distinct group . . . with clearly defined tasks to perform'.[41] One of the most common tasks in which these legal councillors were employed was arbitration between lords who were involved in a dispute. In 1387, for example, when the guardianship of the lands and person of the under-age John, earl of Pembroke, created a complex tangle of administrative and financial problems between Margaret Marshal, countess of Norfolk, who was guardian of the earl's person, and Sir William Beauchamp, who had been granted the custody of some of his estates, it was agreed that 'two of [Beauchamp's] council, with two or three of the council of the said countess and earl', would go around and view the lands in question to determine whether any waste had been committed under Beauchamp's guardianship, and would make arrangements for the future administration of the lands, the two parties agreeing to act 'by advice of both councils'.[42] Indeed, in the powers of arbitration vested in them, councils exercised what was virtually in practice equitabile jurisdiction.[43] Yet despite the prominence of lawyers on nobles' councils, it should not be thought that they developed into primarily legal tribunals. In the Welsh Marches, it is true, where the extent of the independent authority exercised by lords was in any case exceptional, councils do seem to have had the power to administer justice in almost all its forms, often acting as courts of first instance and travelling in eyre around the lordships, but elsewhere councillors remained essentially supervisory and advisory officers.[44] It is worth noting finally that the retaining of legal counsel on a permanent basis, especially when the lawyers in question were the greatest law officers of the realm, gave rise to widespread suspicions that the men in question were abusing their office and prejudicing their impartiality. This applied especially to the king's justices, who, after long years of complaint, were eventually, in 1388, forbidden to take retaining fees from lords.[45]

Councillors, both individually and collectively, were generally men in whom their lords placed great trust. Occasionally this trust was misplaced. In 1393, Roger Wyght of Gloucestershire and his wife Alice complained to the king that William Tanner, whom they had 'lately retained to be of their counsel in divers matters for a yearly pension granted to him by them, had craftily and without legal process entered the manor of Cotes, co. Gloucs., the said Alice's inheritance,' and had not only taken the profits from it but also committed waste on the manor to the value of £106. To add insult to injury, Tanner had even begun wearing Alice's 'hereditary arms', and because of this the case eventually ended up in the court of chivalry.[46] Such cases are rare, however. In most cases, trust seems to have been amply repaid. For the most part, individual officers were probably more important than the council as a body, but where the council as a whole really came into its own was at times when the guiding hand of the lord was absent: when the lord was away on campaign or crusade, for example, or during minorities, when the element of continuity was so important in tiding the young heir and his inheritance over a potentially vulnerable and costly period hence the earl of March's insistence that Sir Hugh Cheyne should continue to counsel only his son after his death). In return, of course, councillors stood to gain greatly from their associations with lords. 'The rank of councillor', as Rawcliffe noted, 'bestowed a tremendous social *cachet*, which in turn brought additional fees, patrons and opportunities for advancement. . . . As an institution, the seignorial council played a major part in cementing the relationship between the lord and his retainer.'[47] In one sense, indeed, the noble council was simply a part of that network of relationships between clients and patrons around which medieval political society revolved. It also played an important role in fostering a lay administrative class in late medieval England, throwing up men – like Thomas Hungerford – with the talent and ambition to succeed, and thus, both politically and socially, to rise. Both the noble household and the noble council demonstrate that at the heart of both political society and social mobility in late medieval England lay the concept of service.

CHAPTER 5

Estates in land

The good management of his estates was a matter of the utmost concern to any lord. Unfortunately, it is virtually impossible to talk of the 'average' great estate in the Middle Ages, for each had been built up in its own way, through a combination of inheritance, marriage, purchase and grant, and each was continually changing in size and composition, as a consequence of economic or familial pressures, individual policy, or political fortunes. Some estates were heavily concentrated in one or two areas (sometimes deliberately, sometimes by chance); others were widely scattered. Nevertheless, some generalisations are permissible. Every lord had his *caput honoris*, his chief and favourite residence at which his household was normally based, and around the *caput* there was often a substantial group of 'home manors', at least some of which would probably be held largely in demesne. Within this area, it was also common for lords to hold additional rights, or franchises, such as private hundreds, 'return of writs' within the area of the honour, or the right to hold markets and fairs in the local town. The remaining lands would often be grouped into honours or receiverships, that is, groups of territorially fairly compact manors which often took their name from what was traditionally the chief castle of the honour, or were sometimes simply grouped by counties or according to some other convenient geographical distinction. There were thus three main levels in the organisation of most great estates: the manor, the honour or receivership, and the central administration revolving around the lord's chief officers and councillors. On lesser estates, of course, there was often no intermediate level, with manors accounting individually to the central officer(s).

Some examples will help to clarify the pattern. The lands of the dukes of Lancaster were concentrated principally in Yorkshire, Lancashire and the North Midlands (with sizeable holdings in Lincolnshire, Derbyshire, Staffordshire, Nottinghamshire and Leicestershire), but there were also holdings in many of the other English counties, with Norfolk and the Welsh Marches especially prominent. This vast agglomeration of rights and properties, worth about £12,000 *per annum* gross by the 1390s, was normally (though practice varied) divided into about ten receiverships.[1] The Yorkshire and Lancashire lands were covered mainly by the two great honours of Lancaster and Pontefract, each worth about £1,500 gross, though there was also a 'receiver of York and Nottingham' who accounted for £680 net in 1376–7. The remaining North Midlands lands were mainly grouped within the honours of Bolingbroke (Lincs.), Tutbury (on the Staffordshire-Derbyshire border), and Leicester, each of which was worth at least £1,000 gross. There was also a receiver for each of the Welsh Marcher lordships: Monmouth (worth over £500 net by the 1390s), and Kidwelly and Iscennen (jointly worth over £650 net).[2] The 'receiver of Norfolk and Suffolk' accounted for £671 net in 1376–7, while the remaining lands in the south, which were spread fairly thinly through Sussex, Hampshire, Somerset, Berkshire, Wiltshire, Dorset, Huntingdonshire and Gloucestershire, were controlled by the 'receiver in southern parts' (though Sussex had a separate receiver in 1376–7). The net value of these southern lands amounted to £367 in 1376–7, but this seems unusually small, and a valuation of 1361 put them at closer to £1,000 gross, which would probably make about £800 net. The only other receivership mentioned in the 1376–7 account is that of Dunstanburgh (Northumberland), based on the magnificent clifftop castle there, which was worth £133 net.

The lands held by the Nevills, a great northern family who eventually (in 1397) rose to an earldom, were much more concentrated, lying almost entirely in Yorkshire and south Durham (see Map 1). The ancient *caput*, from which, before 1397, the Nevills derived their title, was Raby castle in south Durham. This acted as the centre of one receivership for a group of manors straddling the Yorkshire–Durham border. About twenty miles south of Raby was Middleham castle in Wensleydale, a second receivers' centre; it was along Wensleydale that John, Lord Nevill of Raby (d. 1389) concentrated on purchasing land, in addition to which he rebuilt

[105]

Middleham castle and used it frequently as a residence. These two groups of lands placed the territorial power of the Nevills firmly in north-western Yorkshire, but there was also a third group of lands some forty miles south-east of Middleham, around the northern and eastern fringes of York, at the centre of which was the manor of Sheriff Hutton, a third receivers' centre, and the scene of another Nevill castle-building enterprise, this time in the fifteenth century. It is hardly surprising that the first Nevill earl, Ralph, was so delighted to receive from Henry IV in 1399 a life-grant of the honour of Richmond, or that he strove, though unsuccessfully, to convert the life-grant into an entail, for Richmond fitted perfectly between the two main groups of land around Raby and around Middleham, and its acquisition made Nevill, according to C.D. Ross, 'incomparably the richest and most influential lord in the north-western area of Yorkshire'.[3]

Not all great estates were divided into receiverships, however, and this includes some where in many ways such divisions would seem to have been thoroughly logical. From the eleventh century until the early fourteenth, the Mowbrays' lands were essentially in three blocks: firstly, around the traditional *caput* of Epworth castle in the north Lincolnshire 'Isle' of Axholme, from which the Mowbray lords derived their title as lords of Axholme; secondly, a group of manors and castles stretching across central and northern Yorkshire, from Hovingham at the southern tip of the north Yorkshire moors, through Thirsk and Kirkby Malzeard to Nidderdale Chase; and thirdly a group of Midland manors extending into Northampton-shire, Rutland, Nottinghamshire and Warwickshire, but based on the manor of Melton Mowbray in Leicestershire. In the early fourteenth century, as a result of a more than usually fortuitous marriage, they acquired two further blocks, the honour of Bramber in Sussex, based on one of the original five 'rapes' of Sussex, and consisting of a series of valuable properties running from Horsham and St Leonard's Chase in the north of the county to Bramber castle and Shoreham-by-Sea (see Map 4), and the Welsh Marcher lordship of Gower, to the south-west of Swansea (Gower was to be lost to the Beauchamps in 1354, and not regained until 1397). For most of the fourteenth century, therefore, the Mowbray lands, worth around £1,700 in all including Gower, were clearly divided into either four or five territorial groups which would have formed natural receiv-erships, yet they did not apparently introduce any 'honorial' divisions into the administrative hierarchy until after the acquisition of the Brotherton lands, mainly in East Anglia, and worth another £2,800 or so, early in the fifteenth century. Instead, they relied on direct links between the central and manorial administrations.[4] The same seems to have been true for the majority of the manors held by Richard Beauchamp, earl of Warwick, in the fifteenth century (see Map 3). These were for the most part quite heavily concentrated in the Warwickshire/Worcestershire area, though with important outlying groups in Durham, the Welsh Marches, and Devon and Cornwall. Only these latter three groups were organised into separate receiverships, the great bulk of the English manors accounting directly to the central administration.[5]

There was thus room for variation in the administrative machinery adopted. Although many nobles had apparently already adopted a system based on receiverships in the thirteenth century, and although it was probably the most prevalent system among great estates in the fourteenth and fifteenth centuries,[6] it was by no means universal. Nor does it seem that the geographical structure of the estate necessarily determined the machinery used to administer it. The scattered but compact blocks of the Mowbray estate would at first sight appear to be perfectly suited to the receivership system, whereas the concentrated Nevill lands were arguably better suited to central control, but in neither case was what one might think of as the obvious solution adopted. The chief consequence of the decision to use the one system or the other was the effect it had on the level of control vested in the lord's central officers, and especially the receiver-general. As already noted, the power exercised by the Mowbrays' receivers-general was enormous. The Beauchamp receivers-general, according to Ross, 'may be considered the pivot of the whole estate and financial organisation during the time of Earl Richard',[7] which made them more powerful men than the Lancastrian receivers-general – at least within the context of their own administrative machines. Indeed, this was probably the primary consideration governing the lord's choice: how much authority did he want one man to exercise? It is far from improbable that such decisions were made partly on personal grounds.

Each receivership had two principal officials: the receiver, responsible for finance in general and the accounts of his honour in particular, and the steward, responsible for running the honorial court, local appointments, the supervision of leases, and the behaviour of subordinate officers – though in practice receivers and stewards probably co-operated closely on all aspects of their honorial administration. Below them came the reeves and bailiffs, who formed the broad base of the administrative structure at its grass-roots level. Their currency was the manor, the fundamental unit of estate administration. In both size and organisation, manors were almost infinitely variable units. Some were worth only £2 or £3 a year; others, like the earl of Stafford's great manor of Thornbury in Gloucestershire, were worth £400 or more a year. Some were coextensive with villages, others might include only a half or a third of a village, while yet others included half a dozen or more villages. Usually there was one reeve per manor, but large manors, or groups of small manors, were sometimes under the control of a bailiff, an officer who, although the tasks that he performed were not essentially different from those of the reeve, was regarded as of higher status. The reeve's or bailiff's job was to organise the collection of rents and other dues, and to regulate the agricultural cycle of the manor either along the lines established by years of routine or according to orders handed down from above. Once a year, usually around Michaelmas, they had to present their accounts to the steward and receiver of the honour in which their manor was grouped, or directly to the receiver-general and his auditors. Chaucer said of his reeve that 'there was noon auditor coude on him winne', but the proliferation of estate administrators in a clear hierarchy such as that which operated on most estates was essentially designed to build into the system enough checks and controls to ensure that reeves – and others – got away with as little as possible.

The key figures in the lord's central administration were usually the receiver-general, the chief steward, and the auditors – although they might at times be superseded by a man in whom the lord reposed special trust, such as John Wingfield under the Black Prince.[8] To most lords, the receiver-general was their chief financial officer, responsible for collecting the profits of their estates either from the honorial receivers or directly from the reeves and bailiffs, and distributing them according to the lord's wishes – to the household, for example. To help him in this task he had a small number of professional auditors – the earl of Warwick employed three in 1420–1[9] – usually appointed on an annual basis. Together they would make perambulations of the estates, summoning the lesser officers to meet them at convenient spots to have their accounts examined and surrender their profits. The post of chief steward may have been becoming something of a sinecure in the fourteenth and fifteenth centuries: the sort of man (like Thomas Hungerford)[10] who was appointed to the post was often probably valued more for his general counsel and connections than for his dedication to routine administration. Yet if there is a temptation to see the central administration as remote and out of touch with the everyday problems of the manor, it would be unwise to underestimate the amount of quite detailed work that reached it. In 1375, for example, the following writ was sent from John of Gaunt's chancery to William de Nesfeld, 'our steward of Knaresborough':

> We wish and order you to let to farm all the lands and tenements newly-assarted in our lordship of Knaresborough, so that you and the tenants of these lands can make reasonable agreements about them; and that all the tenants who refuse to take the said lands in such manner you should eject from them, and let the lands and tenements go to others who are willing to give more. And concerning our demesne lands, escheats and wastes around the towns of Knaresborough, Auldeburgh and Roucliff, which could be let to farm to our greater profit, and which are not at present, we order you to have them put at their true annual value without sparing anyone in this matter. And besides this, that all the foreign people [i.e. not tenants of the duke] who do not hold from us and who until now have taken common wood and turbary [turf] in our said forest by sufferance of the ministers who were there in the time of my very honoured mother the queen, should in future be prohibited such common [fuel] as reason demands; and also that all our tenants of the said forest who hold any assart should not in future take any common [fuel] because of such tenure, but only on the lands and tenements which belong to them by ancient tenure. At the Savoy, 15 February [1375].[11]

Although written as if from the duke himself, it is never very clear just who was responsible for an order such as this. It may have been a decision of the duke and his council, possibly as part of a general policy of trying to tighten up profit margins and leasing demesnes, it may have been the chief steward and/or the receiver-general, or it may have been done on the initiative of the local steward, with this 'order' serving, in effect, as a ratification. But it leaves no doubt that the lines of communication between local and central machinery did not exist solely to deal with generalities, for these are quite detailed points and show both knowledge of local conditions and a determination to exploit them to best advantage. The lines of communication also existed, of course, in order to keep a check on local ministers. In 1361, for example, some of the tenants of the honour of Denbigh sent a petition to the Black Prince and his council presenting various complaints against a number of the prince's local officers, one of which was that

> also the bailiffs and their underlings out of malice and for their own advantage cause the towns to assemble more often than need be . . . , and charge those who are present to give the names of those who are absent, so that the petitioners cannot till their lands or attend to their husbandry on account of such daily assemblies, which make for the sole profit of the bailiffs and not at all for the prince's . . .

The Black Prince's council duly examined the petition and ordered his steward and receiver of Denbigh to

> find what damage the prince would sustain by granting the requests contained therein, and treat with the petitioners thereon, certifying the prince and his council before the month of Easter [sic] next as to what they consider should be done.[12]

Thus although the procedure was somewhat sluggish, there is a clear example here of the interaction of the three levels of a great lord's estate administration, whereby what must have seemed like a very minor matter to the prince and his council, but was obviously an important one to the ploughmen and husbandmen of Denbigh, was raised, considered, acted upon, and hopefully (the council's eventual decision is not recorded) sorted out.

What part did lords themselves play in the administration of their estates? For the most part, it is very difficult to tell, and many historians have assumed that the answer is very little. It would be rash, however, to assume that because great estates were perfectly *capable* of being run without any direct intervention by the lord (which they undoubtedly were), this is necessarily what happened. No doubt much depended on the inclinations of the lord, as well as on the size of his estate: lesser lords were inevitably more personally involved than greater ones. Greater ones, however, were sometimes closely involved too. Of Richard Beauchamp, earl of Warwick, for example, it has been said that 'his council and officials were not allowed to exercise discretion except in matters of routine. . . . The earl himself expected to be kept informed, even if he were overseas, and it is unlikely that any important decisions were made without reference to him. . . . He retained full and active control in the administration of his great landed inheritance.'[13] Even the greatest lords sometimes more or less retired from military and political affairs for a number of years in order to supervise or overhaul their administrations, as for example John Mowbray, duke of Norfolk, apparently did between 1425 and 1430, or as Edmund, Lord Grey of Ruthin (who was treasurer of England in 1463–4, and thus a man of wide administrative experience) did after 1465.[14] John Smyth (who was writing in the early seventeenth century, at which time he was the Berkeleys' steward and had access to numerous documents which have since disappeared) was clearly convinced that the fourteenth-century Berkeley lords were intimately involved in the management of their estates, and he cites the case of Thomas, Lord Berkeley (d. 1321), personally supervising the drawing up of 800 new leases of land to be held in tail on his Gloucestershire manors and stipulating the inducements (such as the right to take marl from his pits and soil from the highways) which were designed to encourage prospective tenants.[15] Even the Black Prince, an almost permanently absentee landlord in Cheshire, still played an active role in matters of 'grace' or 'patronage', and although he was quite happy to delegate responsibility for policy-making on his lands to a man such as John Wingfield or John Delves, he would nevertheless deal personally with such minor matters as the granting of two oak-trees in Cheshire to a soldier 'for good service in Gascony'.[16]

There is plenty of evidence therefore that at least some nobles took an active interest in estate management, even if it is probably correct to assume that most lords relied heavily on their central officers to do the routine work for them most of the time. That was, after all, what they paid them for, and as the Middle Ages progressed they were paying an ever-growing number. The real growth in the number of estate administrators seems to have come in the thirteenth century, along with the trend towards demesne-farming, but there are no signs of numbers falling away after this – indeed, quite the contrary. At each level of the structure, there were of course many other officials besides those already described: parkers and foresters at the local level; keepers of fees and guardians of franchises at the honorial level; clerks of receipt, clerks of account, and 'supervisors' at the top level. Numbers continued to grow, jobs became more specialised, and procedures became more standardised and more professional. Perhaps the most obvious way in which this happened was in the almost complete separation by the fourteenth century (at least among the servants of great lords) of the household servants and the estate servants. In earlier centuries it was far from uncommon for, for example, the chief steward of the lord's lands also to be the steward of his household, but those days were gone. Accounting and auditing procedures were also tightened up, with the introduction of valors (regular valuations of all or substantial portions of the estate, probably designed as much to check on the activities of local officials of the lord as to maximise revenue from tenants) in the early fourteenth century, and of half-yearly 'views' in addition to the annual audit – the 'view' being a sort of intermediate audit at which local officials were expected to surrender profits accrued so far during the year, partly to provide an infusion of cash for the lord and partly to sort out arrears and other local problems before they had time to become serious.[17] 'Over the period as a whole between 1272 and 1377,' argues Booth, 'the most significant administrative shift affecting Cheshire was towards a fully professional, salaried staff,'[18] and there can be little doubt that the same process was going on all over England, and indeed in English Wales, where the harshness and efficiency of Marcher lordship was one of the recurring themes of the fourteenth century.[19] It is quite possible that a growing number of jobs in estate administration were sinecures, especially at the higher levels, and in this sense service in a lord's administration was yet another avenue through which clients and patrons formed what were essentially political relationships, but this argument should not be overstressed. There was a job of work to be done, decisions constantly to be made, problems to be overcome. Many of these problems were economic, and stemmed from the very different economic circumstances of the fourteenth century as compared with the thirteenth.

The Black Death of 1348–9 cuts dramatically through the economic and social history of fourteenth-century England (and indeed of the whole of Europe), and because its impact was so devastating it makes more sense initially to consider the fourteenth-century economy in two halves. In general, the thirteenth century saw rising population, price and rent inflation, buoyant profits for many landlords, and increasing poverty for substantial numbers of the peasantry.[20] Although trends are by no means uniform, there is a fair amount of evidence to suggest that by the second quarter of the fourteenth century conditions for the peasantry had begun to improve. Rents had stabilised, prices had fallen a little, and as a result real wages had begun to rise. Serfdom, along with demesne-cultivation, had started to decline – or at least it seems that an increasing number of labour services were being commuted for cash payments, though as will be seen this was not necessarily the same thing. It is tempting to attribute this improvement to a drop in the level of population, caused partly by a natural check on a population which had outgrown its means of subsistence, and partly by the appalling series of bad harvests, epidemics, and sheep and cattle murrains which struck England between 1315 and 1322.[21] How many died in these years is not clear: it may have been something like 10 per cent of the population. But although at the time this was undoubtedly a national tragedy, for those who survived it meant at least some alleviation of the pressures which had built up over the thirteenth century. If things were getting better for the peasantry, does that necessarily mean, however, that they were getting worse for landlords? There is some evidence that this was the case: low cereal prices in the 1330s and 1340s, combined with the slow but perceptible rise in wages, did nothing to halt the trend towards demesne-leasing. Rents, however, remained fairly stable, and there are few signs of any serious difficulties for landlords. But this was soon to change.

The Black Death, the most cataclysmic event in medieval European history, arrived in south-western England in the late summer of 1348, and within less than two years had reached out to engulf the whole country, bringing in its wake dreadful suffering, chaos, and an immediate mortality rate such as has probably never been seen before or since. In the long term, bubonic plague was to alter the whole nature of the late medieval economy, but in the short term the landholding classes did not suffer as badly as those below them. For tenants-in-chief, the mortality rate in 1348–9 was 27 per cent, though for the parliamentary peerage it was only 7.75 per cent.[22] Taking the population as a whole it was probably closer to 40 per cent. Once introduced, moreover, bubonic plague became endemic in England, and further outbreaks occurred in 1361, 1369, 1372, 1375, 1390, and, it has been estimated, roughly once every seven years during the fifteenth century.[23] The plague of 1361 was described by some contemporaries as the children's plague (presumably because those who had been born since 1349 had little immunity to the bacteria), but interestingly it was also more lethal for the magnates than that of 1348–9. The mortality rate among the parliamentary peerage was 18.7 per cent, while for tenants-in-chief it was 23 per cent.[24] Among the population as a whole, though, the mortality was certainly not as heavy as twelve years earlier.

Nevertheless, the cumulative effect of four further plagues between 1361 and 1375 may well have produced a further fall in the population of around 25 per cent, and although a degree of immunity must gradually have built up, so that each successive outbreak wreaked less havoc, the population continued to decline until at least the end of the fourteenth century, and probably well into the fifteenth. By 1400, then, if it is correct to assume a population of about five million at the beginning of the fourteenth century, it is unlikely that England contained more than two and a half million people. In purely economic terms, this largely speaks for itself: a labour surplus became a labour shortage, land-hunger turned gradually into land-plenty. For those who survived, the Black Death ushered in what has sometimes been described as the 'golden age of the peasantry'.

Yet this golden age – if it is correct to use such a term about an era which witnessed such widespread suffering – by no means came immediately. Although it would be natural to expect the change from a labour surplus to a labour shortage to result in a fairly rapid escalation of wage rates, the evidence that this is what actually happened is equivocal. In some places there was certainly a sharp rise, for example on the manors of the Westminster Abbey estate, where the average figure for the 1350s shows an increase of 75 per cent over that for the 1340s. For many industrial workers and craftsmen, similarly sudden and substantial rises are also a feature of the 1350s, but comparison with the wages paid on the estates of the bishop of Winchester shows a remarkable disparity: here the increase for the 1350s over the 1340s was only about 3 per cent, and not until the 1370s and 1380s does the level of increase approach 50 per cent. Regional variations in the effect of the plague might help to explain this, but surely that cannot be the whole story. More weight, perhaps, should be given to the Statute of Labourers, that notorious 'landlords' charter' which was first issued as an ordinance by the government in 1349, the very year when England was in the stranglehold of the pestilence, and later reissued as a statute in the parliament of 1351. The essential points of the statute were twofold: firstly that all wages were to be held at their pre-plague levels, and secondly that workers were to remain 'in the places where they ought to serve', rather than move around the country in search of higher wages and cheaper tenancies. And not only were workers forbidden to demand higher wages, landlords were forbidden to pay or offer them. The chronicler Henry Knighton of Leicester Abbey says that when the king heard that some landlords 'had given higher wages to their workmen, he levied heavy fines on abbots, priors, knights of greater and lesser consequence and others, both great and small, throughout the countryside, taking 100s. from some, 40s. or 20s. from others, according to their ability to pay'.[25] Yet the ability of either the government or the landlords to enforce the statute was clearly limited, and although the harsher breed of landlord (of whom the bishop of Winchester may have been one) was perhaps able to wield it with some efficacy, it was difficult to keep moving in a direction which was so clearly contrary to the market forces of the time for any lengthy period, and in the long run all wages were bound to rise.

The trend of prices was not so uniform. Cereal prices, which had remained at a fairly low level between *circa* 1333 and 1350, rose markedly in 1351 and remained at roughly 50 per cent above their pre-plague level for the next twenty-five years. Perhaps this was because *per capita* consumption increased and thus maintained demand, perhaps it reflected the general level of post-plague dislocation and a series of bad harvests, perhaps there was an element of wage-price monetary inflation. However, following a series of good harvests in the mid-1370s prices fell sharply, and, apart from the occasional year of dearth such as 1391, maintained until the end of the century a level which was roughly similar to that of the 1330s and 1340s. With wages and prices now both moving against him, the landlord saw little point in persevering with demesne-cultivation, and it was the last quarter of the fourteenth century which saw the most decisive flight from demesne-farming for the market on most great estates. Yet the trend of rents afforded landlords little comfort either. As land became more plentiful in the post-plague era, they too tended to decline, though not dramatically. For thirty years or so after the Black Death the trend in rents was only slightly downwards, and it was not until the last years of the fourteenth century and the first half of the fifteenth that a more decisive fall occurred. At the same time, rents were becoming more difficult to collect, with arrears mounting, and collective resistance (inspired perhaps by the rising of 1381), becoming more common – and this was an occurrence that was to become even more frequent in the fifteenth century.[26]

From roughly the 1340s until the mid-1370s, it has generally been accepted that landlord incomes did not decline too drastically – perhaps by 10 per cent at most.[27] Various explanations have been put forward as to why this decline was not more marked. For those still engaged in large-scale production for the market, the maintenance of high cereal prices until the mid-1370s must certainly have helped. It may also be true that, even after 1349, England remained a country in which the land: people ratio was unbalanced. It is possible that overpopulation was *so* severe, and land *so* hard to come by, during the first half of the fourteenth century, that even a reduction of 40 per cent or so in the population was not sufficient to correct the imbalance.[28] As far as *good* land was concerned, this is far from improbable. Much of the land which had been taken into cultivation to cope with the hard times of the thirteenth century was marginal at best, and may well have become rapidly exhausted, so that the impression that some land was being abandoned during the first half of the fourteenth century may not indicate as great a degree of relief from land-hunger as might otherwise be imagined. Certainly, the relatively slight decline in rents after 1349, and the fact that good arable land remained expensive and much in demand on the peasant land market,[29] indicates that it was not in such plentiful supply as a 40 per cent drop in population would at first sight imply. It is also highly probable that *per capita* production rose among the peasantry. Whereas before the plague they had been restricted by lack of availability, tenants now found that they could acquire bigger holdings, work longer hours, and thus produce more. Hence the apparent lack of vacant holdings on many of those estates which have been studied – after the dislocation of the initial few years, at any rate. The principal consequence of this increase in *per capita* production was to put more cash into the peasants' pockets, but the secondary consequence was to help to maintain their landlords' income.

Yet in the face of a population decline of around 40 per cent, wage rises averaging 50 per cent or more by the 1370s, and (eventually) declining rents and cereal prices, it is doubtful whether these factors alone were sufficient to maintain landlord incomes at their apparent level, and most historians have concluded that they were accompanied by a severe degree of landlord repression, known as the 'seigneurial reaction'. Put simply, the argument for the seigneurial reaction is that, finding market forces moving against them, landlords in the years after 1349 began to turn the screw on their tenants, extorting greater sums of money from them, insisting in some cases on the reintroduction of labour services which had been commuted for cash during the pre-plague years, and generally acting in such an oppressive way that resentment gradually built up until it found expression in the great rising of 1381. That there was a seigneurial reaction of some kind is not open to doubt – the Statute of Labourers alone is sufficient testimony to that. The more pertinent questions are, was it effective, in which directions and in which years was it pursued most forcefully, and were all landlords able to benefit equally from such a policy?

Recently the emphasis has shifted somewhat away from regarding the seigneurial reaction as principally an attempt to reimpose labour services, towards regarding it as a more widespread movement on behalf of landlords to increase judicial profits from those who lived under their lordship. In particular, court fines were increased substantially. R.H. Hilton noted this trend on a number of West Midland and other estates many years ago, and his evidence has recently been corroborated both by P.H.W. Booth's examination of the Black Prince's administration in Cheshire and C. Dyer's study of a group of south-eastern manors in the years 1340 to 1381.[30] On some manors the increase between the 1340s and the 1370s was over 100 per cent, on others it was no more than 10 per cent – but on each manor the trend was upwards, and it is important to note that with the simultaneous fall in population, even the maintenance of court fines at their pre-plague level would have meant, by the 1370s, a *per capita* increase of close to 100 per cent, so that in fact the rate of increase was usually much greater than the figures imply. That the Black Death was itself a catalyst to landlord efficiency is hardly to be doubted. In many cases it must have involved a process of redefinition and tightening up. Depreciation of stock and equipment during the immediate post-plague years may also have forced landlords to try to recoup necessary investment. But what was perhaps more disturbing for many peasants was that it also seems to have served as a powerful unifying factor among the landholding class, with the labour legislation helping to bind central and local government together to protect their economic interests. Thus it was not just their manorial courts, but also the public courts, which the peasants had reason to fear. The labour legislation ranged the power of the crown squarely behind the landlords, and in 1359 the commissions of the peace (which were staffed by members of the local gentry) were combined with the commissions to enforce the labour laws, thus placing the responsibility for enforcing the legislation in the hands of precisely those whom it was intended to benefit, and associating the government inextricably with the propertied classes. It was also stipulated that the fines which the justices of the peace imposed were to contribute to their salaries, which was no doubt an incentive to keep them high. Further modifications of the Statute of Labourers in the 1360s and 1370s only served to reinforce the powers of local justices. The development of the public courts at this time, according to A. Harding, 'created a new serfdom. . . . The main struggle in 1381 was for civic, not tenurial freedom, because the landlords had got a new public jurisdiction which allowed them to enforce service far more general than the obligations of villein tenure.' They were now, for example, at least in theory, able to force all able-bodied persons to work, and not only to work, but to work at the wages which they specified. 'Entrenched lordly power', concluded Harding, 'had certainly preserved itself through the crises of the fourteenth century, but only by taking on a more political form.'[31] Small wonder, then, that the rebels of 1381, in the words of Dyer, 'recognised the close connection between lordship and government', and saw 'their superiors as involved in a single system of corrupt authority'.[32]

Moreover, there seems little doubt that the pressures exerted by landlords increased perceptibly in the immediate run-up to the 1381 revolt. 'On some manors,' comments Dyer, 'one gains the impression of some administrative slackness in the two decades after the plague, followed by more stringent controls in the 1370s'.[33] This was not simply a consequence of manorial and judicial impositions. The renewal of the war with France in 1369 led to a decade and more of exceptionally high taxation, all the more galling because the 1360s had seen peace and relatively low taxation. Taxation hit the peasantry harder now, for the standard assessment for tenths and fifteenths (these were tax assessments originally based on fractions of the value of movable goods, which was the normal method of raising royal taxation in fourteenth-century England), set in 1334, had not been altered to take into account the decline in population since 1349, and although the taxation of the 1370s was of course imposed by the government rather than by landlords as individuals, the distinction between the two may well have been becoming blurred by now. Naturally, this heavy taxation also meant that peasants had less to give to their landlords, whose demands were simultaneously intensifying. The rising of 1381 was by no means unforeseen. In a famous poem written some time in the late 1370s, John Gower prophesied that the 'common people' would soon rise up against their masters, and in 1377 there was a 'great rumour' accompanied by widespread resistance and near-rebellion among tenants in several of the southern counties.[34] Also in 1377, the knights of the shire presented a petition to the king in parliament protesting that

> in several parts of the realm of England the bondmen and
> landtenants in villeinage, who owe services and customs to lords
> by whatever cause in various lordships, . . . have . . . purchased
> in the king's court exemplifications of Domesday Book, of
> manors and towns in which the said bondmen and landtenants
> dwell, by colour of which, by misunderstanding of them and by

evil interpretation, . . . they have withdrawn and do withdraw their customs and services due to their lords, intending that they should be completely discharged from all manner of service due as well from their bodies as from their tenures abovesaid. . . . And they menace the officials of their said lords to kill them if they distrain them for the customs and services abovesaid, so that the lords and their officials do not distrain them . . . for fear of death, which might easily happen by their rebellion and resistance. And so the said lords lose and have lost great profit from their lordships, to the very great disinheritance and destruction of their estate. . . .[35]

It would be unwise to take such harrowing pictures of seigneurial deprivation at their face value, but the petition does serve as a reminder that the problem of tenurial serfdom, which is in danger of being forgotten amidst the recent emphasis on wider aspects of the seigneurial reaction, was certainly not forgotten in 1381. As Hilton has made clear, there is certainly some evidence that landlords were trying to enforce or even reimpose demands for labour services in the years leading up to the rising,[36] and at least some of the demands for the abolition of serfdom made in 1381 refer pretty unequivocally to tenurial serfdom.

It was perhaps in relation to labour services in particular that lesser landlords were most likely to experience a real drop in their incomes. As the restrictions on peasant mobility in the Statute of Labourers imply, and as the remarks of Henry Knighton make clear, one consequence of the fall in population was to create an element of competition between landlords, for both labour and tenants, and in a competitive situation little fish were more likely to be swallowed by big fish. It was 'on account of the various adversities which . . . the middling men of the realm have long undergone' that Edward III allowed them various tax-concessions in 1357, and recent research into the economic position of the fourteenth-century gentry has helped to provide some clues as to why this was so. Gentry demesnes were on the whole smaller than on the manors held by the magnates, and production for the market was limited. Moreover, the process of commutation of labour services during the first half of the century seems to have gone further on gentry manors than on magnate manors, leaving them heavily dependent on wage labour.[37] This also meant, of course, that they were more dependent on rents, and were less able to cash in on the high agricultural prices of the years 1351 to

1375. As the cost of labour rose, and as rents declined, the gentry must have begun to find themselves squeezed between the rising expectations of the peasantry and the greater purchasing power of their superiors. As far as can be gathered, it was the knights who were behind a series of petitions presented to the parliaments of 1363, 1368 and 1371 complaining of the price of labour, the scarcity of tenants, and so forth.[38] To show definitively that smaller landholders were suffering more than greater ones during the quarter-century following the plague would be impossible; as with the postulated 'crisis of the knightly class' of the thirteenth century, the evidence is too scattered and the sources insufficiently informative. What one can say, however, is that it seems quite likely. By the early fifteenth century, the peers were, economically as well as socially, pretty much in a class of their own.[39] This was certainly not the result of economic factors alone, but they probably played their part in the process.

In seeking to maintain their profit margins, greater landlords not only had greater resources on which to draw (which might help them to weather temporary storms more easily than the gentry), but they also had bigger and more professional administrative machines. If necesssary they might offer higher wages, but they could also enforce higher rents and insist on the performance of labour services. On the earl of Oxford's manor of Laughton (Sussex) a long-running battle of wills between the lord and his tenants reached its climax in the late 1370s, when one Reginald Chiselburgh absolutely refused to keep the lord's pigs in Hawkhurst wood, and a revolt among the ploughmen broke out; Henry Whyte was placed in the stocks for refusing to serve, and John Chiselbergh was attached to do his father's work on pain of 6s. 8d.[40] Seigneurial heavy-handedness is also the keynote of the Black Prince's administration of his lordship of Macclesfield, and not just in the 1370s. In the twenty-five years after 1349, 'the prince's rights of lordship were maintained rigorously and extended wherever possible so that all might be done for his "profit" '. Judicial fines were increased significantly, and arbitrary levies, like those frequently imposed in Welsh Marcher lordships, totalled about £11,000. It was the efficiency and strong central control of the prince's administration which enabled him to behave like this, but inevitably it reaped its own harvest: 'when he died [in 1376] his policy was in ruins and he and his officials had become the prisoners – not of failure, but of their own administrative success.'[41] By the end of the year 1381, many other English landlords may also have been wondering if they had become the victims of their own success. The economic implications of the seigneurial reaction were severe enough, but the social implications were potentially just as damaging. The rising level of court fines, as Booth pointed out, created bitterness not just because it hit people's pockets, but also because in a sense a fine was a way of *not* doing justice. If economic considerations were to prevail at all costs, this might be an equally powerful incentive to disaffection. For those who found servile obligations reimposed on them, it was not just time and money that were lost; there was also the question of the social stigma attached to serfdom, which was no doubt especially galling at a time when in general expectations were rising. Yet economic considerations lay at the heart of the seigneurial reaction, and of the bitterness that it engendered. 'Not just rising expectations', says Dyer, 'but actual achievements, were being exploited by a vigorous seigneurial administration.'[42] The disposable income of the peasantry was increasing, but as it did so the landlords were clawing back an ever greater proportion of it. The alliance of central government and landlords in defence of their economic interests was the keynote of the seigneurial reaction, and the events of 1381 its consequence.

But if at least some landlords – albeit by using any method that was available to them – had succeeded in minimising the decline in their profits for the first twenty-five years or so after the Black Death, the last quarter of the fourteenth century saw a more decisive fall. By now economic forces had turned more sharply against them. The further drop in population of up to 25 per cent in the 1360s and 1370s brought increased alleviation of land-hunger and further lowered rents, the rise in wages by now seems to have become universal, combining with the drop in agricultural prices to make demesne-cultivation much less profitable, and the resentment towards unaccustomed impositions was becoming ever more insistent. On almost every great estate which has been studied in detail, the last twenty years of the fourteenth century witnessed a concerted effort to lease the demesne, so that by 1400 the administrative structure of most great estates had become little more that a rent-collecting apparatus. Whether this was a direct consequence of the 1381 revolt is difficult to say, but although the revolt may not have led directly to the destruction of large amounts of landlord property, it must surely have created an atmosphere of unease about any further attempts to maximise profits. It is surely more than coincidental that the most decisive flight from demesne-farming – and the consequent withering of labour services, also a marked feature of great estates during the last twenty years of the century – occurred during the generation following the rising. But if demesne-leasing was seen as a way of cutting losses, it meant that the great majority of landlords were now dependent on rents for their prosperity, and since rents were also falling, there was no way for profits to go except downwards.[43]

The pattern of fourteenth-century economic trends was thus a fairly consistent one, and the underlying factor throughout the century was the fall in population. Compared with the high profits of the thirteenth century, some landlords may already have been feeling the pinch in the 1330s and 1340s. After the Black Death the problems mounted, especially perhaps for smaller landlords at first, and although for the moment the greater landholders managed to avoid too sharp a reduction in their profits, after *circa* 1375 it was their turn to suffer more severely. However, the evidence for declining profits refers essentially to a reduction in the annual yield of a given area of arable land. A decline in arable income does not necessarily mean a decline in disposable income. As we shall see, there were plenty of other avenues open to landlords in their quest to ensure that they remained as rich as their forefathers.

CHAPTER 6

Property, the family, and money

Larger households, an increasing demand for luxury goods, and the granting of annuities and fees to retainers, all point to a rise in the level of disposable income enjoyed by the peers of late fourteenth-century England. On the other hand, income from arable was declining, and after the crash of the great Italian banks in the 1340s, closely followed by the dislocation caused by plague, there was probably a general contraction of credit facilities in Europe.[1] How then was this greater disposable income obtained? In part it was simply a consequence of the increasing concentration of landed wealth in fewer hands – and hence both a cause and an effect of the general social developments of the time – but it was also open to landlords to take more positive steps to boost their incomes. One of these was to adapt their land to different types of farming.

Changes in land-use are of course a constant part of agricultural management, and without continuous and detailed estate records it is often difficult to differentiate between the ebb and flow of minor alterations and the significant underlying trends. Some underlying trends seem, however, to be unmistakable. One of these was a long-term decrease in cereal production in favour of leguminous crops,[2] but more significant by far (as well as being related to the increase in legumes, for these were often used as winter fodder) was the widespread switch from arable to pasture. This was not merely an English phenomenon. The expansion of sheep-rearing was, according to R.H. Bautier, 'by far the most important argicultural change which took place on a European scale in the fourteenth and fifteenth centuries'.[3] Yet for English landlords the inducements to change from arable to pasture were particularly compelling, for English wool was of high quality, and demand for it, whether in the cloth-manufacturing towns of England's traditional market, Flanders, or in the rapidly expanding home cloth industry of the later fourteenth century, was continuous.

After the Black Death there was an even greater inducement to pasture, for being less labour-intensive than arable-farming it left landlords less vulnerable to the rise in wage rates. Yet the move towards sheep-rearing seems to have been just as marked during the first half of the fourteenth century as during the second. According to R.R. Davies, it was the most important change in the economy of the Welsh March during the fourteenth century, and was just as noticeable during the 1330s and 1340s as during the 1370s and 1380s.[4] A survey of the estates of one of the greatest of all English landholders, the earl of Arundel, in 1349, shows that in this year he had 535 oxen, 47 cows, and 6,549 sheep on his Marcher properties, and 407 oxen, 246 cows, and 8,625 sheep on his Sussex properties.[5] By 1397, the number of sheep on his Sussex properties had increased to 15,350, but his lands in the county had roughly doubled in the intervening period (partly by purchase, and partly by his acquisition of the Sussex and Surrey properties of the Warenne inheritance, which came to him in 1361), so that the extent of the change during the second half of the century was probably not as great as these figures suggest at first sight.[6] Another great fourteenth-century family which expanded its sheep-rearing operation was the Berkeleys. In 1327, on those manors for which records survive, about 90 per cent of the Berkeleys' demesne land was under arable; by 1368, the figure had fallen to about 65 per cent, with much of the rest being used for pasture. Particularly striking is the purchase by Thomas, Lord Berkeley (d. 1361), in the 1340s and 1350s of a series of small properties around Beachley, on the north bank of the Severn, immediately across the river from Berkeley itself (see Map 2). The land around here was largely salt-marsh, excellent for sheep-grazing, and was almost certainly designed to launch the Berkeleys' pastoral economy in a major way. However, the centre of the Berkeleys' sheep-rearing activities seems to have been at the manor of Beverstone, about ten miles east of Berkeley castle on the southern side of the Severn. In 1330, when Lord Thomas bought the manor, he also bought a flock of 1,500 sheep with which to stock it, and three years later 5,775 sheep were being sheared there, from this and the surrounding manors.[7] It was at the same time as this that Elizabeth de Burgh was also adding considerably to her flocks of sheep on her East Anglian manors, so that by 1356 the bailiwick of Clare was producing around 3,000 fleeces *per annum*.[8] Naturally it was not just great landlords who saw the profit to be made from sheep; the flocks held by lesser landlords and peasants also increased considerably during the fourteenth century.[9] Nor is it easy to quantify the profits to be made from pastoral farming, though they must have been considerable. In 1376, for example, the wool from the earl of Arundel's estates in Sussex, Surrey and the Marches was said to be worth over £2,000, even after the deduction of a 25 per cent commission for the earl's agent, the London merchant John Philpot.[10] On average, the farmer was probably able to sell each fleece for about 7½d., so the Berkeleys might have realised about £180 from the sheep shorn at Beverstone in 1333, but from this they would naturally have had to deduct their husbandmen's expenses. Even so, this was a substantial sum, and it is hardly surprising that many landlords turned to pasture in the fourteenth century as a way of compensating for declining arable income.

However, the most direct method of increasing one's landed income was simply to buy more land. It has been suggested by G.A. Holmes that after about 1330, for the higher nobility at any rate, the drive to buy land was slowing up, presumably because of declining returns: 'land', he argued, 'was no longer a good object of deliberate investment', citing as examples the earls of Hereford and Essex and of Warwick.[11] It is not entirely clear whether Holmes was arguing that the magnates virtually stopped investing in land altogether, or that they stopped investing in land except around their own *caputs*, but if what he meant was the former, it is impossible to agree with him. There are in fact numerous examples of nobles great and small investing in land, sometimes in large blocks, sometimes piecemeal, throughout the fourteenth century. Between 1330 and 1376, for example, Richard, earl of Arundel, spent about £4,000 buying some twenty manors in Sussex (see Map 4).[12] Two successive Beauchamp earls of Warwick between the 1340s and the 1390s continued to purchase both manors and smaller parcels of land on a regular basis, not only in Warwickshire and Worcestershire (see Map 3), but also in

Cheshire (where three manors were bought in 1351), Norfolk and Cambridgeshire.[13] William de Bohun, earl of Northampton, seems to have embarked on a deliberate land-purchasing policy in the 1350s, buying a number of lands in Wales as well as about eleven manors near to his favoured residence of Wix in Essex, all from Sir John Neville.[14] The Greys of Ruthin were equally deliberate, buying at least seven manors between *circa* 1360 and 1390 and another twelve in the first sixty years of the fifteenth century, nearly all of them in Bedfordshire where their ancestral lands were concentrated.[15] In the north, the Scropes and Nevills were doing the same. Richard, Lord Scrope of Bolton, was especially active in purchasing land in the 1360s, and while most of the numerous parcels of land that he bought were in Wensleydale and Swaledale, he also bought a house in London and, in 1394, the manor of Pishobury (Herts.) which adjoined land at Bayford which he had inherited from his father. The Nevills' purchasing policy, which was pursued especially by John, Lord Nevill (d. 1389), also concentrated largely on the *caput* (around Middleham and Raby), but in 1396 Ralph Nevill also bought the castle of Wark-on-Tweed from Sir John Montague.[16] Finally, between 1327 and 1355 Thomas, Lord Berkeley (d. 1361), bought about twenty manors, as well as at least twenty-eight lesser parcels of land, most of them adjoining lands which he had inherited or already bought. Most of the manors which he bought were around the ancient Berkeley patrimony in Gloucestershire and Somerset, or in Wiltshire, into which county he was clearly deliberately expanding, but there were also purchases in Suffolk, Essex and Herefordshire.[17]

Naturally there were some who chose not to invest in land. The earls of Stafford, for example, hardly purchased at all, but this was probably because they had inherited so much in 1347 (the Audley and Corbett inheritances both fell in to them by marriage in that year increasing the number of manors they held from about fifteen to over eighty) that further expansion might well have seemed pointless.[18] Yet the Staffords were an exception. The desire to invest in land was an almost universal phenomenon, not only among magnates and peers but also among the gentry and even the peasantry.[19] McFarlane suggested that parvenus to the landholding class were more likely to buy land than older-established families, but while the Scropes of Bolton and the Greys of Ruthin could be thought of as new to the upper echelons of the fourteenth-century nobility, the same could hardly be said of the Fitzalans, Beauchamps, Nevills or Berkeleys.[20] In fact it is doubtful whether, as Holmes implies, economic considerations were uppermost in the minds of magnates when deciding whether or not to purchase – although naturally they played their part. Land meant much more than landed wealth: it meant status, the local weight which went with lordship. Nor is there any very clear evidence that economic trends greatly affected the purchase price of land. McFarlane reckoned that purchase price was normally about twenty times annual net yield in the fifteenth century, though A. Smith has calculated that Sir John Fastolf was buying his extensive properties in East Anglia at a rate of about eighteen times annual yield in the first half of the century, and C. Carpenter thought that there were times in mid-fifteenth-century Warwickshire when the ratio was closer to 10:1.[21] Examples from the fourteenth century are equally varied. In his will of 1375, the earl of Arundel left 400 marks (£266) to buy rents of £20 yearly for the poor people of Shropshire and Sussex (a ratio of only 13:1), but the Montalt inheritance, which Queen Isabella bought for £10,000 in 1327, was subsequently farmed from her by the earl of Salisbury for £400 *per annum* (a ratio of 25:1).[22] It is unfortunately impossible to know what factors influenced such agreements, and they are not necessarily very reliable guides to the annual value of the estates. All that can be said for certain is that there is no evidence to suggest that the purchase price of land declined along with the fall in arable revenues in the later fourteenth and fifteenth centuries, which if it were proven might indicate that demand was falling simultaneously.

More certainly, it can be said that very rarely did magnates sell land, although again there are exceptions. William Montague, second earl of Salisbury (d. 1397), is one. As early as 1355 (when he was only twenty-seven) he sold Sherborne castle to the bishop of Salisbury for 2,500 marks, though this was probably to some extent forced upon him as his title to the castle had been challenged.[23] At the end of his life he was selling land more freely, parting with a number of valuable manors and two private hundreds in Somerset in return for 5,000 marks from John of Gaunt, and giving the Isle of Man to William le Scrope (son of Richard, lord of Bolton) for 10,000 marks in 1392.[24] There are also examples of entire inheritances being sold, such as that of Robert, Lord Montalt, in 1327 (see above), and that of

John, Lord Mohun of Dunster, which was sold (probably at the instance of his wife, though with his agreement) to Elizabeth, Lady Luttrell, for 5,000 marks in 1374.[25] What the earl of Salisbury, Robert Montalt, and John Mohun had in common was that they were childless – as was that John Neville who in the 1350s sold most of his lands to the earl of Northampton. Childlessness was by far the most common reason for landholders at all levels to sell their lands. If the man in question had no heirs at all, the option was doubly attractive. In 1386, for example, the Essex knight Sir Peter Boxstede (who was about to go on campaign to Iberia with John of Gaunt) demised his manor of Boxstede to trustees on the understanding that if he died abroad or failed to return within twelve years they should allow Sir Stephen le Scrope to purchase the manor for 800 marks, the reason being that 'the said Peter has no knowledge who is his right heir of blood'.[26] There can have been few men like Sir Peter; even if they had no children, most landholders had heirs of some sort, and to sell one's inheritance was deliberately to deprive one's heirs – a step which most were reluctant to take. Naturally, not all permanent losses of land were intentional. When Walter, Lord FitzWalter, was captured in France in 1370, he mortgaged his castle and lordship of Egremont (Cumberland) for £1,000 in order to pay his ransom. Unfortunately, the person to whom he mortgaged it was the king's mistress Alice Perrers, whose lands and goods were forfeited to the crown in 1377, and despite a protracted legal battle FitzWalter failed to recover Egremont, which eventually passed to the esquire John Windsor, nephew and heir of Alice's husband Sir William Windsor.[27] As a general rule, though, landholders were careful in the legal arrangements which they made regarding their lands, and tenacious in defending them, and as long as they both had children and avoided being captured in war, there was little chance of them selling their land. Those from whom magnates and peers bought land were more commonly lesser men, such as knights and esquires. It is possible that the difficulties experienced by lesser landholders after the Black Death allowed some of the greater ones to profit from their misfortune, but it is impossible to quantify any such trend and it would probably be dangerous to over-exaggerate its significance.

An aggressive land-purchasing policy was naturally accompanied by consideration for the territorial configuration of the estate. Indeed, if there is an element of truth in Holmes's suggestion that magnates stopped buying land after *circa* 1330, its significance lies in the fact that purchasing policy for the most part now seems to be concentrated on the consolidation and expansion of the core of the inheritance. Besides fulfilling the desire simply to acquire more land, every one of the examples given above of magnates purchasing land also fulfilled this secondary purpose, to maintain and increase the lord's influence within his chosen 'country'. For the Fitzalans, this meant primarily Sussex; for the Beauchamps, western-central Warwickshire and eastern Worcestershire; for the Nevills, north-western Yorkshire; for the Berkeleys, south-western Gloucestershire, north Somerset, and western Wiltshire; for the Scropes of Bolton, Wensleydale and Swaledale (see Maps 1–4). John of Gaunt's acquisition of the three rich Somerset manors of Curry Rival, Langport and Martock, together with two private hundreds in the same county, from the earl of Salisbury in the early 1390s had a similar aim in view. He granted all these lands to John Beaufort, his eldest son by Katharine Swynford, and John and his successors continued the policy of acquiring lands in the county. In 1407 he received the neighbouring (and both large) manors of Queen Camel and Kingsbury, together with a number of other, smaller properties in the county, as a result of the settlement following the death without children of Edmund Holland, earl of Kent.[28] Further lands in Somerset were purchased, and then in 1444 an enormous expansion came with the death of John, Lord Tiptoft, when Edmund Beaufort (who was by now duke of Somerset – John had been created earl of Somerset in 1397) persuaded Henry VI to grant to him, in lieu of an exchequer annuity, about a dozen manors in the county which had been held by Tiptoft and which were worth over £400 *per annum*. Within the space of fifty years, therefore, through a mixture of purchase, inheritance, and royal favour (as well as good luck), the Beauforts had effectively carved out a Somerset 'country' for themselves, making them the greatest landholders in the county and fully justifying their title (see Map 2).[29]

The Beaufort expansion in Somerset was untypical only inasmuch as they started from nothing and built so rapidly. Most lords were already well established in their 'countries' at the time when they entered their inheritances. Obviously some estates were much more concentrated than others, but in general the later Middle Ages in England seems to have witnessed a more concerted attempt by landholders to rationalise and consolidate their holdings – and this applies to gentry as much as to peers.[30] Changes in the laws and customs concerning property undoubtedly helped with this process,[31] and the adverse economic trends may have encouraged it, because compact estates, and the officers who administered them, were more easily supervised than scattered ones. What the Beaufort story also demonstrates clearly is that the dual process of acquisition and consolidation was not achieved solely – indeed, in many cases not achieved mainly – by purchase. Rapid and substantial increases in the size of the estate were much more likely to be secured as the result of a marriage or by royal grant, and there is clear evidence that territorial considerations were often at the heart of such transactions. The Mauleys, for example, who were almost exclusively Yorkshire barons, built up their holdings in the county substantially during the thirteenth and fourteenth centuries through a series of marriages to Yorkshire heiresses, the climax of such a policy coming in 1371 when Peter, sixth Lord Mauley, and his eldest son simultaneously married the two daughters and co-heiresses of Sir Thomas de Sutton, by which they acquired Bransholme castle and the manor of Sutton-in-Holderness, as well as some smaller properties, a splendid augmentation of the lands they already held in the area around Beverley (see Map 1).[32] The Morleys of Norfolk (not to be confused with the Mauleys, although both families were summoned to parliament continuously through the fourteenth century) held a similarly concentrated estate in the area to the west of Norwich, and not surprisingly they nearly all married into other Norfolk landholding families. For them, the most important marriage of the fourteenth century was that of Robert, Lord Morley (d. 1360), to Hawise, sister and co-heiress of John, Lord Marshal of Hingham, as a result of which he and his heirs acquired the manors of Hingham, Hockering, Morton, and Swanton (now Swanton Morley), and the hundreds of Forehoe and Eynesford, all of which were in the same twelve-mile radius to the west of Norwich and clearly established the Morleys as the dominant landholders in the area.[33] The estate of the la Zouches of Harringworth was less compact. Although the *caput* was clearly at Harringworth (Northants), there was also a substantial group of lands in the Arden area of south Warwickshire, acquired by marriage in the thirteenth century, and there were outlying properties in Devon and Somerset. It is interesting therefore that the marriage of

William, Lord la Zouche (d. 1352, aged seventy-six), was to Maud, daughter of John, Lord Lovel of Titchmarsh, who brought to her husband the manors of Thorpe Arnold (in Leicestershire, but only a few miles north-west of Harringworth), and several properties in south Warwickshire, principally Weston-in-Arden and Wolverton. The marriage seems to have been cleverly designed to add to both main groups of existing holdings.[34]

On a much greater scale, as befitted their station, were the activities of the Percys in the north. The expansion of the Percy lands in the fourteenth century, during which they were transformed from middle-ranking Yorkshire barons into one of the greatest English families of their age, is probably the most remarkable success-story of the period, and bears witness to the ruthlessness and single-mindedness with which great landholders might pursue their territorial ambitions (see Map 5).[35] Before the fourteenth century, the Percys were essentially Yorkshire lords. They already held eighty-six parcels of land in the county at the time of Domesday Book, and although other properties had been acquired (most notably the Sussex honour of Petworth, by marriage, in the twelfth century), their landed base remained firmly in Yorkshire, especially in the East Riding. During the fourteenth century, however, their land-acquisition policy was directed very largely towards Northumberland. The methods which they used included straight purchase, marriage, royal grants, taking advantage of rights of feudal over-lordship, and not a little sharp practice. They first established a foothold in the county when Henry, Lord Percy (d. 1314), bought the great honour of Alnwick, which included the castle and at least eleven manors, from Anthony Bek, bishop of Durham, in 1309–10. The purchase was probably financed by a loan from some Italian merchants, and there is a tradition that Bek acted dishonestly in selling Alnwick as he was supposed to be holding it in trust for a minor of the Vesci family, though this allegation has never been properly substantiated. The next Percy lord, another Henry (d. 1353), added substantially to this foothold. In 1327 he indented to serve the new king, Edward III, in peace and war in return for an annual fee of 500 marks, which fee was to be replaced by the castle and honour of Warkworth and all the other lands in Northumberland held by Sir John Clavering, which, since they were held in tail male and Clavering had no sons, were due to escheat to the king at

Clavering's death. In 1331, however, it was agreed in parliament that such peace-time indentures were to be repealed, and, 'for the good service that the said Sir Henry has done to him, and will do in time to come', the king granted Percy the Clavering lands quit of any conditions.[36] They fell in to him when Clavering died in the following year, and included not only Warkworth with three attached manors, but also the manors of Rothbury, Newburn and Corbridge with their attached lands, along the upper Tyne and the Coquet. Two years later Henry also managed to substantiate his claim to the manor of Thirston on the Coquet, and, as a reward for his support for Edward Balliol, the English claimant to the Scottish throne, he was granted by Edward III the castle, constableship, and forest of Jedburgh, the custody of Berwick castle, and 500 marks a year from the customs of the town of Berwick. When the earl of Dunbar deserted the English cause, Percy was also given his barony of Beanley (just west of Alnwick) and other properties of the earl in Northumberland. Within twenty-five years, therefore, the Percys had established themselves as the greatest landholders in Northumberland. Their rise to such prominence is largely explained by the continuous Anglo-Scottish warfare of the period and the vital part which they played in it.

For the next forty years there was little further expansion, but the last quarter of the fourteenth century was to see a further massive increase in the Percy lands in the north. Henry, Lord Percy, who succeeded his father in 1368, became earl of Northumberland in 1377, and died in rebellion against Henry IV in 1408, is best known as the man who was instrumental in placing Henry Bolingbroke on the throne in 1399 and then turning against him four years later, but in his pursuit of his territorial ambitions in Northumberland and elsewhere he was to prove himself every bit as opportunistic as in his political life. By the time he succeeded his father, the Percy power-base had already shifted decisively northwards. Alnwick and Warkworth were now the most common familial residences, and Alnwick was becoming the family's normal place of burial. Throughout his life, Henry pursued a policy of purchasing manors and smaller parcels of land in Northumberland when they became available: the manors of Fawdon and Bilton, for example, were purchased, and in 1395 he acquired four manors in the county which had become detached from the barony of Alnwick in the twelfth century and held since then by the Milton family, granting to the Miltons in exchange various lands in Yorkshire. But the major acquisitions he made were achieved by other means. In 1373, for £760, he bought from the king the custody of the Northumberland estates of David Strathbogie, earl of Athol (d. 1369), together with the marriages of Strathbogie's two daughters and co-heiresses. He promptly married the two girls to his second and third sons, Thomas and Ralph, as a result of which the Strathbogie barony of Mitford (in the Morpeth area) as well as substantial lands of the barony of Tynedale (to which the girls were also heiresses) fell in to the Percys after 1399, when both of Henry's younger sons had died.[37] Henry's greatest coup, however, was to persuade Gilbert Umfraville, earl of Angus, who was old and childless, to make over about half of his inheritance, including the castle and barony of Prudhoe on the Tyne, with at least nine attached manors, to him in 1375. It is not clear why Umfraville did this – Percy probably bought the lands from him – but it meant that Umfraville was depriving his half-brothers of their inheritance. Not content with this, Henry then, following Umfraville's death in 1381, married his widow, Maud, by which he gained even greater lands. Maud not only held a life interest in the Umfraville lands (which enabled Percy to make good his title to them immediately), but she was also in her own right heiress to the enormous barony of Cockermouth in Cumbria (which included over thirty manors in that county), and to the barony of Langley in Northumberland, comprising six manors, by virtue of the childlessness of her brother Anthony, Lord Lucy. In 1383, in return for a promise by Henry that he would quarter the Lucy arms with his own, these vast lands were entailed on him and Maud and their heirs male, the effect of which was to deprive the rightful heirs of their title to them.[38]

In the lawless border society of fourteenth-century Northumberland, there were windfalls as well. In 1379, for example, the manor of Lucker escheated to Percy when its holder, David de Lucker, died, and his heir was found to be his uncle Henry, who had been outlawed fifteen years earlier for the murder of one of the wardens of the Scottish March.[39] And Henry Percy's eldest son, Hotspur, showed no sign of abandoning his father's territorial policy, for shortly before his death in 1403 he purchased several manors in Northumberland from Sir Richard Arundel. By the time the Percys were brought to ruin (albeit temporarily) as a consequence of their rebellions against Henry IV, they held four castles, five baronies, and some seventy manors in Northumberland, all acquired during the previous hundred years. Having also been granted the sheriffdom of the county for life in 1385 – and, of course, being earl as well – Henry Percy must have dominated the county to an extraordinary degree. Good luck had played its part in this, but it was essentially through a judicious marriage policy, royal service, consistent purchasing, and an unscrupulous attitude to the rights of others, that such a massive territorial power-block, which, when combined with their York-shire estates, was to create such problems in the north for Henry IV, had been created.

Landholders' desire for territorial consolidation was naturally recognised by the king, and was consistently taken into account by him whenever possible. There are innumerable examples of grants of small amounts of lands, single manors and so forth, conforming to this pattern, but more telling, and in the long run more formative, was the distribution of those great estates which fell in to the king. Two examples will suffice: the dispersal of the Warenne inheritance after 1347, and the granting out of the Arundel, Warwick and Gloucester estates forfeited to Richard II in 1397. When John de Warenne, earl of Surrey, died without legitimate children in 1347, the question of who would succeed to his estates had already been a matter of controversy for twenty years and more.[40] The earl of Arundel had a claim to them by virtue of the fact that his father had been married to Warenne's sister Alice, but there were other in-terested parties too, notably the king, and Warenne's mistress Isabel de Holland, and his bastards, to whom he had tried to persuade the king to allow them to pass. In the event, both his mistress and his bastards were to be cut out of the inheritance by the king in favour of himself and Arundel. There were five main blocks of land: the honours of Reigate and Lewes, which adjoined each other on the Surrey–Sussex border; the Welsh Marcher lordship of Bromfield and Yale (worth about £900 a year net), together with a number of other properties on the border of Shropshire and Wales; some twelve manors, three hundreds, and other lands in Somerset, Dorset and Wiltshire, worth about 800 marks a year, to which Warenne's title was a little suspect as he had acquired them as a result of an exchange with Thomas, earl of Lancaster, in 1318–19 and only had them confirmed following Lancaster's forfeiture in 1322; a group of about fifteen manors in south Yorkshire centred on the castles of Conisbrough and Sandal, and including the towns of Wakefield, Halifax and Dewsbury; and about ten manors in Lincolnshire, with the towns of Stamford and Grantham. Lewes, Reigate, and the Welsh lands were granted to Arundel, complementing perfectly his existing holdings in both regions (the honour of Arundel, and the Welsh lordships of Oswestry, Chirk and Clun, with the town of Shrewsbury). The West Country lands were taken by Edward III and granted to William Montague, earl of Salisbury, as had been promised to his father at the time of his elevation to the earldom in 1337.[41] It was in the West Country that the Montagues were already strongest. The Yorkshire lands were also taken by the king and used to form the initial territorial endowment of his fourth son, Edmund (later duke of York). The Lincolnshire lands were held in dower by Warenne's widow, Joan de Bar, until her death, but in 1363 they too were added to Edmund's estate.

A clear territorial logic also underlay Richard II's distribution of the forfeited Appellant estates in 1397. The principal beneficiaries were those who had helped the king to defeat his enemies, notably William le Scrope, earl of Wiltshire, Edward, earl of Rutland, Thomas Mowbray, earl of Nottingham, and John Holland, earl of Huntingdon.[42] From the earl of Arundel's lands, Mowbray was granted the honours of Lewes and Reigate (which adjoined his own Sussex honour of Bramber: see Map 4) and the castle and town of Castle Acre in Norfolk, together with some smaller properties in the county, which complemented the East Anglian lands which he stood to inherit from his grandmother, the new duchess of Norfolk. From the earl of Warwick's lands, he received six manors in Warwickshire in a line stretching from Berkswell (west of Coventry) to Brailes (near Banbury), which fitted perfectly with his existing holdings in the county, consisting of eight manors running in a parallel line slightly to the east, from Thurlaston (near Rugby) to Chipping Warden and Weston (north-east of Banbury).[43] Warwick's Durham honour of Barnard Castle, however, was given to le Scrope, and was clearly designed to extend the north Yorkshire heartland of the Scrope estates, which reached along Wensleydale, Swaledale, and the upper Tees, and which William could expect to inherit from his now aged father in the near future. Le Scrope was also granted Arundel's powerful castle of Holt in Clwyd, precisely the area where the king had been building up le Scrope's power during the previous few years (and in the following year he was granted custody of the lordship of Denbigh when the earl of March died).[44] Rutland meanwhile was granted all of Gloucester's lands in southern Yorkshire, including the large and valuable manor of Burstwick-in-Holderness, which again fitted well with the lands which he could expect to inherit from his father, the duke of York. The logic of the 1397 grants is thus to be found not in the desire by Richard to destroy forever the possibility that the three great inheritances of his opponents might be reunited[45] (they were in fact put together again perfectly easily in 1399), but in the desire to reinforce the existing regional strengths of his friends. The method adopted – by dividing them according to the existing honours or receiverships – was as traditional as it was convenient.

The advantages of consolidation were so clear that some landholders were even keen to make temporary arrangements. When Peter, fourth Lord Mauley, retired from public life in 1332 he handed over the central portion of his inheritance (in the North and East Ridings) to his son, but he was prepared to allow his outlying share of the barony of Doncaster, with the manor and town, to be held by John de Warenne for the latter's life, as long as it reverted to the Mauleys after his death.[46] Presumably this was at Warenne's request, for Doncaster was adjacent to his own south Yorkshire lands. Right up to the last years of her life, Richard II's mother, Princess Joan, was trying to consolidate her lands in Cardiganshire by exchange.[47] Some exchanges, like the extensive swap of lands in Yorkshire, Wales and the West Country which was agreed in 1318–19 between Thomas, earl of Lancaster, and John de Warenne, were probably for political and personal reasons as much as for administrative convenience (the two earls had virtually gone to war with each other following Warenne's abduction of Lancaster's wife in 1317), but there were no doubt administrative advantages to be gained too.[48]

There was nothing new in the fourteenth century about the desire to conslidate holdings. More pertinent was the question of how consolidation was to be effected and whether it could be maintained, and here landholders were helped by the changes which occurred during the later Middle Ages in the laws and customs concerning the transmission of property. These changes were both complex and gradual – indeed, in many ways they were no more than the logical continuation of the way in which feudalism had been developing for centuries.[49] Nevertheless they were of immense significance, and their significance extends far beyond the effect they had on landholders' ability to consolidate their lands. Essentially, what happened was that as a result of the gradual acceptance of certain legal devices (notably the entail, the jointure, and the enfeoffment to use) which were designed specifically to circumvent the rigidities of feudal custom, feudal tenants were increasingly able to avoid the exaction by their lords of the obligations which were technically consequent upon their vassalage, as well as to regulate the transmission of their lands in accordance with their own wishes, either during their lifetime or after their death. 'Feudal tenants' includes every landholder in England apart from the king, for the king was the only person in England who truly *owned* land.

The rigidities of early feudal tenure had to a large extent disappeared already by the late thirteenth century, but two significant restrictions remained. Firstly, landholders were still liable to feudal incidents, of which by far the most important was wardship and marriage; and secondly, they could not bequeath their lands as they wished, for land held feudally followed feudal rules of inheritance, which meant primogeniture. Entails, jointures, and enfeoffments to use provided landholders with ways of getting round these restrictions. Entails were popularised by the clause *De Donis Conditionalibus* in the 1285 Statute of Westminster. As the title of the clause suggests, the entail was in essence a conditional gift. The condition attached to it was that as long as the grantee and his descendants continued to have direct heirs (i.e. legitimate issue of his body), they continued to be the legal holders of the land, but once the grantee's direct line failed, the land reverted to the heirs general (i.e. the primogenitary heirs) of the grantor. Thus the essential difference between land held in tail and land held in fee simple was that the former could not be inherited by collaterals.[50] Naturally, it was also stipulated that entailed land could not be alienated for a period longer than the life of the grantee, since to sell the land outright would be to nullify the reversionary rights of the heirs general. This was the basic entail, or fee tail, or estate tail (the terms are interchangeable), but further conditions could be added. If land was granted in tail male rather than simply in tail, then only if the grantee's family continued in the direct *male* line would the land remain with them. Also, by employing the entail with remainder (or with a series of remainders), a landlord could create second, third, or (theoretically) any number of further estates in the land, which were to come into operation after his death (or after the death of the original grantee). What he did was to entail the land upon himself, with remainder to his desired beneficiary. The advantage of this was that the original landholder continued to enjoy the profits of the land while he lived (a simple entail would not achieve this), while at the same time, by virtue of the remainder, he could dispose of it after his death in accordance with his wishes, and, by virtue of the entail, maintain the reversionary rights of his heirs general. This was one way in which landholders could evade the feudal restriction on bequeathing property.

The object of *De Donis*, as specifically stated in the statute, was to protect the rights of primogenitary heirs by forbidding alienation for a period longer than the life of the grantee or his direct descendants, and although in the short term it facilitated the process by which land could be granted to persons *other* than the primogenitary heir, this was only because landholders were now aware that in the long term there was a good chance that the land would return to the direct line of the original grantor. In a more general sense, entails gave a landholder more choice in the disposal of his property, and they might also provide confirmation of title to land. In theory, too, entails were protected from forfeiture in the event of the holder being convicted for treason, though in practice this custom was not always followed.[51]

The jointure was simply a joint tenancy in survivorship by a landholder and his wife, normally achieved by the husband granting his lands (or some of them) to trustees who would then grant them back to him and his wife jointly. In order to protect the heirs of their marriage from the possible consequences of a second marriage should the wife be widowed, jointures were normally combined with an entail. Jointures first became popular in the second half of the thirteenth century, and by the fourteenth century were very common. There were two main advantages. The first was the avoidance of feudal incidents through the retention by the wife of the lands after her husband's death, thus (for as long as she lived) denying to the superior lord his rights of wardship over the lands. Secondly, jointures provided for the security of the wife after her husband's death, and they were thus frequently negotiated as part of the marriage contract. In theory, widows had always been entitled to their dower thirds of their husbands' lands, but there was often considerable haggling over dowers, with widows under pressure to take less or to commute their dower rights for cash. The security of the widow was also threatened by the increasing popularity of entails and enfeoffments to use, which might reduce the inheritance from which the third was to be taken. Although she might still be under pressure from her family, with a jointure the widow was at least secure at law.[52]

The enfeoffment to use (or 'use' as it is commonly called) was in essence a trust. The landholder (the 'feoffor') granted his lands, in fee simple, to a group of trustees (the 'feoffees'), who thus became the legal holders of the land. By prior arrangement, however, the profits of the land would be made over by the feoffees to whomsoever the original grantor nominated (the 'cestui-que-use') and after his death they would grant it to another party – again, naturally, according to his wishes. Frequently the landholder would nominate himself as the first cestui-que-use, which enabled him to continue enjoying the profits while he lived, simultaneously nominating his intended beneficiary post mortem. He had thus succeeded in bypassing feudal inheritance law, for technically the land was never actually inherited. The great advantage of the use was its flexibility: time limits could be set on its operation, and any number of secondary conditions could be attached. Naturally, feudal obligations could also be evaded, for since a landholder did not legally hold any land that had been enfeoffed by him at the time of his death, his superior lord had no claim to its wardship, and it could continue to be held by the feoffees on behalf of the heir until he came of age. while the profits would either be made available to him or allowed to accrue for his future benefit.

The entail, the jointure, and the use revolutionised fourteenth-century landholding. De Donis certainly did not create entails, but by securing the reversioner's rights it made them much more popular, so that by the late fourteenth century most of the land in England was held in tail rather than in fee simple. Jointures were equally popular, and soon came to form a standard part of most marriage contracts. Acceptance of the use took a little longer, partly because, being the most radical of the three devices (at least in the short term), it was closely controlled by superior lords, and partly because, being a legal fiction and thus not enforceable at common law, many landholders themselves were probably wary of it. Numerous examples of all three devices can, and have, been cited, and naturally different landholders were inclined to use the new freedom which they had acquired in different ways. Nevertheless it is possible to make some generalisations, though it is very important to distinguish between the long-term and the short-term intentions of landholders. In the long term, the primary consideration of the great majority of landholders was to maintain the integrity of their estates. In the short term, there were three principal considerations: the evasion of feudal incidents (especially wardship), the funding of projects close to the landlord's heart, and the desire to make ample provision for his immediate family, that is, his wife, his sons, and his daughters. Some examples will demonstrate this.

Just before departing on campaign to France in 1345, Thomas Beauchamp, earl of Warwick, undertook an extensive reorganisation of his estates, the object of which was to make proper provision for his numerous children in the event of his death. He had four sons and four daughters, though his youngest son, William, was intended for the church and thus did not figure in these arrangements.[53] The largest portion of his lands (Warwick castle with seven manors in Warwickshire, the lordships of Barnard Castle in Durham and Painscastle in the Welsh March, and six manors in other counties) was jointly entailed upon himself and his eldest son, Guy, with successive remainders to each of his younger sons, in tail male. A further four manors were entailed upon the earl and his wife in jointure with remainder to Guy, four manors in Cornwall were entailed upon the earl and his wife with remainder to his second son, Thomas, and two manors and a hundred in Rutland were entailed upon the earl and his wife with remainder to his third son, Reynbrun. Each of these latter three grants was also in tail male, and in each it was specified that should the son upon whom they were initially remaindered die without male issue, successive remainders should be vested in the other two sons, in order of age. Finally, Elmley castle and eight manors in Worcestershire, together with four manors in Gloucestershire and one in Warwickshire, were en-feoffed to trustees for a term of twelve years on condition that they should make over to the earl a rent of £373 *per annum* from the lands, which was to be set aside to provide marriage-portions for his daughters. Elizabeth was to get £1,200, Matilda and Philippa 1,000 marks each, and Katharine £200. If the earl died before the twelve years had passed, the trustees were to continue to hold the lands until they had accumulated the £2,733. 6s. 8d. necessary to provide these marriage-portions, whereupon it 'should be lawful for his [primogenitary] heirs to enter upon and hold the said castle and manors for ever'.

Before his death in 1369, Earl Thomas was to have cause radically to revise these arrangements, but his intentions at the time are perfectly clear. In the short term, he was providing security for his wife, marriage-portions for his daughters, and lands for his younger sons. If this alone had been his aim, he could of course have done it quite easily without the need to employ jointures, entails, or uses, but the difference was that he could now do so without prejudicing the long-term integrity of the inheritance. By entailing each group of lands on each of his sons in succession, he was ensuring that if one or more of his sons should predecease him, what he held would still be divided among those who remained, and by granting the lands not just in tail, but in tail male, he was ensuring that at no time in the future could the lands be partitioned between co-heiresses. At the same time, the twelve-year use which he created for his daughters' marriage-portions was specifically designed to ensure that even should he die they would still be properly provided for, for the effect of this was to remove the lands in question from the inheritance of his primogenitary heir until the appropriate sums had been accumulated. After this, however, the lands would return to his heir. Warwick had no doubts about whom he wanted to succeed him: one of his sons, failing whom one of his grandsons. Though he cared greatly for the welfare of his daughters, he had no desire to see his inheritance parcelled out among grand-daughters.

In this, he was far from untypical. In theory, by employing either the entail or the use, landholders were now perfectly able to cut their daughters out of the inheritance, and thus, if their daughters were their heiresses (i.e. if they had no sons), to keep the estates intact by entailing them on, for example, a nephew, or a brother. In practice, they hardly ever did so. It is here that we see the crucial difference between the long-term and short-term intentions of landholders. The great majority of landholders undoubtedly placed the welfare of their immediate children at the top of their list of priorities. They were quite happy to see their lands divided between daughters, even if it meant the dissipation of the inheritance. At the same time, though, the prevailing (and growing) fashion for tail male was bound in the long term to deprive female descendants of their inheritances. A classic case is that of the Berkeley inheritance (see Table 3). In January 1349 Thomas, Lord Berkeley (d. 1361), surrendered the central portion of his estates (the castle, manor and hundred of Berkeley, with ten manors of the ancient patrimony and a number of appurtenant rights) to feoffees and received it back from them in tail male, with remainder to his eldest son, Maurice, Maurice's wife, and their heirs male. Since Maurice was already his heir, the only reason Thomas can have had for doing this would have been a desire to ensure that at no time in the future was the ancient barony of Berkeley partitioned between co-heiresses, or in any other way alienated (the prevalence of the plague probably encouraged him to act at this time).[54] Thomas was duly succeeded by Maurice in 1361, and Maurice by another Thomas in 1368; but when this Thomas died in 1417, his heir general was his only child, Elizabeth, who was married to Richard Beauchamp, earl of Warwick. As a result of this entail, however, made nearly seventy years earlier, the heir to the barony of Berkeley was not Elizabeth but her cousin James, nephew of Thomas (d. 1417), the senior surviving heir male of Maurice, and although Elizabeth and her husband (and indeed their three daughters and *their* husbands) fought long and hard to recover what they considered to be their rightful inheritance, they were forced to make do with a compromise which left James with the major portion of the inheritance (as well as the right to a parliamentary summons).[55]

The twin themes of provision for one's children and maintenance of the integrity of the inheritance are also revealed in the

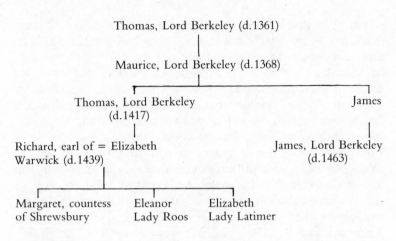

Table 3 *The Berkeley inheritance in 1417*

will of Hugh, earl of Stafford (d. 1386), only by employing a use rather than an entail he was able to take the process a step further. Before his death Stafford had enfeoffed to trustees a very substantial portion of his lands, with which they were to fulfil three requests: the pensions of his retainers were to continue to be paid for the terms of their (the pensioners') lives, a dowry was to be provided for his daughter, and each of his three younger sons was to be given an annuity of £100 and be granted £100 worth of land – but the crucial condition attached to this final request was that they were only to hold these lands for the terms of their lives, after which they were to revert to the earl's primogenitary heir and his descendants.[56] As can be seen from this, it was the flexibility of the use which was its chief advantage over the entail. Almost any object that the landholder desired could be achieved through it. The payment of pensioners' annuities was one which was frequently stipulated, as was the payment of the landholder's debts. Building projects, often of a religious nature, and other forms of religious endowment, were also commonly provided for. Henry of Grosmont, for example, gave lands worth several thousand pounds (including the honours of Bolingbroke and Tutbury) to feoffees just a week before he died, with the intention that they should use the profits from them to complete his endowment of St Mary's College, Leicester. King

Edward III similarly enfeoffed extensive lands which he had purchased to a group of his closest advisers less than a year before he died, to complete the endowment of his three favoured religious houses. Not surprisingly, heirs sometimes challenged these grants, and usually some sort of compromise was reached;[57] but as time went on and uses became increasingly accepted as an integral part of English property law, it became very difficult to overturn such arrangements.

In those very few cases where the object of the landholder's arrangements was substantially to disinherit an heir general who was also his child, there was naturally an even greater likelihood that his dispositions would be challenged. It must be emphasised that such cases are extremely rare, but one striking example comes from the early fourteenth century. In 1310–11, John, Lord Grey of Wilton, entailed the castle and lordship of Ruthin with the cantred of Dyffryn Clwyd, and no less than twenty-one manors, mostly in Bedfordshire and Buckinghamshire, on his son (by his second marriage) Roger, thus detaching them from the inheritance of his eldest son (by his first marriage) and heir general, Henry. R.I. Jack estimated that the lands entailed on Roger were worth about £850 *per annum*, while those left for Henry were worth only £280 *per annum*; as he points out, it is probably the most remarkable example in the Middle Ages (at least at this level of society) of the employment of a device which so drastically disinherited an eldest son. Nor is it surprising to find that after his father's death in 1325 Henry resisted the settlement strongly, not only at law but also by violence. He did manage to win a few manors back (no more than two or three), but in 1328 he was forced to recognise the validity of his father's entail. As a consequence, the Greys of Wilton were never again the force that they had been, or might have become. The new Greys of Ruthin, however, descended from Roger, and further massively boosted by the acquisition of much of the Hastings inheritance in 1390, went from strength to strength, until in 1465 Edmund Grey of Ruthin, Roger's direct descendant, was created earl of Kent.[58]

Why John, Lord Grey, did what he did in 1310–11 is a matter for speculation – it probably had much to do with personalities. In another case in which the Greys were involved, their acquisition of part of the Hastings inheritance, there is a clearer picture of the motivation involved. In 1372, when still childless and about to set off on campaign to Gascony, John Hastings, earl of Pembroke, made arrangements for the inheritance of his vast comital estates should he fail to return from the war. His chief aim in doing so was specifically to disinherit his heir general, Reynold, Lord Grey of Ruthin (son of Roger), with whom he had quarrelled violently during the previous two years. To achieve this, he placed almost all his estates (with the king's permission, which was granted in return for the lordship of Pembroke) in the hands of feoffees, with instructions, in the event of his death without children, to grant them to his cousin William Beauchamp. He then sailed away to Gascony.[59]

At this point, a complication arose. Pembroke did indeed fail to return from France. He was captured by the Castilians and imprisoned by them for three years, and died in April 1375 while on his way back to England to collect money for his ransom. Shortly after his departure in 1372, his wife Anne had given birth to a son, John, who was naturally the heir to the earldom and all the estates, so for the moment William Beauchamp's hopes were dashed. In 1389, however, not even having reached his majority, the young John Hastings was killed at a tournament. This raised a new problem: had the birth of the heir in 1372 invalidated the enfeoffment made earlier that year, or had it merely rendered it dormant? In other words, was William Beauchamp the heir to the Pembroke lands in 1389, or was Reynold, Lord Grey?[60] As it turned out, the matter never came to court. In all probability neither William nor Reynold could feel too sure about the outcome should the matter go to law, and they decided to come to an agreement. Beauchamp took the castle and lordship of Abergavenny and about twenty-five manors, and Grey took the rest, a further thirty-five or so manors.

Although few men acted in such extreme fashion as did John Hastings simply out of personal dislike, his action demonstrates vividly that new freedom of choice which was available to the fourteenth-century landholder; and since that freedom was very unlikely to be used to undermine the rights of his children, the real element of choice available to him was often between collaterals. Thus while the *rights* accorded to collaterals were naturally falling away (since they could not inherit entailed land), the *opportunities* for at least some of them, as for younger sons, were there to be grasped. John Hastings wished his lands to go to William Beauchamp not because William was his cousin, but because the two men were friends and he considered that Beauchamp would prove a worthy successor to his title.[61] The story of William Beauchamp is worth pursuing further, for he was a younger son, and his rise to prominence and wealth (though no doubt merited by ability) was very largely dependent on that new element of choice which landholders had acquired through the entail and the use. William was the fourth son of that Thomas, earl of Warwick, who in 1345 had reorganised his estates to make provision for his children. At that time William had been intended for the church, and thus sent to Oxford, but when two of his elder brothers (Guy, the eldest, and Reynbrun) died within a few months of each other in 1361, he was removed from the university, so that he would be able to inherit the earldom in case his last surviving elder brother died as well. Initially he was given only a few lands by his father, but shortly before his death in 1369 Earl Thomas completely revised his arrangements. He created a use whereby about ten manors (mostly in Worcestershire) were to be granted in tail male to William, thus transforming him from a poorly-endowed younger son into a notable West Midland landholder, and simultaneously depleting the inheritance of his elder brother (Thomas, who became the fourth earl) by about 400 marks per annum (see Map 3).[62] Once William had also inherited Abergavenny and further manors in 1390–1, his estate was approaching comital size (Abergavenny was worth at least £500 a year net, and his thirty-five or so additional manors can hardly have been worth much less than £750 a year). He was duly summoned as a peer of parliament from 1392 until his death, and within thirty years his son Richard had been granted an earldom (that of Worcester), though he died in the following year. William's wife Joan was still alive, however, and continued to hold these lands until her death in 1435, whereupon they reverted (in accordance with the entail of 1369) to the earl of Warwick – and not only these lands, but also those acquired by William (his share of the Hastings inheritance). Thus over a period of ninety years in all, the great Beauchamp inheritance

[147]

had done service not only to three successive earls but also to their cadets (and one in particular), but at the end of that time, when the cadet branches died out in the male line, everything had been reunited once more – and with interest.

The control over their inheritances which these new legal devices afforded to fourteenth-century landholders was certainly remarkable, but it was by no means absolute, and they were not without their attendant problems. The legal position of the enfeoffment to use, for example, was equivocal to say the least, for being a legal fiction it was not justiciable at common law, and not surprisingly heirs general were sometimes inclined to challenge dispositions which severely depleted their inheritances. There was also the possibility that feoffees might act fraudulently, though most landholders chose their feoffees carefully and this was very uncommon.[63] Nevertheless, the problem of whether or not uses could be enforced at law probably made some landholders remain suspicious of them. The entail and the jointure were also somewhat unpredictable in their effects. If extensive lands were granted in jointure, for example, the effect might be to remove these lands from the heir's inheritance for a very long time, thus severely reducing his wealth, stature and influence. Hence the prominence of several of those tough old dowagers, such as Marie de Saint Pol, countess of Pembroke, or Margaret Marshal, countess of Norfolk, who are such a feature of late medieval England. For example, the first adult lord of the Mowbray family to enter upon the Brotherton and Segrave inheritances (to which they had acquired the titles in 1338 and 1353 respectively, and which were worth about twice as much as the Mowbray patrimony itself) was Duke John in 1413, and the reason was the longevity of the widows who held jointure and dower rights in the lands.[64] Entails, too, might deprive primogenitary heirs of substantial portions of their inheritances for several generations, and in such circumstances the knowledge that the land would eventually return to the main line of the family was not always sufficiently comforting. Resources were limited, and needs had to be balanced against each other. Hugh, earl of Stafford, evidently considered that his duty extended to providing for his children, but no further. It was up to *them* to make provision for *their* children.[65] Most heirs general were not as lucky as his, however, and were reduced to waiting until cadet branches died out naturally before their inheritances could be reunited.

Another problem for many landholders was the decline in their feudal revenues which followed from the ability of their tenants to use these devices to evade feudal incidents – especially wardship, which was potentially the most profitable of them. In this sense, all great landholders were in an ambivalent position, for they were both lords and tenants. Thus while they wished to avoid the consequences of wardship as far as their own heirs were concerned, they were simultaneously eager to maximise the profits which they might receive from the wardship of their tenants' lands. In 1339, for example, the 'great men' of the realm complained in parliament 'that remedy be ordained in this parliament concerning men who when dying make alienation of their lands . . . by fraud to deprive the chief lords of the wardship of them'.[66] J.M.W Bean has argued that it was only shortly after this date that uses became common among tenants-in-chief (who held land directly from the king), whereas they were already common among mesne tenants, and this may explain why the 'great men' thought that they were being defrauded by their lessers at this time. There are also signs that, once the Black Death had brought home to them the likelihood that their incomes were about to suffer an even more serious decline, they made greater attempts to claw back what they could. John of Gaunt, for example, sent out a circular to all the 'guardians of fees and franchises' in his receiverships in late 1374 ordering them to make inquiries about all wardships, marriages and escheats which might pertain to him within their spheres of jurisdiction, and to continue reporting to his council on the matter twice every year. The Black Prince was also much concerned with the problem, as demonstrated by a number of cases in the 1350s and 1360s.[67] While this suggests anxiety, it is difficult to know how successful such measures were, but Booth has argued that the Black Prince's 'rights of lordship were maintained rigorously and extended wherever possible', and Astill found that great lords kept a close eye on uses in late fourteenth-century Leicestershire, which was probably why, although wardship was greatly resented by the local gentry, not many of them were able to employ uses in order to evade it.[68] Since feudal and judicial profits tended to be greater in large lordships than in smaller ones, the greater landlords stood to lose most from the implementation of these devices. If, however, they were successful in restricting the gentry's employment of them (as at least some of them appear to have been), and if at the same time they were able to deprive the king of the wardship of their own lands, they naturally had much to gain.

The position of the crown requires special attention, for alone among English landholders the king was always lord and never tenant. Thus he could only lose from any widespread ability to evade feudal incidents. Bean argued that it was only from *circa* 1340 that tenants-in-chief began to employ the use with any regularity, and that the chief responsibility for the decline in the crown's feudal revenues must thus be laid largely at the feet of Edward III. Why, he asked, was Edward III apparently happy to forgo his rights in this way?[69] There are probably three reasons. Firstly, because tenurial customs were already moving in this direction, and had been for a long time; although the concessions that Edward was prepared to allow to his great landholders were undoubtedly substantial, it would have required a considerable act of will on the part of the crown to resist the changes that were taking place. Secondly, and most importantly, the whole basis of crown finance was changing in the fourteenth century. Increasingly, what mattered was taxation, not the king's 'ordinary' (including feudal) revenues. What Edward was doing, probably quite consciously, was to trade marginal revenues for the co-operation and good will through which he hoped to gain greater ones – especially, of course, through support in parliament, where taxation was granted. Thirdly, it would be wrong to exaggerate the decline in the king's feudal revenues. Tenants-in-chief certainly had no automatic right to create enfeoffments to use. When the earl of Pembroke set up the use by which he hoped to disinherit Lord Grey in 1372, he gave the king the valuable lordship of Pembroke (worth about £300 *per annum*) for the right to do so. For a licence to create a use which settled lands on his younger sons in 1383, Henry, earl of Northumberland, paid £350 to Richard II.[70] Such licences served a double purpose: not only did they bring in revenue, they also enabled

the king to keep a check on the passage of land held directly
from him, and thus to maintain control over it. Moreover, evasion of wardship through uses did not extend to personal
wardship and marriage. It only deprived the king of the
wardship of the lands, and substantial profits could still be made
from selling or otherwise exploiting the wardship and marriage
of the heir or heiress in person. There also remained a surprisingly large number of tenants of all classes who failed to, or
decided not to, or were not permitted to, take advantage of these
devices. Some were no doubt refused licences. Others probably
remained suspicious of them, and there were perhaps some who
simply failed to make proper arrangements before their deaths.
The great March inheritance, for example, fell into the hands of
the crown twice during the last twenty years of the fourteenth
century. On the first occasion it was (after some initial
wrangling)[71] committed in the winter of 1383–4 to the wardship
of four high-ranking magnates for a joint annual rent of £4,000,
payable to the royal exchequer. On the second occasion, in 1398,
it was parcelled out to the king's current favourites in an attempt
to strengthen their territorial and financial power-bases.[72] On
each occasion the earl died suddenly and may not have got round to
making alternative dispositions.

Finally, it is important to remember that the adoption of these
devices could have positive benefits for the chief lord of the fee,
for since entailed lands could not be inherited by collaterals, it
meant that when they were entailed *directly* by, for example, the
king, on to one of his subjects, there was a much greater chance
that they would escheat to the crown before too long and could
accordingly be re-granted to another deserving candidate. Because they were held in tail rather than in fee simple, the comital
inheritances of the earl of Norfolk (in 1306) and the earl of Suffolk (in 1382) fell in to the king. That of Norfolk, probably
worth about £3,000 *per annum*, was used by Edward I to endow
Thomas of Brotherton, his elder son by his second marriage.[73]
That of Suffolk was transferred almost wholesale by Richard II
to his favourite Michael de la Pole, who also acquired the title in
1385. In each case, had the lands been held in fee simple, they
would have passed to collaterals and thus out of the crown's
control. In this way, the entail could increase the resources

available to the king and help him to maintain control over the composition of his nobility. This is one of the reasons for that increasing politicisation of promotions to the higher nobility which has already been discussed.[74]

To quantify the gains made by landholders from their ability to evade feudal incidents would be impossible, but there are indications that these could be very substantial. Although the wardship of the March inheritance fell in to the king in 1381, he was under pressure from some of the nobility not to grant it out to courtiers who might exploit it (by asset-stripping, for example), but instead to grant it to persons who would safeguard the interests of the minor and preserve the revenues until he came of age. It was with this in mind that the entire inheritance was put in the guardianship of those four high-ranking magnates (the earls of Arundel, Warwick, and Northumberland, and John, Lord Nevill of Raby) in February 1384, for a joint annual rent of £4,000. Yet despite such a seemingly high rent, the four lords apparently performed their task so well that, according to the chronicler of Wigmore (the Mortimer *caput*), over the remaining eight or nine years of the young earl's minority not only were 'castles, houses and other dwelling places . . . well maintained', but a sum of no less than 40,000 marks was accumulated from the profits of the estates and made available to Roger Mortimer when he came of age.[75] The reliability of the chronicler's estimate is obviously open to question, but the whole episode is indicative of a widespread change in attitudes to wardship in the later Middle Ages. In 1339, and again in 1376, petitions were submitted to the king in parliament requesting that the wardship of lands in the king's hands should be granted to the friends or kinsmen of the minor in question rather than to royal favourites or simply to the highest bidder, who would naturally be more inclined to exploit the lands for all they were worth.[76] Moreover, even in cases where uses had not been created, the king was sometimes, as a mark of favour, prepared simply to waive his right to wardship over the lands, as well as the wardship and marriage of the heir. Such favours were by no means common, no doubt because they were of such value to the family concerned.[77] But the general consequence of this changing attitude to wardship was that minorities might not necessarily be as debilitating as they had once been. Indeed, as with the March minority of the 1380s, they might afford an opportunity for recuperation and revenue accumulation.

This chapter began with the assertion that despite falling profits from arable in the fourteenth century, the disposable income of most peers was greater at the end of the century than it had been at the beginning. Hopefully, the reasons why this was so are now becoming clearer. By adapting his land to changing economic circumstances (by leasing the demesne, and by switching from arable to pasture), the landholder was to a certain extent able to mitigate the adverse effects of price and wage trends. By acquiring more land, especially in a concentrated form around the *caput honoris*, he was both increasing his sources of revenue and making his lands easier to manage. By employing the new legal devices which were available to him, he could both maintain the integrity of his estate in its more consolidated form and go some of the way towards evading his feudal obligations to superior lords. And by tightening up his administrative structure, he could both extract more from the peasantry under his lordship, and try to minimise his own loss of feudal revenues. But along with all these developments, the fourteenth century also witnessed in many cases a marked increase in the alternative sources of revenue available to landholders.

It has already been suggested that the basis of crown finance altered fundamentally during the fourteenth century, so that by the end of the century English kings were heavily dependent on taxation. What this meant was that although in the end fourteenth-century kings may not have been richer than their predecessors, the turnover of cash and tallies in the exchequer certainly increased, and this benefited the nobility because, in one way or another, more and more of this increased turnover found its way into their pockets. Some did so directly. In June 1340, for example, 'as a gift', Edward III granted the earl of Arundel £1,000 from the second year of the ninth recently granted in parliament.[78] Such unashamed misappropriation of supply was uncommon, however. More usually, 'public money' was transferred to the nobility in the form of wages of war or annuities, normally (at least in theory) in return for military service. As is well known, wages of war were not always paid very promptly, but this may only have encouraged commanders to make what they could of the system. Some were undoubtedly dishonest, as for example John, Lord Nevill, who in 1372 contracted with the king to take 600 men to the relief of Brest, received payment for that number, but ended up only taking about 100 with him and, apparently, pocketing the wages of the rest. This case is known to us because the details emerged at the time of Nevill's impeachment in 1376, but many other similar cases probably never became public.[79] It also seems to have been common for commanders to offer their subcontracted soldiers rates of pay well below those which they received for their men from the crown, again presumably pocketing the difference.[80]

More direct transfers of wealth from the king to the nobility came in the form of pensions, fees and annuities. According to P. Contamine, the late medieval French royal budget became increasingly a 'budget of noble assistance'.[81] Much the same thing was happening in England. An early example comes from the years 1316–17, when Edward II tried to buy the support of nineteen of his leading magnates with promises of retaining fees totalling about £4,000 in peace-time and considerably more in time of war.[82] Edward III, under whom royal taxation scaled new heights, was even more generous to his supporters. As already seen, five out of the six new earls created in 1337 were granted sums of £1,000 or 1,000 marks at the exchequer to support their new-found dignity. These were ostensibly in lieu of landed endowments, but some of them continued to be taken for many years, and Edward was equally liberal with his retaining fees. Thomas, earl of Warwick, and Ralph, earl of Stafford, were each granted 1,000 marks at the exchequer, in 1347 and 1353 respectively, both for life, and Henry of Grosmont was also receiving £1,000 from the royal exchequer in the late 1340s.[83] Lesser peers also benefited substantially: Henry, Lord Percy, Henry, Lord Ferrers of Groby, Reginald Cobham of Sterborough, Geoffrey Scrope of Masham, Thomas Bradestone, John de Beauchamp, and Geoffrey de Say were all granted annuities by Edward ranging between 200 marks and 500 marks in the 1330s and 1340s,[84] and there were many more besides. Usually there were conditions attached to the grants (often of a military nature), but this should not blind us to the fact that life-grants were essentially a way of buying and rewarding political support. As such, they became habitual, a permanent channel through which members of the nobility expected a proportion of the crown's income to be diverted in their direction. In the mid-1360s, Edward III's annuity bill was probably in the region of £13,000.[85] By 1399, Richard II's was probably closer to £25,000. This was partly because, to those whom he liked, Richard was of a generous (many thought over-generous) disposition. To Michael de la Pole, for example, he granted 400 marks annually 'of special reward' in 1383, over and above the fees which he would normally take as chancellor anyway.[86] Among those receiving annuities in 1395–6 were the earl of Nottingham (200 marks), Richard of York, the king's godson (350 marks), Edmund, duke of York (500 marks), and Thomas Holland, son of the earl of Kent (200 marks).[87] The earls of Huntingdon and Buckingham each received 1,000 marks a year at their creations in 1377, and when Buckingham was elevated to a dukedom in 1385 he and his brother Edmund (who also became a duke in that year) each received a further £1,000 a year. But what really swelled the royal annuity bill in the 1390s was Richard's policy of retaining king's knights and esquires. By 1397 he was already retaining about 250 knights and esquires, at a cost – theoretically, at least – of about £10,000 a year. By 1399, his gentry retainers alone were probably costing the king at least £15,000 a year, and his policy was continued by his successor. Within six months of Henry IV's coronation, his council estimated that royal annuities cost the exchequer some £24,000 a year. By the middle of the reign the figure may well have been close to £30,000 – and this excludes some £8,000 worth of annuities charged to the revenues of the duchy of Lancaster throughout the reign. At this rate, annuities were accounting for close on a third of all royal revenue, and although they were not paid as often as they were promised, to judge from the bitter complaints in parliament kings were well advised not to allow arrears to accumulate for too long.[88]

And of course it was not only from the crown – indeed, not principally from the crown – that the gentry benefited in this respect. The figure of 200 or so knights and esquires retained by John of Gaunt in the early 1380s was thoroughly untypical, but retaining was widespread in fourteenth-century England (and became more so in the later years of the century). It has often been assumed that most peers spent about 10 per cent of their income on retaining fees, but this was probably very much a minimum. R.E. Archer has estimated that Thomas Mowbray's grants in land, cash and offices accounted for about 40 per cent of his income in the late 1390s, although it dropped to more like 20 per cent under his successor.[89] The significance of this calculation is that it includes lands and offices as well as cash grants, thus, in an age when the number of sinecures was increasing, providing a much more realistic picture of the degree of transference of wealth from peers to gentry than any calculation based on fees alone. Moreover, peers sometimes granted annuities to other peers, and naturally these tended to be larger than those which they granted to knights or esquires. In 1365, for example, the Black Prince granted to Richard, earl of Arundel, 'and his heirs for ever', £400 worth a year of rent from his lands in Chester.[90] In general, the number of fees and annuities changing hands in late fourteenth-century England is symptomatic of a higher level of disposable income, and it had important economic as well as political consequences for all classes of noblemen. For a knight, whose average landed income was probably in the region of £50 to £100, a retaining fee of £20 (or £40 or £60, which is what the king frequently offered) was a very substantial addition. Even for the earl of Arundel, rich as he undoubtedly was, £400 a year was a lot of money. Moreover, since the size of retaining fees was to a large extent governed by the status of the recipient, their effect was to accentuate existing economic and social divisions. The chief beneficiaries of retaining were the county gentry, and it further widened the gap between them and the parish gentry.

It comes as no surprise to find that those who exude the greatest signs of wealth are often those whose careers were most closely linked to the service of the crown. Some made their fortunes in the war – like Sir John Fastolf and those other profiteers from ransoms and booty described by McFarlane.[91] The profits of war sometimes came in stranger ways as well. In May 1397, for example, Richard II gave £1,000 in compensation to Thomas Holland, the new earl of Kent, because it had been agreed that he would be appointed as king's lieutenant of Ireland for nine years, but then the king decided that he would appoint the earl of March to the post instead. The £1,000 was Holland's compensation for the breaking of the original indenture.[92] But the problem about going to war was that a soldier was as likely to lose a fortune as to make one. A surer road to prosperity lay in government service. C.D. Ross, in his study of the Yorkshire baronage, singled out four peers in the county whose disposable incomes seem to have been especially large: John, Lord Nevill; Richard, Lord Scrope of Bolton; Thomas, Lord Furnivall; and William, Lord Roos.[93] What they had in common was that they were all crown servants at the highest level. Nevill was for five years steward of the royal household. So was Scrope, as well as holding the chancellorship twice and the treasurership once. Roos and Furnivall were both treasurers of England under Henry IV. As buyers of land, builders of castles, patrons of religious houses, and lenders of money, they were outstanding among their generation. Richard Scrope, for example, was not only a buyer of land on a vast scale, he also rebuilt Bolton castle in splendid fashion, at a cost of roughly £12,000 spread over twenty years (1378–97). Ross estimated his landed income to be about £600 a year, so clearly he must have had substantial alternative sources of income. It may be, as McFarlane suggests, that he made his fortune as a war-captain,[94] but the timing is suggestive of something else. Scrope was treasurer of England in 1371–5, steward of the royal household in 1377–8, and chancellor in 1378–80 and again in 1381–2. It was a long time, in 1378, since he had been to war. The perks of office, by their very nature, are hidden from us, but if the charges of malpractice laid against the king's steward and chamberlain (John, Lord Nevill, and William, Lord Latimer) in the Good Parliament are anything to go by, they were potentially enormous.[95] It is far more likely that Bolton castle represents the profits of a decade in the highest echelons of the royal administration.

Even a year or two at this level could reap rewards that a lifetime of careful husbandry could not. Thomas, Lord Furnivall, was Henry IV's treasurer for just two years, during which time he was in a position personally to lend sums totalling £6,362 to the crown.[96] And for a man who spent forty years and more at the heart of English government, the wealth that could be accumulated was quite fabulous. After his death in 1376, it was discovered that Richard, earl of Arundel, had no less than 90,359 marks in hard cash (*deniers secks*) in his various castles and houses about the country (of which half was in the *haut tour* of Arundel castle), not counting additional sums due to him from various of his ministers and others.[97] Arundel was a great landholder and probably a thrifty one too, but he was also a lifelong royal councillor and servant. In the years 1348–56, W.M. Ormrod found, he was one of the most regular witnesses to royal charters. His record in this respect during the 1360s is astonishing. Of the 130 great charters issued by the king between April 1360 and December 1369, Arundel witnessed 126 (the next most frequent witness was Gaunt, with 72).[98] In other words, he was almost constantly at court, and without doubt a man of great influence in royal government. Not surprisingly, the wealth which he accumulated in the royal service was often used to make loans, some to his fellow nobles, but on a much greater scale to the crown. Some of his loans were enormous, as was the interest paid on them. In 1370, for example, he advanced (probably) 20,000 marks to the king, receiving £20,000 in return.[99] Twenty-five or 33 per cent interest on loans to the crown seems to have been quite common at this time, but 50 per cent seems excessive, and may represent either the government's desperation, or Arundel's bargaining strength, or both. Arundel's wealth was exceptional, but he understood well enough, as did many of his contemporaries, that there was money to be made in all sorts of ways in the service of the king.

Another source of disposable income for nobles who had sons to marry off was the new fashion for dowries in cash rather than in land, which had been gaining ground since the thirteenth century. The *maritagium* (dowry in land) had by no means disappeared even by the late fourteenth century, but the marriage-portion (dowry in cash, paid to the groom's father) seems to have been more popular from quite early in the century. Portions varied greatly in size, partly dependent, it seems, on the size of the jointure simultaneously offered by the groom's father, but more importantly on the status of the groom. G.A. Holmes estimated that among the higher nobility in the fourteenth century between 1,000 marks and £1,000 was average, but some went a lot higher than that. When the earls of March and Arundel agreed in 1354 to marry the former's son to the latter's daughter, Arundel was to pay £2,000.[100] These were admittedly great families, but why Thomas, Lord Berkeley (d. 1361), should have felt it necessary to offer £2,900 *and* the reversion of Langley Burrell manor (Wilts.) for his daughter Joan to marry Reginald Cobham in 1343 is by no means clear. Although a favourite of the king's, Cobham was only a banneret at the time and had not even received his first summons to parliament yet.[101] Thomas was a wealthy man, however (Smyth calls him 'Thomas the Ritch'), and perhaps Cobham drove a hard bargain. More typical was the 1,000 marks which Thomas received from Hugh, Lord Despenser, when he married his son Maurice to Hugh's sister Elizabeth in 1338. But whatever the reasons governing the size of individual portions, they could undoubtedly enhance a landholder's spending power – and naturally they not only contributed to the rise in the general level of disposable income among the nobility, but were also symptomatic of it.

The royal 'budget of noble assistance' thus worked in a whole variety of ways. The consequence of the development of regular taxation in fourteenth-century England was not simply to allow the king to pay his contract armies. It also allowed him to buy the support of the nobility, and, indirectly, it allowed the magnates to buy the support of the gentry. In this way, it also had important implications for the exercise of political power.

CONCLUSION

Political society in fourteenth-century England

In late medieval England, every great lord had his 'country'. It was here that his chief castle stood, where the core of his estates was concentrated, and where the leaders of local society looked to him to provide a focus for their service and aspirations. What, then, did a lord expect from his country? Naturally, he expected that he and his family would be given pride of place in the local social hierarchy. He expected the inhabitants of the region to pay their dues and support his lifestyle. He expected to be consulted on matters of importance concerning the region – and because his 'country' was part of a county, that included matters which affected the shire as a whole. More specifically, he expected the region to provide manpower for his retinues when he went on campaign, and at least part of his local retaining was probably geared specifically to that end.[1] He expected political or military support at home, either when he was engaged in a quarrel with one of his neighbours, or in a more general crisis.[2] He also expected to be able to raise money in a hurry when he needed it, either through impositions such as those laid by the Black Prince on Cheshire to finance his wars, or through loans from local towns, religious houses, and landholders.[3] And he expected the king (or greater lords than himself) to recognise his position in the region, and not to make grants or appointments which deliberately or implicitly undermined his authority there. Hence, for example, the earl of Northumberland's fury when Richard II appointed Thomas Mowbray as warden of the East March in 1389.[4] In other words, he expected it to be recognised that within his 'country' he exercised the political, military and seigneurial authority that was vested in him as its chief representative, and as a peer of the realm.

A considerable portion of a lord's wealth was directed towards achieving these ends, and the essential means by which he did it was through the employment, retention, and general patronage of those who came below him in the social and political hierarchy of the region – the county gentry. If half or more of his income was normally spent on his household (which in itself served as a social and political focus for the region, as well as a continual advertisement of his status there), most of the rest was spent on the maintenance of his following. The nominal 10 per cent which most lords apparently spent on retaining fees was very much a minimum: including the lands and offices which they granted out to their followers, the true figure must usually have been at least double this and in some cases much more. To buy the support of the gentry was just as important as to maintain a splendid lifestyle. When William, Lord Hastings, was granted the stewardship of the honour of Tutbury by Edward IV, he used its resources not so much to make himself a wealthier man as to extend his influence in the North Midlands – patronising the already prominent members of the local gentry, avoiding interference but at the same time securing loyalty. As I. Rowney puts it, he ' "bought" a clan rather than constructed an affinity'.[5] Kings did likewise. In the first six months of his reign, Henry V granted annuities totalling £1,100 to eighty-six members of the Lancashire gentry, about half the total value of his estates in the county. Richard II promised £5,000 a year to his Cheshire archers alone, payable from the profits of the county. Indeed, it sometimes seems as if, in the words of M.J. Bennett, 'the earls of Chester and the dukes of Lancaster were administering their estates in the north-west largely for the benefit of the local gentry'.[6] Yet they would not, of course, have indulged in such a policy had they not hoped that in reality it was they who would be the beneficiaries, and in some cases they were handsomely repaid. The support which Henry IV received from the gentry of Yorkshire and the North Midlands, for example, was a crucial factor in his eventual defeat of the Percys, and was a direct consequence of the retaining policy followed both by his father, John of Gaunt, and by Henry himself during the early years of his reign.[7]

The territorial policy followed by most magnates was directed towards the same end, that is, the entrenchment of the lord within his 'country' by the deliberate expansion of the nucleus of his estates. In many cases this involved an active purchasing policy: the Berkeleys, Scropes of Bolton, Greys of Ruthin, Nevills, Percys and Fitzalans are among the most striking examples of a successful land-purchasing policy around the *caput* in the fourteenth century. In other cases (the Mauleys, for example), the acquisition of estates contiguous with the patrimony was achieved through a consistent policy of marrying into neighbouring families.[8] Royal grants of forfeited or escheated lands, or (occasionally) of crown lands, were also usually designed to fill out existing territorial strengths. Obviously, a lord's influence within his 'country' was not in direct proportion to his territorial holdings. Moreover, the building up of a real local following was always a slow process, and frequently owed as much to traditions of loyalty and service as to territorial strength. The Greys of Ruthin, for example, although they had held some fourteen manors in Bedfordshire and Buckinghamshire since the 1320s, only really began to make themselves felt in local affairs there in the last quarter of the fourteenth century, by which time their holdings in the two counties had certainly grown (to twenty-one manors by 1400), but more importantly they had put down roots and forged links with several of the leading gentry families of the region.[9] Nevertheless, a strong territorial interest within his country was vital to any lord, not merely for economic reasons, but also for the seigneurial authority which came with land, for the opportunities which his landed holdings afforded him of establishing or strengthening his ties with other landholders in the region, and for the sense of common identity and purpose which it fostered between him and them.

Those families which were most strongly identified with their 'countries' were frequently those which had been established there the longest, and in this context it is worth emphasising those factors at work in late medieval England which enabled landholders to maintain the long-term integrity of their estates. The statute of *Quia Emptores* (1290), for example, by putting an end to subinfeudation in fee simple, encouraged lords instead to reward their followers with grants of land for life (or, occasionally, in tail), which meant that the lands were not permanently alienated. The entail, which placed (at least in theory) a perpetual restriction on future heirs' right to alienate, was also important in maintaining the unity of groups of estates. In some ways, the entail was merely a more formal way of ensuring what was already a prevalent practice among medieval landholders: it was a common contemporary maxim that, while a man might dispose as he wished with lands which he himself had acquired during his lifetime, he should pass on intact to his eldest son whatever lands he had inherited from his father. What was especially significant in this context, however, was the growing popularity of grants in tail male in late medieval England, which (as with the Berkeley inheritance in 1417) could in the long term prevent the break-up of the inheritance between female co-heirs. The enfeoffment-to-use could also (as, for example, by the earl of Stafford in his will of 1386) be used to achieve similar ends.[10]

Once again, though, it is important to distinguish between the long-term and short-term intentions of landholders. In the long-term, their primary intention was clearly to keep the core of the familial estates intact. In the short term, however, familial or personal considerations frequently worked in a contrary direction. A good example in an area where there seems to have been a real 'sphere of influence' (and where it might thus be expected that there were strong reasons for maintaining the integrity of the estates) is that of the Courtenays (see Table 4). The influence which the Courtenays, as earls of Devon, exercised in their county was undoubtedly considerable, and it was here that their lands were concentrated. In 1340, when the second Earl Hugh came into his inheritance, it consisted of about twenty manors in Devon, based on the baronies of Okehampton and Plympton, four in Somerset and Dorset, and a further seven or so elsewhere. Before his death in 1377, Hugh added (probably by purchase) about fifteen more, thirteen of which were in Devon and Somerset. He thus conformed to the pattern of acquisition

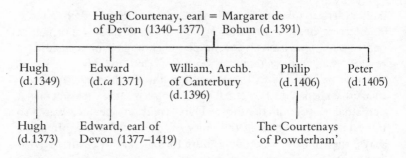

Table 4 *The Courtenays, 1340–1419*[12]

around the *caput* (his chief seat at this time was at Tiverton, close to the Devon–Somerset border). Yet when Hugh's heir, his grandson Edward, became earl in 1377, he found his inheritance depleted by nearly a quarter in order to provide for his two surviving uncles,[11] for Hugh had granted to Philip and Peter the entailed remainders (successively) of at least ten manors, not in distant counties such as Berkshire and Buckinghamshire where he still held land in 1377, but in the heart of Courtenay country. Five of the ten were in Devon, four in Somerset, and one in Dorset (though none of them was parcel of the Okehampton or Plympton baronies). Philip and Peter Courtenay became influential men at court,[13] and now that they were substantial landholders in Devon as well as close kinsmen of the earl they also became influential men in the county. In 1393, a Devonshire landholder petitioning to parliament because he claimed to have been unlawfully ejected from his manor of 'Bygelegh' by Philip Courtenay, declared that 'the said Sir Philip is so great in this country, that no poor man dares to pursue the law against him, nor to tell the truth against him in the same county'.[14] Whether or not he would have approved of this particular action, it was no doubt part of Earl Hugh's intention when detaching these substantial portions of the inheritance for his younger sons that they would help to maintain Courtenay influence in the region.

The successive Lords Berkeley also had a quite clearly defined 'country' and followed an undoubted policy of territorial consolidation in the fourteenth century (for the Berkeley and Courtenay holdings in the West Country, see Map 2). They too, however, were prepared to make substantial inroads into their holdings in order to provide for younger sons. Maurice, Lord Berkeley (d. 1326), detached four manors in Gloucestershire and Somerset for his second son (Maurice 'of Stoke Giffard'), and further small lands in the same counties for his third son, John. Thomas, Lord Berkeley (d. 1361), granted to his younger son John (by his second marriage) about ten manors in Gloucestershire and Somerset, probably about a fifth of his whole estate, thus enabling John to establish the prominent local gentry family known as the Berkeleys of Beverstone.[15] Once again, though, the ancestral core of the patrimony (the castle and barony of Berkeley) was kept intact, and indeed entailed upon Thomas's heir in tail male.

Thus with both the Berkeleys and the Courtenays (as with many other families), two different aspects of territorial policy are clearly detectable. The real core of the inheritance (often the barony from which the family took its title) was preserved intact in the male line. Younger sons, however (assuming the lord had any), were deliberately established as landholders within the family's 'country', often (though not always) with lands acquired by the lord during his own lifetime. The 'country' was, therefore, to some extent at any rate, a resource to be shared amongst and jointly presided over by the family group. There is a sense in which the entail can be seen in the same light. By placing restrictions on the rights of future heirs to alienate the land, the entail too recognised the collective interest of the family as well as the right of the individual at the head of the family to do with his property as he wished. It was the family as much as the individual landholder who benefited from the new freedom from feudal property law in the late Middle Ages – though in the great majority of cases that meant the immediate family.

In the end, then, for most landholders, the interests of their children were just as important as the long-term interests of the dynasty, and territorial policy was a matter of balancing these two overriding concerns in the best way possible. The same interests prevailed at the highest level. It is sometimes asked why the kings of France, having acquired such great lands in the thirteenth century, regularly parcelled out large *appanages* to their younger sons. Why did they not keep the lands in the primogenitary line, thus ensuring the overwhelming territorial power of the crown? The answer is that they were acting like most great lords did, providing for *all* their children, establishing a familial system of government in their territories. And when the cadet branches failed, the lands reverted to the crown.[16] On those occasions when the lands failed to revert, historians have often been quick to point to the folly of such grants, arguing that to establish cadet branches of the royal house as major territorial powers within the kingdom was bound to lead to trouble in the long run (Valois Burgundy is the obvious example in late medieval France), and the same point can perhaps be made about the grants made by some English magnates. The Courtenays of Powderham, for example, descended from that Sir Philip Courtenay to whom his father had entailed a substantial portion of his grandson's inheritance, became a powerful family in fifteenth-century Devonshire and staunch opponents (in alliance with the Bonvilles) of Thomas Courtenay, earl of Devon (d. 1458).[17] But to blame the quarrels of his great-great-grandchildren on Earl Hugh would be as foolish as to say that Edward III's dynastic policy was responsible for the Wars of the Roses.

There is no reason to suppose that the fourteenth-century kings of England regarded the establishment of peers in their 'countries' as anything but entirely natural, and indeed advantageous to the monarchy. With the centralisation of government at Westminster, kings and their households were by now spending more and more of their time in the south-eastern quarter of England,[18] which made it doubly necessary to have reliable deputies in the shires. At the same time, the more sedentary noble household of the fourteenth century meant that most peers were also spending more time in their 'countries' (rather than at a number of different residences), and in general the attitude of successive kings was to boost and uphold the local influence of their peers by those means which were available to them, namely, grants of land and office, and appointments to commissions.[19] Edward III was especially generous in this respect. Palatinate rights were granted to the Black Prince in Cornwall in 1337 (he already held them in Cheshire), and to Henry of Grosmont in Lancashire in 1351 (later transferred to John of Gaunt).[20] Between 1344 and

1351 the king also granted life shrievalties to four peers. That of Warwickshire and Leicestershire was granted to the earl of Warwick (who was already hereditary sheriff of Worcestershire) in 1344. In the same year the shrievalties of Shropshire and Staffordshire, which had been held jointly for over a century, were separated. That of Shropshire was granted for life to Richard, earl of Arundel, the greatest landholder in the region, while that of Staffordshire was granted in the following year to Henry of Grosmont, the heir to the great Staffordshire honour of Tutbury (to which he succeeded later in the year, when his father died). In 1351 the shrievalty of Cambridgeshire and Huntingdonshire was granted for life to John, Lord Lisle of Rougemont.[21]

These grants may have been intended to help the recipients to recruit soldiers for the war, for they were all noted commanders. The men of Shropshire had a high military reputation and were strongly represented in royal armies, and Henry of Grosmont certainly recruited considerable numbers of men from Staffordshire for his retinues.[22] As the complaint of the men of Shropshire (about the great 'meschief' which Arundel's tenure of the life shrievalty had done them) in 1376 indicates, however, the grants can hardly have failed to augment the local authority of the recipients in other ways as well.[23] There were some regions in which kings were prepared to devolve extraordinarily wide powers, though there were usually good reasons for this. It was the need to defend the Scottish border, for example, which accounted for the immense authority (and very large fees) granted to those northern lords (most notably the Percys) who held the wardenships of the Scottish Marches.[24] Indeed, it was the prolonged Scottish warfare of the fourteenth century which really raised the Percys and the Nevills to the forefront of national politics at this time, just as the situation on the Welsh Marches had brought several local families to national prominence in the twelfth and thirteenth centuries (the Fitzalans and Mortimers, for example), and similarly accounts for the virtual independence from royal control of the Welsh Marcher lordships.

Naturally, problems might follow from the conferment of such extensive powers on great lords. It was the Percy power in the north, augmented on a regular basis by the crown, which enabled them to hold out for so long against Henry IV in the early years of the fifteenth century.[25] As a general rule, though, it is difficult to see how kings could have acted otherwise than they did. To ignore or attempt to undermine the authority exercised by a peer in his 'country' was far more likely to cause trouble, as was any attempt by the king to intrude a new power into a region which a great lord traditionally regarded as his own – as for example with the series of lands and offices (culminating in 1397 with the dukedom of Exeter) granted by Richard II to his half-brother John Holland in the West Country in the 1380s and 1390s. In fact, Holland seems to have won 'very little dependable support in the West Country' (as demonstrated by his vain attempt to stir up support there for his rebellion in 1400), but the earl of Devon nevertheless regarded his intrusion as a major threat to his own authority in the region.[26] Unlike the Percys in the north, Holland's lordship had not had time to take root in Devonshire. It is worth remembering that all those great territorial rivalries of the fifteenth century – the Percys and Nevills in the north, the Courtenays and Bonvilles in the south-west, and the Harringtons and Stanleys in the north-west are the most famous – were between families who had long been established in their respective regions.

On the whole, kings were best advised not to interfere with territorial patterns of power – and this applies to the gentry as well as to the peers, as both Richard II and Henry VI found to their cost when they tried to pack local offices with their own supporters.[27] On the other hand, there were occasions when they could hardly avoid it, for to them fell the responsibility of settling the major territorial disputes of the magnates. Probably the two most famous property disputes between great families in the fourteenth century were those concerning the lordship of Gower, disputed throughout the century by the Mowbrays and the Beauchamps, and the lordship of Denbigh, acquired by the Mortimers in 1327, forfeited by them and granted to the Montagues in 1330, restored to the Mortimers in 1354–5, but still claimed by the Montagues in Richard II's reign.[28] On the two occasions when the lordship of Gower actually changed hands (from Mowbray to Beauchamp in 1354, and from Beauchamp back to Mowbray in 1397), the motivation behind the decisions was essentially personal, and the same is true of the decision to restore Denbigh to Roger Mortimer in 1354.[29] In their desire to control the passage of land within the kingdom and to provide inducements and rewards for their supporters, kings were often guilty of bending the law in their own, their families', or their favourites' favour. Property disputes, great and small, were constantly being decided at court (or at least through influence at court), and the landholder who found himself the victim of such a judgment probably had little option but to wait, like the abbot of St Albans when contesting a manor in Hertfordshire against Edward III's mistress Alice Perrers, 'until kinder fortune smiled upon him'.[30] But while the responsibility for making judgments was unavoidable, vindictiveness was unnecessary. When Richard II decided in Thomas Mowbray's favour in 1397, he not only ordered the earl of Warwick to hand over Gower, he also ordered him to repay to Mowbray all the issues and profits of the lordship over the previous thirteen years (reckoned to total 8,000 marks). To do this, Warwick was forced to place seventeen of his Midland manors in trust, to be held to the use of Mowbray, for a period of eleven years.[31]

Richard's interference with the property rights of his lords has often been seen as one of the chief causes of his downfall, but other fourteenth-century kings were by no means blameless on this score,[32] and it is worth asking why it was so controversial an issue during Richard's reign. Part of the reason no doubt lies in his vindictiveness towards his opponents, but there are also indications that he tried on occasion to resist the greater freedom of control over their property which Edward III had been prepared to allow to many landholders. The case of the March inheritance between 1381 and 1384, for example, which led to the dismissal of Chancellor Richard, Lord le Scrope, in 1382, really turned on the issue of who was to have the wardship of the estate during the minority of the heir. It is quite possible that fifty years earlier few would have objected to Richard's original plan to parcel out the custody of the inheritance to a group of courtiers, but ideas on wardship had changed as a result of Edward III's willingness to allow his tenants-in-chief to evade some of their feudal incidents, and it was no doubt this to which le Scrope referred when he refused to seal the king's charters, declaring that they were against the custom of the realm.[33] When the March, Norfolk and Lancaster inheritances fell in to the king in 1398–9, he again distributed the custody of them amongst his favourites. Nor was his attitude to the entail and the enfeoffment-to-use above suspicion, at least not when it was in his interests to try to overturn them. He used every means at his disposal to try to regain the lands which Edward III had enfeoffed to the use of his three favourite religious houses, and in 1397 he declared forfeit not only the lands which his opponents held in fee simple, but also those which they held in tail or had enfeoffed to others – going much further in the process than those same opponents had gone in 1388.[34] There is no reason to suppose that Richard *systematically* tried to do away with such devices – any such policy would surely have met with irresistible opposition from the propertied classes – merely that he chose to ignore their effect when it suited him to do so. He also, of course, quite blatantly broke his word, most notably in revoking the licences which he had permitted Bolingbroke and Mowbray to grant to their attorneys before they departed into exile in 1398, the effect of which would have been that they and their families, rather than the king and his favourites, would have enjoyed the profits of their great inheritances.[35]

It was this disregard for the rights of real property which cost Richard II his throne, just as it had cost Edward II his throne seventy years earlier when he allowed the Despensers to acquire vast estates in south Wales and elsewhere by methods which appalled contemporaries. It was the king's responsibility not only to settle disputes between his lords, but also to ensure that no lord should be allowed to convert that local power with which he was entrusted into a weapon for the enforcement of his own will to the detriment of his fellow landholders in the region. Yet once again Edward III was by no means blameless on this score either: his eldest son, the Black Prince, for example, was allowed to manipulate the law of property in his palatine county of Cheshire to a degree that (in the words of P.H.W. Booth) 'made it clear to the community that the prince's government's favour was not just a prerequisite for advancement but a necessity for holding on to what they already had'.[36] Herein lay another danger in allowing too much local power to lords – the danger that the gentry might become alienated – for what they looked for from those above them was essentially 'consensus politics'. In general, though, Edward III's failures in this respect seem to have been more in the nature of faults of omission than of active participation. His father and his grandson went much further than this: with the Despensers in the 1320s, and the royalist nobles in the years 1397–9, both Edward II and Richard II ranged the power of the crown squarely behind the unlawful activities of their principal supporters.[37]

Beyond the vague notion of consensus politics, the gentry looked to those above them in the social hierarchy for three things. Firstly, they hoped for financial remuneration of some sort, whether in cash, land, or office, any of which could make a substantial addition to their income. (This is where the king and the greater magnates had an advantage, for they could and did offer bigger financial inducements to the gentry.) Secondly, they looked for avenues through which to make their careers. It was only really through service and connections that careers *could* be made in the Middle Ages. There were no career structures in the modern sense. Jobs in royal or noble administration, military commands, positions in local government, or at court, or in a lord's household, were dependent primarily on personal connections. This is not, of course, to say that merit was not rewarded, but without connections a man with ambition was unlikely to get into a position where his abilities would be noticed. That lords deliberately, and usually successfully, advanced the careers of their supporters is beyond doubt. In most of those regional gentry societies which have been studied, for example, the real leaders of local society were men closely bound to the service either of the king or of the great lord of the region.[38] The system worked at the highest level too. For example, C.D. Ross has pointed out how many Yorkshire lords held high crown offices during the reigns of the first two Lancastrian kings. (After 1422, however, when although still a Lancastrian the king was a minor and could not take a positive lead in advancing men from his 'country', the number fell away markedly.) Here was the greatest landholder in Yorkshire patronising his local supporters.[39] It is a reminder, moreover, that what we think of as 'public' administration in medieval England was really – in its higher echelons, at any rate – little more than an extension of the personal connections which underlay private administrations.

Thirdly, a knight or esquire wanted to 'belong' to the regional establishment. If he had quarrels with his neighbours, he expected his lord to help him to sort them out, possibly by arbitration, possibly by using his influence at higher levels (at court, for example, or in the shire administration or the judiciary).[40] In a more general sense, though, a great lord could act as a political focus for the gentry of his 'country', influencing local appointments and elections, offering opportunities for advancement, embracing and reflecting within the dynamics of his affinity the tensions and structures of local politics and peace-keeping. This is not meant to suggest that the gentry were at the beck and call of the magnates C. Richmond is surely right to argue that we should beware of seeing the retainers and other followers of a great lord as 'Pavlovian dogs, jumping at the chance of a fee'.[41] They were quite capable of making up their own minds on the issues of the day. Indeed, the growth of retaining in the fourteenth century is in itself indicative of what G.L. Harriss has characterised as 'the growing shift of power at local level from the nobility [i.e. the peerage] towards the gentry'.[42] The peers needed the gentry as much as the gentry needed the peers. Nevertheless, it is important to recognise that the gentry *did* need the peers. Affinities were systems – political systems, peace-keeping systems, career systems – and, to adapt Richmond's metaphor, most men shrank from biting the hand that fed them. Of course, by far the most sensible line for any lord to take in his 'country' was to use his authority to bolster and maintain the existing power-structure, rather than to try to undermine it by raising new men or outsiders above the local bigwigs; but that does not mean that he lacked the authority to advance some careers more than others, and men knew well that service and loyalty would be rewarded in the same measure as they were offered.

What gave the affinity its strength was the fact that it was a partnership of the governing, a mutual alliance, for mutual benefit, of those who mattered in the region. And it was the recognition of local power-structures, combined with the force of tradition, which in large part explains the stability of most noble affinities in the late Middle Ages.[43] Yet to argue that the magnate affinity at its best was a product rather than a catalyst of the regional establishment clearly begs a further question. At what level did the regional establishment operate? J.R. Maddicott and others have argued recently that county gentry communities were becoming more politically and regionally conscious in the fourteenth century. Their need to act together in the presentation of community petitions (which became more common from the 1320s) and in negotiations over taxation and other matters which affected the county as a whole, together with their increasing control of office-holding in the shire, welded them into a real 'county community'.[44] If this was the case, then, might it be possible for a great lord to harness this growing regional identity to his own interests, and effectively, by forming an alliance with that dominant elite which claimed to represent the shire, become himself the respresentative of his shire? After all, it would surely be wrong to suggest that administrative boundaries played no part at all in influencing political structures. Nearly all peers were also appointed regularly to the crown commissions issued for the counties in which their major territorial holdings lay. Might this too give them a wider influence than that which they exercised over their actual territorial holdings, a sense of identity not just with their 'countries' but with the shire as a whole?[45] And might it be, as McFarlane suggested many years ago, that with the greater freedom of choice allowed to a lord through indentures of retainer, 'an enterprising magnate could therefore reach out beyond the frontiers of his fief, and, by indenting with his neighbours for their services, bring whole districts, sometimes an entire county, under his control'?[46]

There were different ways in which great lords might hope to impose their authority on the affairs of their counties. C. Carpenter has argued that what really enabled the earl of Warwick to extend his influence throughout Warwickshire in the 1420s and 1430s was his ability to form a 'coalition' of the lesser peers' affinities in the county, such as the Ferrers of Chartley and the Mowbrays, and in effect to subsume them within his own great affinity.[47] John of Gaunt seems to have done much the same thing in Yorkshire and the North Midlands in the 1370s and 1380s – among the peers in this area whom he retained were

Lords Roos, Nevill, Dacre, de la Pole (this was before they acquired the Suffolk inheritance), le Scrope of Bolton, Welles, and Grey of Codnor, as well as numerous knights and esquires from the region.[48] The devolution of county-wide powers such as palatinate rights and the shrievalty were also important. Yet power inevitably had to be exercised in alliance with the gentry, especially those 'county gentry' whose leadership of local society was becoming ever more entrenched in the later Middle Ages, and it was therefore necessarily dependent on their acquiescence. In some counties, under certain lords, this may well have been forthcoming: in Devon under the Courtenays, for example, in Northumberland under the Percys, in Warwickshire (and perhaps Worcestershire too) under Richard Beauchamp, and in Westmorland under the Cliffords (though it is worth noting that all these counties were remote from Westminster, which no doubt encouraged devolution of power). Richard, earl of Arundel, may have entertained similar ambitions in the mid-fourteenth century, but his methods do not seem to have won him many friends among the gentry. His major territorial holdings were in Sussex and Shropshire (see Map 4; he was continuously acquiring new lands in Sussex), in both of which counties he secured grants from Edward III which enabled him to extend his influence in the county. Shortly after his death the commons of Surrey and Sussex complained to the king that, having been granted the sheriff's tourns in the rapes of Arundel and Chichester, the earl had established a 'novele Court appelle Shire-court a Arundell', to which he had transferred pleas of the county. In the same year, the people of Shropshire also complained that the earl's life tenure of the county's shrievalty (which he held from 1345 until 1376) had done them great 'meschief'.[49] The implication seems to be that despite his territorial strength in the two counties, as well as Edward III's acquiescence in his influence there, he had been unable to carry the local gentry with him.

To think of the magnate 'sphere of influence' as normally embracing a county would surely be wrong, and indications to this effect are more often than not likely to be an illusion of the records. The problem is that it is often difficult to *demonstrate* the exercise of local influence except through reference to administrative records, and frequently that means shire records (parliamentary elections, the connections of the shire's office-holders, and so forth). To show that magnates competed to intrude their supporters into the chief shire offices *might* indicate that they aspired to a position of dominance in county-wide politics, but it might just as likely indicate that they were hoping to further their more localised interests, to advance their own supporters, or simply to demonstrate that they were men of standing in the region. Most peers, even most earls, when they spoke of their 'countries', certainly did not mean counties. Most counties were like Norfolk and Suffolk, where a number of peers had substantial holdings, but none held sufficient to be assured of a dominant place in the politics of the county. And as to the gentry (even the county gentry), while the offices which they held, and the demands of central government, sometimes forced them to act as the representatives of their 'county communities', they were probably for the most part concerned with rather more localised issues than the administrative records tend to suggest. This at least is the conclusion of most of those historians who have studied regional gentry societies in recent years.[50]

To try to be too precise about the extent of a lord's 'country' would be pointless. The important point to recognise is that the lordly 'sphere of influence' was a fundamental political entity in medieval England, and this was a situation which was both acknowledged and encouraged by the crown. In the past, some historians have perhaps been guilty of overemphasising the 'national' role of the lords and underestimating their local role. It is important, for example, not to exaggerate the amount of time that most peers spent at court. The witness lists to the great charters (on which the names of peers were usually recorded if they were present) may be individually unreliable as indications of time and place of witnessing, but collectively they can be used to give a general indication of which peers were active in court and government circles, and what they reveal is that only a handful were. In the 1360s there were 130 great charters issued, of which only ten peers witnessed twenty or more. In the years 1372–82, the years of Edward III's senility and Richard II's minority when one might have expected more of the peers to come to court in order to bolster the government, there were 126 great charters issued: twelve peers witnessed twenty or more of them, but five of these were men who held high office in the royal household or administration, and were only witnessing regularly during their periods of office.[51] With a few exceptions, fourteenth-century peers certainly did not regard the royal court as a home from home. When they were not campaigning, or travelling, or undertaking specific duties elsewhere on their own or the king's business, the normal place for them to be was in their 'countries'.

This is not to deny that more nobles were probably finding themselves drawn to the royal court in the later Middle Ages than had been the case in earlier centuries, for that is almost certainly true, but what was it that took them there? The essential function of the court, as has often been pointed out, was to serve as a point of contact. For many nobles, though – gentry as well as peers – there were good financial reasons to attend the king. In the earlier Middle Ages, when feudal incidents were exacted more rigorously, many nobles were often permanently indebted to the crown. By the late fourteenth century, with the development of the crown's 'budget of noble assistance', and with both annuities and war wages frequently in arrears, the reverse was often true. It may be that this tended to create competition between nobles for payment. In mid-fifteenth-century France (where admittedly the granting of crown pensions to nobles had gone rather further than it had in England), Jean Juvenal des Ursins advised Charles VII: 'when you cease to pay the said pensions, the lords will be more contented than they are at present; for it's all these jealousies that produce covert hatreds, and each one thinks that he deserves to have more than another. . . .'[52] It has been suggested that the kings of late medieval England sometimes deliberately used pensions and annuities as a way of keeping lords dependent on the crown,[53] but this is unlikely: they were probably more concerned to relieve the exchequer of its obligations. Nevertheless, the need to secure their arrears, and actually to convert their grants into cash, may well have drawn more lords to court, for there was nothing automatic about the payment of annuities. For each instalment a warrant for issue would have to be secured, which might well involve influence and pressure being exerted. It is surely not coincidental that it was in 1376–7, when he was about the court more, and in a position of greater authority than he had been during the previous few years, that John of Gaunt managed to secure his £6,255 of arrears for wages of war.[54]

For some nobles, regular attendance at court was a consequence of active participation in royal government. The king's council, for example, became increasingly noble in composition in the fourteenth and fifteenth centuries, though the number of peers or knights who sat on it at any one time was quite small (rarely more than ten or so). It is also true that more laymen, and fewer clerics, were holding high posts in the royal household and other crown departments in the fourteenth and fifteenth centuries.[55] There is a tendency to think of these royal servants – or 'courtiers' – as having different interests from the rest of the nobility (the class from which they were almost invariably drawn), but the distinction is by no means a very clear one. 'Courtiers' came to court for much the same reasons as nobles did: to maintain the links between court and country, to secure their pensions, and to try to win the king's backing for matters of immediate importance to them and their followers, as well as to have some say in greater matters and generally to counsel, serve, and simply 'attend' the king. It is no doubt true that those who actually held positions in the royal household or the government were, because they had more to lose, potentially more amenable to the royal will than those who did not, but most lords were also courtiers to some degree, and most of the courtiers who mattered were also nobles.[56]

The most common reason why most peers came to court in the later Middle Ages was almost certainly to attend parliaments, which were held on average about once a year in the fourteenth century. As is well known, however, many of the peers were far from assiduous in their attendance at parliaments. It was not uncommon for half or more of those who received individual summonses not to bother to come[57] (though on occasion the king tried to put pressure on them to attend: in 1363, for example, Walsingham records that Edward III held a parliament 'a quo nullus magnus potuit se absentare').[58] The development of parliament from an extension of the *curia regis* into something like a national assembly – from an 'occasion' into an 'institution', as it has been put – was probably the most important political legacy of the late Middle Ages, and the emphasis commonly placed by baronial reformers on the necessity for regular meetings of parliament is sufficient testimony to the fact that they recognised its crucial role. Yet the general level of lordly indifference to most meetings of parliament hardly accords with the view that the peers as a group were overwhelmed by the desire to involve themselves in high politics. This is not to deny that both peers and gentry were concerned about matters of policy. It would be quite wrong, as C. Richmond has pointed out, to reduce politics to patronage.[59] Financial and commercial policy, law and order, and above all diplomatic and military policy, were matters which often concerned them deeply. But if it is true that 'every baron was a politician',[60] it is also probably true that most of them were primarily concerned with local rather than national politics. And with regard to the gentry, this is doubly true. There were certainly times (1376, for example) when the knights of the shire played a highly significant role in national politics, but if we look at the sort of issues on which the commons as a group developed recognisable 'policies' in the fourteenth century – livery and maintenance, or the role of the justices of the peace, for example – they have an unmistakably 'local' flavour.

That broad responsibility for decision-making at the national level fell to the king, his ministers, and the peers, was not something which the commons tried or wished to deny. This was not because of any definable powers which the peers held, or because the knights of the shire could be persuaded to act as their mouthpieces, but simply because of their inherently greater authority on the national scene, and their more direct access to the king.[61] The commons claimed no executive authority: when they asked for continual councils or commissions of reform to be set up, it was the lords whom they expected to sit on them. Their role in government was not so much constitutional as 'occasional and corrective'.[62] In the end, it is difficult to disagree with McFarlane when he says that 'the real politics of the reign . . . were inherent in [the king's] daily personal relations with the magnates'.[63]

In the end, though, we might also ask, 'how many of the magnates?' Was it really national politics which mattered most even to most of the peers? For the very greatest of them – some, at least, of the earls and dukes – national politics was both a natural preoccupation and a duty, and obviously for those with ambition the court was the natural place to go. We are frequently reminded, though, that many knights and esquires tended to shun involvement in politics,[64] and it would be surprising if the same were not true of the peers. Naturally, they were bound to be involved in national affairs to some extent: to further their military careers, for example, and to attend parliament. But for many of them, as for the gentry, national politics was largely an extension of local politics. Access to the king meant primarily an additional means of furthering their interests in their 'countries'. And for most of them, it was mainly for their local authority that the king valued them: because he had no standing army, he needed them to raise troops for him in their shires; because he lacked the sort of administrative apparatus which the twentieth century takes for granted, he needed them to provide leadership and continuity in the regions. Early Tudor England, it has recently been said, was 'a federation of noble fiefdoms'.[65] So was fourteenth-century England. The essential prerequisities of noble power were the wealth which they enjoyed, and the lordship of land and men which they exercised in the regions, and it was to the maintenance of these, along with their privileged lifestyle of course, that their energies and expenditure were largely directed. In the connections they fostered, the religious houses they patronised, the bequests they made in their wills,[66] and the familial and territorial policies which they pursued, they were continually cultivating and enriching that regional authority which was the bedrock of their status in the realm.

Abbreviations

All works are cited in full in the Bibliography.

Annales	*Annales Ricardi Secundi et Henrici Quarti,* ed. H.T. Riley
BIHR	*Bulletin of the Institute of Historical Research*
BL	British Library
Black Prince's Register	*Register of Edward the Black Prince*, 4 vols
CCR	*Calendar of Close Rolls*
CFR	*Calendar of Fine Rolls*
CIPM	*Calendar of Inquisitions Post Mortem*
CPR	*Calendar of Patent Rolls*
Dugdale, *Baronage*	Sir William Dugdale, *The Baronage of England*, 2 vols
EHD	*English Historical Documents*
EHR	*English Historical Review*
GEC	*Complete Peerage*, ed. G.E. Cockayne
POPC	N.H. Nicolas (ed.), *Proceedings and Ordinances of the Privy Council*, 2 vols
P & P	*Past and Present*
PRO	Public Record Office
RP	J. Strachey *et al.* (eds), *Rotuli Parliamentorum*, vols ii–iii
TRHS	*Transactions of the Royal Historical Society*
Westminster Chronicle	B. Harvey and L.C. Hector (eds), *The Westminster Chronicle 1381–1394* (1982)

Notes

PREFACE

1 *The Westminster Chronicle 1381–1394*, ed. L.C. Hector and B.F. Harvey (1982), 396.
2 T.H. Marshall, *Citizenship and Social Class* (1950), 92.

INTRODUCTION

1 Maurice Keen, *Chivalry* (1984), 16 and *passim*.
2 Nicholas Orme, *From Childhood to Chivalry: The Education of the English Kings and Aristocracy 1066–1530* (1984), 183 and *passim*, for this and what follows.
3 In 1366, for example, Edward III paid £4 to one Edward Palmer for the king's youngest son, Thomas of Woodstock, aged nine at the time, 'to be instructed in the science of grammar' (F. Devon (ed.), *Issue Roll of the Exchequer Henry III to Henry VI* (1837), 189). Palmer was presumably a professional teacher, but the fact that he received a one-off payment strongly suggests that he had been employed on a temporary basis and for a specific purpose, not that he was Thomas's regular guardian or tutor.
4 Orme, *Childhood to Chivalry*, 18, and for what follows, 182–210.
5 *Ibid.*, 163–70.
6 *Ibid.*, 144; K.B. McFarlane, *The Nobility of Later Medieval England* (1973), 228–47; V.H. Galbraith, 'A new life of Richard II', *History* (1942), 227; M.T. Clanchy, *From Memory to Written Record* (1979).
7 Quoted in Orme, *Childhood to Chivalry*, 49, 55.
8 Keen, *Chivalry*, 83–101 and *passim*.
9 Maurice Keen, 'Chaucer's Knight, the English aristocracy, and the Crusade', in J.W. Sherborne and V.J. Scattergood (eds), *English Court Culture in the Later Middle Ages* (1983).
10 Froissart, *Oeuvres*, ed. Kervyn de Lettenhove (25 vols, 1867–77), xiv, 314.
11 Though in fact the 'Normans' included a small number of Bretons and Flemings who had also come over with the Conqueror. For

these figures and what follows see W.J. Corbett in *Cambridge Medieval History*, v, 507ff, and E. Miller and J. Hatcher, *Medieval England: Rural Society and Economic Change 1086—1348* (1978), 15–19.

12 Miller and Hatcher, *Medieval England*, 16; GEC, *sub* Cornwall.

13 F. Barlow, *William Rufus* (1983), 170.

14 Henry II, for example, spent thirteen years of his reign in England, fourteen and a half in Normandy, and seven in Anjou and Gascony (E. King, *England 1175–1425* (1979), 122). Richard I spent less than a year in England during his reign.

15 Robert J. Wells, 'Recruitment and Extinction among the English Nobility from 1216 to 1300', unpublished M.Litt. thesis, University of St Andrews (1984), appendix I.

16 Barlow, *Rufus*, 165.

17 GEC, *sub* Cornwall; W. Kapelle, *The Norman Conquest of the North* (1979), 142ff.

18 J.C. Holt, *Magna Carta* (1965), 318–19.

19 Miller and Hatcher, *Medieval England*, 169, based on the list compiled by I.J. Sanders, *English Baronies: A Study of Their Origin and Descent 1086–1327* (1960).

20 Holt, *Magna Carta*, 321; C. Johnson (ed.), *Dialogus de Scaccario* (1950), 95–6 and 95 n. 1.

21 King, *England 1175–1425*, 44; but 'the median income for a barony was £116, for some of these estates were very large'. Painter estimated that only seven members of the English baronage regularly received more than £400 a year around 1200 (S. Painter, *Studies in the History of the English Feudal Barony* (1943), 170–1).

22 Wells, 'Recruitment and Extinction', 37–8 and *passim*.

23 For a useful general discussion see Miller and Hatcher, *Medieval England*, 165–79; for Domesday knights see Sally Harvey, 'The knight and the knight's fee in England', *P & P* (1970).

24 N. Denholm-Young, *Collected Papers on Medieval Subjects* (1946), 56–67; McFarlane, *Nobility*, 268.

25 Barlow, *Rufus*, 163.

26 A hide was very variable in size, between 40 and 120 acres. For contrasting opinions on the question of knightly status, see Harvey, 'Knight and knight's fee', and R.A. Brown, 'The status of the Anglo-Norman knight', in J.C. Holt and J. Gillingham (eds), *War and Government in the Middle Ages* (1984).

27 Keen, *Chivalry*, 23ff.

28 P.D.A. Harvey, 'The English inflation of 1180–1220', *P & P* (1973); P. R. Coss, 'Sir Geoffrey de Langley and the crisis of the knightly class in thirteenth-century England', *P & P* (1975); D.A. Carpenter, 'Was there a crisis of the knightly class in the thirteenth century? The Oxfordshire Evidence', *EHR* (1980).

29 Miller and Hatcher, *Medieval England*, 170.

30 For this and what follows see especially G.T. Lapsley, *Crown Com-*

munity and Parliament in the Later Middle Ages (1951), 63–110, and J. R. Maddicott, 'Magna Carta and the local community 1215–1259', *P & P* (1984).

31 N. Denholm-Young, *Seignorial Administration in England* (1937), 76.

32 Maddicott, 'Magna Carta and the local community'.

33 Keen, *Chivalry*, 143–53, on which this paragraph is largely based.

34 *Ibid.*, 145

35 For distraint of knighthood, that is, the imposition of monetary fines on potential knights who declined to assume the honour, see M.R. Powicke, *Military Obligation in Medieval England* (1962); the first distraint of knighthood was in 1224.

36 F.L. Ganshof, *Feudalism* (3rd edn, 1964).

37 For serfdom in medieval England see P.R. Hyams, *Kings, Lords and Peasants in Medieval England* (1980). For the effects of the Norman Conquest on the English peasantry see H.R. Loyn, *Anglo-Saxon England and the Norman Conquest* (1962), 343ff.

38 Hundreds were local administrative areas; some shires contained only five to ten hundreds, but larger ones often had more, sometimes up to fifty or sixty.

39 D.W. Sutherland, *'Quo Warranto' Proceedings in the reign of Edward I 1278–94* (1963).

40 R.R. Davies, *Lordship and Society in the March of Wales 1282–1400* (1978).

41 Good general histories are Miller and Hatcher, *Medieval England*, and M.M. Postan, *The Medieval Economy and Society* (1972).

42 J. R. Maddicott, 'The English peasantry and the demands of the crown', *P & P Supplement* (1975).

43 For a summary of the debate see J.L. Bolton, *The Medieval English Economy 1150–1500* (1980), 105ff.

44 D. Oschinsky (ed.), *Walter of Henley and Other Treatises on Estate Management and Accounting* (1971).

45 E.A. Kosminsky, *Studies in the Agrarian History of England in the Thirteenth Century* (1956).

46 R.H. Hilton, *The Decline of Serfdom in Medieval England* (Studies in Economic History, 1969).

47 However, the demands for the abolition of 'serfdom' in 1381 probably meant rather more than just manorial serfdom; see below. pp. 117ff.

48 Quoted in Keen, *Chivalry*, 154.

1   KINGS AND THE TITLED NOBILITY

1 But for the duke of Brittany's part in the revolution of 1326, see N. Fryde, *The Tyranny and Fall of Edward II 1321–1326* (1979), 183f.

2 The oldest of them was Aymer de Valence, earl of Pembroke, born some time between 1270 and 1275 (J.R.S. Phillips, *Aymer de Valence Earl of Pembroke 1307–1324* (1972), 8); Gilbert de Clare was allowed

livery of his lands in November 1307 despite being only sixteen; all the others were aged twenty-one or more.

3   J.R. Maddicott, *Thomas of Lancaster 1307–1322* (1970), 12–13, 22, 27.

4   Fryde, *Tyranny and Fall*, 107–8.

5   Excluding the duke of Brittany and the earl of Ulster, neither of whom were of political significance in England. John, duke of Brittany and earl of Richmond, died in 1334; the new earl of Ulster, William de Burgh, died in 1333, aged twenty-one, without male heirs.

6   For his estates and his unhappy personal life see E.R. Fairbanks, 'The last earl of Warenne and Surrey', *Yorkshire Archaeological Journal* (1907).

7   M. Prestwich, *The Three Edwards* (1980), 157.

8   K.B. McFarlane, 'Had Edward I a "policy" towards the earls?', in *Nobility*, 248–67.

9   Quoted in J.E. Powell and K. Wallis, *The House of Lords in the Middle Ages* (1968), 326.

10 R. Douch, 'The career, lands and family of William Montague, earl of Salisbury', *BIHR* (1951).

11 K. Fowler, *The King's Lieutenant: Henry of Grosmont, First Duke of Lancaster 1310–1361* (1969).

12 W.M. Ormrod, 'Edward III's Government of England, c. 1346–1356', unpublished D.Phil. thesis, University of Oxford (1984), 110–14, using the witness lists from the great charter rolls for the period 1348–56, shows that those who were most active at court and in government were the earls of Lancaster, Northampton, Stafford, Warwick, Arundel, Huntingdon and (after 1354) March. Suffolk, surprisingly, does not seem to have witnessed many charters at this time, while Oxford (again surprisingly), Salisbury, Devon, and Hereford and Essex 'remained for various reasons outside the king's circle'. My own analysis of the great charter rolls from April 1360 to December 1369 shows that the most active of the earls and dukes at this time were Arundel, John of Gaunt, Edmund of Langley, and Thomas de Vere, the new earl of Oxford, who had succeeded his father in 1360, followed by Warwick, Salisbury, Suffolk (though he virtually stopped witnessing charters after 1363), and, when he was not in Ireland, the duke of Clarence: PRO C53/145–52, and see below, pp. 175–6.

13 B.P. Wolffe, *The Royal Demesne in English History* (1971), *passim*.

14 *CPR, 1334–8*, 400.

15 *CIPM*, x, 171f.

16 *CPR, 1334–8*, 409, 415–18; Wolffe, *Royal Demesne*, 50–60; see also BL Harleian MS 700, ff. 1–6, which lists the knights' fees and advowsons held by Earl Humphrey at his death in 1373; his knights' fees totalled 247, and he held the advowsons of forty religious houses.

17 *RP*, ii, 56; at the time of the grant, Denbigh was said to be worth 1,000 marks a year, but this was almost certainly an undervaluation. See Davies, *Lordship and Society*, appendix, where the gross valuations were consistently over £1,000.

18 G.A. Holmes, *The Estates of the Higher Nobility in Fourteenth-Century England* (1957), 17. Montague's defence, that the original grant to Mortimer had only mentioned the castle of Denbigh and thus did not include the rest of the lordship, was surely thoroughly specious, especially since the grant to Montague in 1330 specified that 'the said Roger held heritably of the gift of the king . . . the castle, town, manor, and honour of Denbigh, and the Cantreds of Ros, Reywynok, and Kaermer, and the Commote of Dynmael, with the appurtenances . . . . ' – that is, clearly the whole lordship (*RP*, ii, 56; *CPR, 1354–8*, 159).

19 CPR, *1334–8*, 426–7; Holmes, *Estates*, 29, shows that Montague and Gaunt agreed to a compromise whereby they split the lands; for the original arrangement between Warenne and Lancaster, see Fairbanks, 'Last earl of Warenne and Surrey'.

20 At the time of his creation, Thomas Despenser was also granted some lands forfeited by the earls of Arundel and Warwick, but his third of the Clare inheritance still formed the chief element in his landed estate (GEC, *sub* Gloucester).

21 In fact Stafford had abducted Margaret in 1336, but it is quite probable that the abduction was collusive (Powell and Wallis, *House of Lords*, 324). Edward III retained Stafford in 1348 with an annual fee of 600 marks; this was enlarged to 1,000 marks in 1353 following his promotion, but this was explicitly a retaining fee, not an endowment-substitute, and there was no suggestion that it might be converted into land (*CPR, 1348–50*, 183). Some idea of the size of Stafford's estate can be gained from the list of knights' fees compiled at the death of his grandson Edmund, who inherited the earldom in 1395 and died in 1403: these totalled 279, with the advowsons of thirty-two religious houses (BL Harleian MS 700, ff. 6–13). Following the acquisition of the Audley and Corbet inheritances in 1347, the Stafford estate underwent little expansion in the second half of the fourteenth century. Compare with the Bohun estate in 1373 (n. 16 above).

22 The Stafford and Bohun inheritances were both of good comital size, but even they were dwarfed by the March inheritance after 1368. At his death in 1425 Edmund, the fifth Mortimer earl of March and grandson of the Edmund who married Philippa in 1368, held 552 knights' fees and the advowsons of forty-seven religious houses (BL Harleian MS 704, ff. 1–16).

23 William, count of Juliers in the Low Countries, was made earl of Cambridge in 1340, partly because he was Queen Philippa's brother-in-law, and partly because he was a useful ally against France. John de Montfort, the new duke of Brittany, was allowed

his deceased brother's earldom of Richmond – again largely because he was a useful ally – in 1341, but he was deprived of it again in the following year, when it was granted to the king's son John of Gaunt. Not until 1372 was it restored to Montfort's son. In 1366 the earldom of Bedford was granted to Enguerrand de Coucy, a French lord who had been captured by the English and ended by marrying Edward III's daughter Isabella. He renounced his earldom in 1377 when, after Edward's death, he returned to the French allegiance. The earldom of Richmond carried a substantial Yorkshire estate with it, but those of Cambridge and Bedford were largely honorific titles, backed by annuities of £1,000 and 1,000 marks respectively from the king. The earls of Kent were John, son of Edmund, earl of Kent (who had been executed by Mortimer in March 1330), who was restored to his father's title at the age of nineteen in 1349, only to die three years later; and Thomas Holland, who married Joan, the 'Fair Maid of Kent', John's sister, and was allowed to assume the title *jure uxori* in November 1360; he died just one month later.

24 Apart from a brief interlude in 1264–5, when the future Edward I was in the custody of Simon de Montfort, who took the title for himself, the earldom of Chester had been in the hands of the king or his heir since 1254. The grant of the earldom of Cornwall to Gaveston in 1307 was quite exceptional, for it was normally reserved for a cadet of the royal family. The principality of Wales, created in 1301 for the future Edward II, had not been granted to Edward III before his accession, possibly because he was too young, but from now on it was to become the traditional patrimony of the heir to the throne.

25 Fowler, *King's Lieutenant*, 225–6.

26 Maud had been married in 1352 to William, duke of Bavaria and count of Holland and Zealand, but it was a miserable marriage. In 1357 William began to go insane, and in the following year he had to be interned in Quesnoy castle, where he lived, by now quite insane, for another thirty-one years (Fowler, *King's Lieutenant*, 120–1).

27 John of Gaunt had been granted the earldom of Richmond at the age of two; for the earldom of Cambridge see n. 23 above.

28 For the details of the distribution of the Warenne lands, see Fairbanks, 'Last earl of Warenne and Surrey'. Essentially, Arundel took the Sussex, Surrey and Marcher estates, Edmund of Langley took the Yorkshire and (in 1363) Lincolnshire lands, and Salisbury took the West Country lands (but see above, n. 19).

29 Wolffe, *Royal Demesne*, 242–3.

30 The story is told in the somewhat unreliable edition by T. Johnes of Froissart's chronicles (vol. i, 623), but most historians have agreed that it fits well enough with the known facts (Holmes, *Estates*, 24; A. Goodman, *The Loyal Conspiracy* (1971), 89–90).

31 *CPR, 1377–81*, 60.

32 For the dispute over Gower, see Rowena E. Archer, 'The Mowbrays, Earls of Nottingham and Dukes of Norfolk, to 1432', unpublished D.Phil. thesis, University of Oxford (1984), 16f.

33 For some of the ideas expressed in this paragraph I am indebted to Professor Ralph Griffiths for allowing me to quote from his paper, 'The Crown and the Royal Family in Later Medieval England', delivered at St Andrews University on 5 November 1985.

34 For a good general discussion of politics in the last years of Edward's reign see G.A. Holmes, *The Good Parliament* (1975).

35 The Arundel estates had been swollen not only by the acquisition of a large part of the Warenne inheritance after 1347, but also by a consistent policy of acquisition in Sussex on the part of this earl's father, who died in 1376 leaving £60,000 in cash (L.F. Salzman, 'The property of the earl of Arundel, 1397', *Sussex Archaeological Collections*, (1953), 33–4).

36 The fact that this was very much an honorary title is shown by its restriction to the life of Guichard (the first English earldom to be so restricted); it was backed with 1,000 marks from the exchequer, raised to £1,000 in 1378 (Powell and Wallis, *House of Lords*, 384).

37 Archer, 'The Mowbrays', 50–4, 69, 75.

38 They were the sons of Joan of Kent's first marriage, to Thomas Holland; after his death in 1360 she married the Black Prince. John Holland's promotion in 1388 may in fact have been advocated by the king's opponents, possibly as a reward to Holland for his political support in 1387–8 (Anthony Tuck, *Richard II and the English Nobility* (1973), 79–80). For the problems encountered in endowing Holland with sufficient land see C. Given-Wilson, 'Richard II and his grandfather's will', *EHR* (1978), and Martin Cherry. 'The Courtenay earls of Devon: the formation and disintegration of a late medieval aristocratic affinity', *Southern History* (1979).

39 *CPR, 1385–9*, 113, 115.

40 J.S. Roskell, *The Impeachment of Michael de la Pole, Earl of Suffolk, in 1386* (1984).

41 J.J.N. Palmer, 'The parliament of 1385 and the constitutional crisis of 1386', *Speculum* (1971), 490.

42 C. Given-Wilson, *The Royal Household and the King's Affinity* (1986), 132–5.

43 Given-Wilson, 'Richard II and his grandfather's will'.

44 He was the son of Richard's half-brother Thomas Holland, and had succeeded his father as earl of Kent in April 1397.

45 C.D. Ross, 'The Yorkshire Baronage, 1399–1435', unpublished D.Phil. thesis, University of Oxford (1950), 6–13.

46 Above, p. 40; but he also received some lands forfeited by Warwick and Arundel (GEC, *sub* Gloucester). In 1349 the Despenser inheritance was valued at £1,580, though this may only refer to two-thirds of the whole. *See CPR. 1348–50*, 293–4, where the meaning is not quite clear.

47   *CPR, 1396–9*, 82.
48   GEC, *sub* Worcester.
49   *CPR, 1408–13*, 142, 147; A.J. Elder, 'A Study of the Beauforts and Their Estates, 1399–1450', unpublished PhD thesis, Bryn Mawr College (1964), 57–8, 77, 100.
50   *Annales*, 233.
51   Archer, 'The Mowbrays', 28.
52   The same four had also been given the custody of the great March inheritance following the death in Ireland of Roger Mortimer in July 1398 (*CPR, 1396–9*, 408; *CFR, 1391–9*, 293–7, 303).
53   Archer, 'The Mowbrays', 77–8: 'the general tenor of Richard's directions was the seizure of Norfolk's inheritance for the crown's enrichment.'
54   William le Scrope, earl of Wiltshire, had already been executed during the course of the revolution; Beaufort, Rutland, Kent and Huntingdon were allowed to keep their earldoms but not their higher titles.
55   This is particularly true of the growing popularity of the entail, which was legalised by Edward I in the statute of Westminster II (1285); see below, pp. 137ff.

2   THE PEERAGE

1   McFarlane, *Nobility*, 268–9.
2   *Ibid.*, 142–3.
3   The lists of summonses are printed in *Reports of the Lords Committees Touching the Dignity of a Peer of the Realm*, vol. i (1829).
4   See above, pp. 11ff; Wells, 'Recruitment and Extinction', appendix II, basing his figures on an analysis of tenurial barons, military summonses, and conciliar and parliamentary summonses, estimated that of the 206 'baronial' families in 1216, 77 had become extinct or suffered derogation by 1300, while a further 88 had emerged to join this upper stratum of the nobility, making 217 in 1300. It was during the next century that, with the stricter definition of a parliamentary summons coming to be used to determine nobility, the real thinning of the ranks occurred: by 1350 the number of 'noble' families had fallen to 147, and by 1400 it had fallen to 73.
5   Even though the statute of April 1341 was revoked by the king six months later, it is clear that from this time onwards the right of peers to trial by their peers was in practice accepted; see B.C. Keeney, *Judgement by Peers* (1949).
6   For examples of livery laws and sumptuary legislation, see *EHD*, iv, 1116, 1153; for a recent discussion of late medieval courtesy books see J.M. Thurgood, 'The Diet and Domestic Households of the English Lay Nobility 1265–1531', unpublished M.Phil. thesis, University of London (1982), 189–90.
7   For what follows see Powell and Wallis, *House of Lords, passim*.

8 *Ibid.*, 436.
9 McFarlane, *Nobility*, 175.
10 *Ibid.*, 172.
11 I say that they *could* have been considered his heirs general because in 1344–5 the third earl had entailed most of his lands to Gúy with successive remainder to each of his younger sons, which technically disbarred Guy's two daughters from these lands (see below, pp. 141–2). The entail, of course, makes the 'extinction' and 'new creation' of 1369 even more 'theoretical.'
12 He inherited not only his father's title and most of his lands, but also his hereditary sheriffdom of Worcestershire and his hereditary chamberlainship at the exchequer: GEC, *sub* Warwick.
13 Powell and Wallis, *House of Lords*, 315, 366, and *passim*.
14 McFarlane, *Nobility*, 269.
15 The banneret was a battlefield commander who would normally bring with him a larger retinue than a knight, was entitled to the use of a square banner rather than the triangular pennon of the knight, and received wages while on campaign of 4s. a day rather than the knight's 2s. In royal wardrobe account books of the early fourteenth century, for example, there are separate lists of *baneretti* of the household, and *milites simplici* of the household (Given-Wilson, *Royal Household*, 205).
16 Powell and Wallis, *House of Lords*, 349–51.
17 *Ibid.*, 392, 403. See, for example, the letter of appointment of the continual council to govern the country during Richard II's minority in 1377: the council was to consist of 'two bishops, two earls, two barons, two bannerets, and four bachelors [i.e. knights]' (*EHD*, iv, 122).
18 *CPR, 1381–5*, 398; in fact this was probably a deliberate ploy to keep Camoys out of parliament, possibly because there were suspicions that the king had been interfering with parliamentary elections (Given-Wilson, *Royal Household*, 247).
19 His grandfather had, however, been summoned, between 1313 and 1336.
20 PRO EIOI/401/16, m. 26. The ten were: Thomas Trivet, Simon Burley, Hugh Segrave (never summoned); Thomas Percy, William Beauchamp, Aubrey de Vere (not summoned until the 1390s, by which time all three had either inherited much greater estates or been promoted to earldoms); John Lovell, John Roos, John Devereux, and John Montague (all receiving summonses at this time).
21 *CPR, 1334–8*, 346.
22 Powell and Wallis, *House of Lords*, 425.
23 Beauchamp was created, in tail male, a 'peer and baron of the realm of England, under the style of lord of Beauchamp and baron of Kydermunster (Kidderminster)' (*CPR, 1385–9*, 363); see also Powell and Wallis, *House of Lords*, 403.
24 *Nobility*, 172–6; McFarlane implicitly recognised this shift of

emphasis when he changed his terminology from 'new summonses' (1300–50) to 'new creations' (1350–1500). Although his adoption of modern peerage law exaggerated his figures for extinction and recruitment, he used the same rules throughout and his figures for the first and second halves of the fourteenth century are thus directly comparable.

25 See below, pp. 137ff.

26 For the economic gap between peers and gentry by 1436 see T. B. Pugh, 'Magnates, knights and gentry', in S.B. Chrimes, C.D. Ross, and R.A. Griffiths (eds), *Fifteenth Century England 1399–1509* (1972), 97–101.

27 See above, pp. 59–60.

28 The Mortimers, Percys, Nevills, Courtenays, Mowbrays, Montagues, Staffords, Hastings, and Despensers; see Chapter 1 above.

29 As J.S. Roskell, 'The problem of the attendance of the lords in medieval English parliaments', *BIHR* (1956), pointed out, many lords were far from punctilious in attending parliament, but inevitably those who attended most frequently were those who were most actively involved in politics, and it was to these men that the king really looked for support.

30 H.L. Gray, 'Incomes from land in England in 1436', *EHR* (1934), 619.

31 A *valor* of the Black Prince's lands at his death in 1376 totalled £9,982 (P.H.W. Booth, *The Financial Administration of the Lordship and County of Chester* (Chetham Society, 1981), 173–5).

32 See, for example, Edward III's grant of 400 marks *per annum* to Reginald Cobham when making him a banneret in 1335 (above p. 62).

33 Gray 'Incomes from land', 619.

34 Pugh, 'Magnates, knights and gentry', 97–101.

35 See, for example, G.G. Astill, 'The Medieval Gentry: A Study in Leicestershire Society, 1350–1399', unpublished PhD thesis, University of Birmingham (1977), 43–5; C. Carpenter, 'Political Society in Warwickshire *c.* 1401–1472', unpublished PhD thesis, University of Cambridge (1976), 34; S. Wright, 'A Gentry Society of the Fifteenth Century: Derbyshire *circa* 1430–1509', unpublished PhD thesis, University of Birmingham (1978), 11; K. Naughton, 'The Bedfordshire gentry in the thirteenth and fourteenth centuries', *Leicester University Occasional Publications* (1973), 23.

36 For the Mauleys see GEC, *sub* Mauley; Dugdale, *Baronage*, *sub* Mauley; C.L. Kingsford, 'The Barons de Mauley', *EHR* (1896); C.D. Ross, 'The Yorkshire Baronage, 1399–1435', unpublished D. Phil. thesis, University of Oxford (1950), 310f.

37 This was Peter VI's second marriage, contracted *circa* 1371; his first marriage was to Elizabeth, daughter of Nicholas, Lord Meinill, and widow of John, Lord Darcy, another Yorkshire baron; she died in 1368. At the same time that Peter VI married Constanza, he mar-

ried his eldest son (another Peter, who predeceased his father and thus never succeeded to the title) to Constanza's sister Margery; the two sisters were co-heiresses to their father's lands, and clearly father and son were leaving nothing to chance in their attempt to acquire these lands, which fitted neatly with the group of lands which they already held in the East Riding.

38 This Peter always styled himself Peter, *eighth* Lord Mauley, since he succeeded his grandfather (see n. 37 above).

39 Maud, widow of the last Lord Mauley, was assessed at £266 for the income tax of 1436 (Gray, 'Incomes from land', 618). Assuming, as Gray does, that this represented the normal dower third of her late husband's estates, this makes £800 for Peter VII at his death. The approximate rectitude of this figure is confirmed by Maud's inquisition *post mortem* in 1438, which valued her estates at £290 (Ross, 'Yorkshire Baronage', 448).

3 THE GENTRY

1 Pugh, 'Magnates, knights and gentry', in Chrimes *et al.* (eds), *Fifteenth Century England*, 97.

2 G.E. Mingay, *The Gentry* (1976), 13–14.

3 See above, pp. 14–19.

4 *CPR, 1381–5*, 462.

5 Mingay, *Gentry*, 4: it is interesting to note that when Richard II granted to John de Kyngeston, 'who is challenged by a French knight', the right to bear arms, the king not only 'receives him to the estate of a gentleman', but also 'makes him an esquire'. This was in 1389, well before gentlemen had acquired the right to be armigerous, but after esquires had (*CPR, 1388–92*, 72).

6 Carpenter, for example, working from the 1436 Warwickshire income tax returns, found that the knights enjoyed an average income of £164 each, compared with the esquires' £52 and the gentlemen's £12 – though the *median* income of each group would surely have been lower ('Political Society', 35).

7 M. J. Bennett, *Community, Class and Careerism: Cheshire and Lancashire Society in the Age of Sir Gawain and the Green Knight* (1983), 82–3; N.E. Saul, *Knights and Esquires: The Gloucestershire Gentry in the Fourteenth Century* (1981), 34–5; P.W. Fleming, 'Charity, faith and the gentry of Kent 1422–1529', in A. J. Pollard (ed.), *Property and Politics: Essays in Later Medieval English History* (1984), 36–7; Astill, 'Medieval Gentry', 17; Carpenter, 'Political Society', 18, 22–5, 42–5, 85; Wright, 'Gentry Society', 9–10.

8 Gray 'Incomes from land', 607–39; for comment see Pugh, 'Magnates, knights and gentry', 97f, where it is shown that Gray considerably underestimated the economic gulf between the peers and the 183 'richer knights', who enjoyed incomes around the £200 mark and who, Gray suggested, might have formed a separate 'elite

gentry' group between the peers and the rest of the knights and esquires. The tax was not levied on those who held less than £5 worth of land per annum.

9   There were thirty-nine counties (excluding Monmouth) in medieval England. Larger counties (Kent, for example) obviously had more gentry families, while smaller ones had fewer.

10 Fleming, 'Charity, faith and gentry of Kent', 36.

11 As suggested by Dr D.L. Morgan in his paper on the fifteenth-century English gentleman delivered to the Fifteenth-Century Colloquium at Nottingham University, September 1984.

12 Bennett, *Community, Class and Careerism*, 68–9, 82, 241.

13 Wright, 'Gentry Society', 6–9; Fleming, 'Charity, faith and gentry of Kent', 36; Saul, *Knights and Esquires*, 33–4.

14 Astill, 'Medieval Gentry', 144, 184; Wright, 'Gentry Society', 9; Naughton, 'Bedfordshire gentry', 40–7, 53; Saul, *Knights and Esquires*, 259; Carpenter, 'Political Society', 42–5.

15 Maddicott, 'Magna Carta and local community', 45; Naughton, 'Bedfordshire gentry', 45–7.

16 Ross, 'Yorkshire Baronage', 424; Naughton, 'Bedfordshire gentry', 27, 47; Carpenter, 'Political Society', 105.

17 Wright, 'Gentry Society', 10; Carpenter, 'Political Society', 85–8, 95.

18 Fleming, 'Charity, faith and gentry of Kent', 36–7, talks of the 'clannish nature' of many Kentish gentry families, though as he explains this was probably accentuated by the county's peculiar 'gavelkind system, a partible inheritance custom which allowed . . . cadet branches to remain in the same locality along with the senior line, but with an ever-decreasing share of the patrimony'.

19 Fleming, 'Charity, faith, and gentry of Kent', 36; Astill, 'Medieval Gentry', 43, 339; Wright, 'Gentry Society', 11–13; Naughton, 'Bedfordshire gentry', 23; Carpenter, 'Political Society', 22–5, 35, 92.

20 Wright, 'Gentry Society', 63, 94; Naughton, 'Bedfordshire gentry', 20, 24.

21 Fleming, 'Charity, faith and gentry of Kent', 42–52.

22 Cherry, 'Courtenay earls of Devon', 71, 97.

23 For what follows. see Bennett, *Community, Class and Careerism*, especially 26–33; see also Booth, *Financial Administration of Chester*, 6–9, who also argues that there was in Cheshire 'a potent combination of a socially cohesive community with a judicially privileged institution [the county court].

24 Bennett, *Community, Class and Careerism*, 18, 220–2; Booth, *Financial Administration of Chester*, 116–41.

25 Cherry, 'Courtenay earls of Devon', 76f.

26 Carpenter, 'Political Society', 89–94, 98, 149–50.

27 According to Carpenter (see her map), Warwickshire was divided into five principal regions, based partly on magnate affinities and partly on gentry associations.

28 Wright, 'Gentry Society', 114–20; Astill, 'Medieval Gentry', 81, 129, 201; and for the importance of kinship in Kentish gentry society see above, n. 18.

29 Saul, *Knights and Esquires*, 258; J.R. Maddicott, 'The county community and the making of public opinion in fourteenth-century England', *TRHS* (1978), 43.

30 See, for example, Maddicott, 'Magna Carta and local community', *passim*.

31 Maddicott, 'County community and public opinion', 30, 39; Saul, *Knights and Esquires*, 259; Booth, *Financial Administration of Chester*, 8; Booth, however, thought that the power of the county court in Cheshire was exceptional by comparison with other counties.

32 Astill, 'Medieval Gentry', 158–71, 190–2; Maddicott, 'County community and public opinion', 41–2.

33 Although royal justices and magnates were also frequently appointed, they seem rarely to have attended (Carpenter, 'Political Society', 176; Wright, 'Gentry Society', 136). See also Ormrod, 'Edward III's Government of England', where it is argued that during the 1350s there was a real attempt by central government to control local administration, but in the 1360s these efforts slackened and the gentry really began to dominate institutions such as the sessions of the justices of the peace (199–201, 321–3).

34 See above, p. 73; on local control of shire offices in general see Naughton, 'Bedfordshire gentry', 46–53; Carpenter, 'Political Society', 38; Saul, *Knights and Esquires*, 258–9; Wright, 'Gentry Society' 173; Maddicott, 'Magna Carta and local community', 26f.

35 Bennett, *Community, Class and Careerism*, 72.

36 *John of Gaunt's Register 1379–1383*, ed. E.C. Lodge and R. Somerville, ii, 6–13; Ross, 'Yorkshire Baronage', 394; Archer, 'The Mowbrays', 307–9.

37 Given-Wilson, *Royal Household*, ch. 4.

38 C. Carpenter, 'The Beauchamp affinity: a study of bastard feudalism at work', *EHR* (1980); Cherry, 'Courtenay earls of Devon, Archer, 'The Mowbrays', 279–80.

39 Given-Wilson, *Royal Household*, ch. 4; Bennett, *Community, Class and Careerism*, 73–4; *POPC*, i, 109.

40 Bennett, *Community, Class and Careerism*, 127, 133.

41 Mingay, *Gentry*, 9–10.

42 For Bedfordshire, compare Naughton, 'Bedfordshire gentry', 20–2 and map, with the list of Grey of Ruthin lands given in R.I. Jack, 'The Greys of Ruthin 1325 to 1490: A study in the Lesser Baronage', unpublished PhD thesis, University of London (1961), appendix; Wright, 'Gentry Society', 25; Carpenter, 'Political Society', 28, 89–90.

43 Booth, *Financial Administration of Chester*, 6–9; Bennett, *Community, Class and Careerism*, 68, 241; Bennett estimates that the gentry held 75 per cent of land in the Cheshire/Lancashire region.

44 Archer, 'The Mowbrays', 271–2, 313–14.

45 Saul, *Knights and Esquires*, 257; Astill, 'Medieval Gentry', 314; Wright, 'Gentry Society', 354.

4 HOUSEHOLDS AND COUNCILS

1 PRO DL 28/3/1, m. 4.

2 PRO EIOI/400/28, mm. 1–2.

3 McFarlane, *Nobility*, 110–11; R.G.K.A. Mertes, 'Secular Noble Households in England 1350–1550', unpublished PhD thesis, University of Edinburgh (1981), 213, 222.

4 Elder, 'Beauforts and their Estates', 130; John Smyth, in his *Lives of the Berkeleys*, 3 vols, ed. J. Maclean (1883), i, 309, says that Thomas, Lord Berkeley (d. 1321), had a 'household and standinge domesticall family . . . lodged in house' consisting of over 200 persons, but it is clear that this included many more than one should think of as real household servants: among them were 'husbandmen, hindes, and others of lower condition' – in other words, tenants who might have been invited to the castle for occasional feasts, but who were certainly not full-time employees of the lord.

5 Quoted by D. Starkey in S. Medcalf (ed.), *The Context of English Literature: The Later Middle Ages* (1981), 244.

6 Astill, 'Medieval Gentry', 288; Mertes, 'Secular Noble Households', 16.

7 For what follows see Mertes, 'Secular Noble Households', 76f; for the organisation of the royal household, which was run along similar lines though obviously on a grander scale, see Given-Wilson, *Royal Household*, ch. 1.

8 *EHD*, iv, 1138–9.

9 Holmes, *Estates*, 64; PRO DL 28/3/1, m. 8.

10 Fleming, 'Charity, faith, and gentry of Kent', in Pollard (ed.), *Property and Politics*, 42.

11 *Ibid.*, *passim*; H. Johnstone, 'Poor-relief in the royal households of thirteenth-century England', *Speculum* (1929); J.M. Thurgood, 'The Diet and Domestic Households of the English Lay Nobility 1265–1531', unpublished M.Phil, thesis, University of London (1982), 227–8.

12 PRO EIOI/400/28, m. 2d.

13 Thurgood, 'Diet and Domestic Households', 235–7.

14 See above, pp. 2–5

15 S. Armitage-Smith, *John of Gaunt* (1904), 447–9; Gaunt's landed income was probably around £12,000 gross, or *circa* £10,000 net, at this time, but he was also receiving several thousands of pounds each year from the exchequer for his custody of Aquitaine, and from the king of Castile, who had bought out his claim to the Castilian throne in 1388.

16 PRO DL 28/3/1; this again excludes fees and annuities, as well as

building expenses, out-of-court payments, and some incidental expenses, to make it comparable with the 1394-5 figure.

17 Smyth, *Lives of the Berkeleys*, i, 306.

18 Mertes, 'Secular Noble Households', 221; Thurgood, 'Diet and Domestic Households', 55-73.

19 I am grateful to Bridget Harvey of St Andrews University for supplying this information from her research into the Berkeleys in the fourteenth century.

20 Holmes, *Estates*, 110-11.

21 Mertes, 'Secular Noble Households', 202-7.

22 Thurgood, 'Diet and Domestic Households', 34-40, 69-87.

23 Mertes, 'Secular Noble Households', 171, 315.

24 Thurgood, 'Diet and Domestic Households', 189, 235-7.

25 R. Allen Brown, *English Castles* (2nd edn, 1976), *passim*; Thurgood, 'Diet and Domestic Households', 32, 233; Mertes, 'Secular Noble Households', 16-17, 168-9.

26 Mertes, 'Secular Noble Households', 234f.

27 C. Given-Wilson, 'Purveyance for the royal household 1362-1413', *BIHR* (1983); some nobles were clearly aware that purveyance might create local shortages, as witness the following letter from the Black Prince to his father and mother in 1352, asking them not to purvey in the neighbourhood of Byfleet manor (Surrey) for a while, 'inasmuch as the prince and his brother [Gaunt] plan to stay a great deal at the manor of Byfleet, and when he is absent his household will be there' (*Black Prince's Register*), iv, 54.

28 *RP*, ii, 269; *ibid.*, iii, 15, 146, 158, 410.

29 Mertes, 'Secular Noble Households', 215-19.

30 *Ibid.*, 133-40, 310.

31 Denholm-Young, *Seignorial Administration*, 28; and see generally C. Rawcliffe, 'Baronial councils in the later Middle Ages', in C.D. Ross (ed.), *Patronage, Pedigree and Power in Later Medieval England* (1979).

32 *Black Prince's Register*, iv, 263 and *passim*.

33 Booth, *Financial Administration of Chester*, 74-5.

34 Archer, 'The Mowbrays', 114-16, 171, 224.

35 *CPR, 1364-7*, 169.

36 J.S. Roskell, *The Commons and Their Speakers in English Parliaments 1376-1523* (1965), 121.

37 Given-Wilson, *Royal Household*, 201-2.

38 Cherry, 'Courtenay earls of Devon', 80-1.

39 Rawcliffe, 'Baronial councils', 100-1.

40 PRO DL 28/3/1, mm. 3, 6.

41 Rawcliffe, 'Baronial councils', 90-4.

42 *CPR, 1385-9*, 350-1.

43 E. Powell, 'Arbitration and the law in England in the late Middle Ages', *TRHS* (1983), 66; Rawcliffe, 'Baronial councils', 91.

44 Davies, *Lordship and Society*, 168 and *passim*.

45 J.R. Maddicott, 'Law and lordship: royal justices as retainers in thirteenth and fourteenth century England', *P & P Supplement* (1978).

46 *CPR, 1391–6*, 294, 380.

47 Rawcliffe, 'Baronial councils', 104–5.

5 ESTATES IN LAND

1 For what follows see R. Somerville, *History of the Duchy of Lancaster*, i (1953); Fowler, *King's Lieutenant*, 225–6; PRO DL 28/3/1; and for the distribution of the Lancastrian lands see the map in Armitage-Smith, *John of Gaunt*.

2 For these valuations of Marcher lordships see Davies, *Lordship and Society*, appendix.

3 Ross, 'Yorkshire Baronage', 6–14.

4 Archer, 'The Mowbrays', 4, 75, 116–17.

5 C. Ross, 'The estates and finances of Richard Beauchamp, earl of Warwick', *Dugdale Society Occasional Papers* (1956), 6.

6 Denholm-Young, *Seignorial Administration*, 68.

7 Ross, 'Estates and finances', 7; see above, pp. 99–100, for the Mowbrays.

8 See above, p. 99.

9 Ross, 'Estates and finances', 10–11.

10 See above, p. 100.

11 *John of Gaunt's Register 1372–1376*, ed. S. Armitage-Smith, ii, 292.

12 *Black Prince's Register*, Chester, 410.

13 Ross, 'Estates and finances', 13–14.

14 Archer, 'The Mowbrays', 206–7; Jack, 'Greys of Ruthin', 320–1.

15 Smyth, *Lives of the Berkeleys*, i, 157–60.

16 Booth, *Financial Administration of Chester*, 77.

17 For valors see McFarlane, *Nobility*, 213–14, and R.R. Davies, 'Baronial accounts, income and arrears in the later Middle Ages', *Economic History Review* (1968).

18 Booth, *Financial Administration of Chester*, 67.

19 Davies, *Lordship and Society*, passim.

20 See above, pp. 22ff.

21 For the events of 1315–22 see I. Kershaw, 'The great famine and the agrarian crisis in England 1315–22', *P & P* (1973); for the early fourteenth-century economy in general see Miller and Hatcher, *Medieval England*; B. Harvey, 'The population trend in England between 1300 and 1348', *TRHS* (1966); and A.R. Bridbury, 'Before the Black Death', *Economic History Review* (1977).

22 King, *England 1175–1425*, 15.

23 For the later fourteenth-century economy see especially J. Hatcher, *Plague, Population and the English Economy 1348–1530* (1977).

24 *Ibid.*, 23; King, *England 1175–1425*, 15.

25 *EHD*, iv, 90, 562.

26 C. Dyer, 'A redistribution of incomes in fifteenth-century England?', *P & P* (1968).

27 Holmes, *Estates*, 114; C. Dyer, 'The social and economic background to the rural revolt in 1381' in R.H. Hilton and T.H. Aston (eds), *The English Rising of 1381* (1984), 29; Hatcher, *Plague, Population and English Economy*, 32.

28 Bridbury, 'Before the Black Death', and 'The Black Death', *Economic History Review* (1973).

29 Dyer, in Hilton and Aston (eds), *English Rising*, 22.

30 *Ibid.*, 28–9; Hilton, *Decline of Serfdom*, 41–2; Booth, *Financial Administration of Chester*, 109–10.

31 Harding, in Hilton and Aston (eds), *English Rising*, 187.

32 Dyer, in *ibid.*, 38–9.

33 *Ibid.*, 27–8.

34 R.B. Dobson (ed.), *The Peasants' Revolt of 1381* (1970), 97–8; Faith, in Hilton and Aston (eds), *English Rising*.

35 *RP*, iii, 21.

36 Hilton, *Decline of Serfdom*, 40.

37 Saul, *Knights and Esquires*, 211–14; R.H. Britnell, 'Minor landlords in England and medieval agrarian capitalism', *P & P* (1980); Astill, 'Medieval Gentry', 30.

38 Saul, *Knights and Esquires*, 238.

39 See above, Chapter 2.

40 *Victoria County History of Sussex*, ii, 181.

41 Booth, *Financial Administration of Chester*, 107–10, 123–4, 138–41.

42 Dyer, in Hilton and Aston (eds), *English Rising*, 36.

43 Holmes, *Estates*, 117–18; Hatcher, *Plague, Population and English Economy*, 36–7; Hilton, *Decline of Serfdom*, 43.

6 PROPERTY, THE FAMILY, AND MONEY

1 See for example H.A. Miskimin, *The Economy of Early Renaissance Europe* (1969).

2 Astill, 'Medieval Gentry', 31; see also R.H. Bautier, *The Economic Development of Medieval Europe* (1971), 200.

3 Bautier, *Economic Development of Medieval Europe*, 199.

4 Davies, *Lordship and Society*, 115.

5 Shrewsbury Record Office, Acton of Aldenham Collection no. 1093, box I.

6 L.F. Salzman, 'The property of the earl of Arundel, 1397', *Sussex Archaeological Collections* (1953), 38–41; unfortunately there are no figures for the earl's Marcher properties in 1397, but there are strong indications that the number of sheep on his lands here continued to increase also, especially on his Marcher lordship of Clun. (See, L.O.W. Smith, 'The Lordships of Chirk and Oswestry 1282–1415', unpublished PhD thesis, University of London, 1970, 143–7.)

7 Smyth, *Lives of the Berkeleys*, i, 302, 326; Bridget Harvey, 'The Berkeleys in Fourteenth-Century Gloucestershire' (unpublished MA Honours Dissertation, University of St Andrews, 1983), 17, 22–3.
8 Holmes, *Estates*, 89–90.
9 A.R. Bridbury, 'Before the Black Death'; Dyer, in Hilton and Aston (eds), *English Rising*, 22.
10 Salzman, 'Property of the earl of Arundel', 34.
11 Holmes, *Estates*, 113–14.
12 Salzman, 'Property of the earl of Arundel', 33; A. Goodman, *The Loyal Conspiracy* (1971), 108.
13 *Warwickshire Feet of Fines*, ed. L. Drucker (Dugdale Society, 1943), iii (1345–1509), no. 1972; W. Dugdale, Warwickshire (1730 edn), i. 494; *Black Prince's Register*, iii, 40; *CIPM*, xii, 326; Goodman, *Loyal Conspiracy*, 138f.
14 *CPR, 1350–4*, 252–61; *ibid., 1354–8*, 607; *ibid., 1370–4*, 265.
15 Jack, 'Greys of Ruthin', 180–1, 359f.
16 Ross, 'Yorkshire Baronage', 1–13, 223f.
17 Smyth, *Lives of the Berkeleys*, i, 325–31.
18 For the Stafford patrimony in 1323, see *CIPM*, v, 131; in 1372, see *ibid.*, xvi, 432–54; in 1403, see BL Harl. MS 700, ff. 6–13.
19 Astill, 'Medieval Gentry', 59; Wright, 'Gentry Society', 44–50; Saul, *Knights and Esquires*, 229; Dyer, in Hilton and Aston (eds), *English Rising*, 22.
20 McFarlane, *Nobility*, 83–4.
21 *Ibid.*, 56–7; Carpenter, 'Political Society', 102; A. Smith, 'Litigation and politics: Sir John Fastolf's defence of his English property', in A. Pollard (ed.), *Property and Politics: Essays in Later Medieval English History* (1984), 60.
22 Salzman, 'Property of the earl of Arundel', 35; GEC, *sub* Salisbury.
23 *CCR, 1354–60*, 181.
24 GEC, *sub* Salisbury; Armitage-Smith, *John of Gaunt*, 449.
25 R.E. Archer, 'Rich old ladies: the problem of late medieval dowagers', in Pollard (ed.), *Property and Politics*, 25–6.
26 *CCR, 1385–9*, 137–8; for childlessness as a reason for gentry selling land, see also Astill, 'Medieval Gentry', 59, and Wright, 'Gentry Society', 59.
27 For some of the details of this thoroughly complicated case see *CCR, 1374–7*, 274–7, *CPR, 1385–9*, 204–5, and PRO SCI/214/10685; capture in war also sometimes led to the straightforward sale of land, as with Reynold, Lord Grey of Ruthin, captured by Owen Glendower in 1400, and consequently forced to sell about seventeen of the manors which he had recently acquired from the Hastings inheritance, in order to pay his ransom (Jack, 'Greys of Ruthin', 180, 190, 359f). See also McFarlane, *Nobility*, 126–8.
28 Edmund's sister Margaret was John Beaufort's first wife.
29 Elder, 'The Beauforts and their Estates', 57–68, 82, 86, 162.

30 Wright, 'Gentry Society', 46; Naughton, 'Bedfordshire gentry', 17–19; Astill, 'Medieval Gentry', 39; Saul, *Knights and Esquires*, 227–8.
31 See below, pp. 137ff.
32 See above, pp. 67–8.
33 GEC and Dugdale, *Baronage, sub* Morley.
34 *Ibid., sub* Zouche.
35 For what follows see *The Percy Chartulary*, ed. M. T. Martin (Surtees Society, 1911); J.M.W. Bean, *The Estates of the Percy Family 1416–1537* (1958), 3–11; and Ross, 'Yorkshire Baronage', 96–124.
36 *RP*, ii, 62.
37 *CPR, 1370–4*, 329; *Victoria County History of Northumberland*, vii, 236.
38 *CPR, 1381–5*, 392; according to Ross, 'Yorkshire Baronage', 103, the right heirs included the Meltons, Harringtons, and FitzWalters.
39 *Victoria County History of Northumberland*, i, 234, 239.
40 Fairbanks, 'Last earl of Warenne and Surrey'; one of the crucial documents of the case is in *CPR, 1345–8*, 221; *CIPM*, ix, 43, has most of the earl's lands at his death.
41 *CPR, 1334–8*, 426; and see above, p. 39.
42 The last three had been granted dukedoms in 1397, but for convenience they are referred to by their comital titles.
43 In fact these manors had been among those surrendered by Warwick to Mowbray in June 1397, when the king ordered Warwick not only to hand over Gower to Mowbray, but also to restore to Mowbray the issues of the lordship for the preceding thirteen years, reckoned at 8,000 marks (Archer, 'The Mowbrays', 18).
44 For the development of le Scrope's power in north Wales, see Given-Wilson, *Royal Household*, 168.
45 As suggested by Tuck, *Richard II and the English Nobility*, 184.
46 *CPR, 1330–4*, 262, and GEC, *sub* Mauley.
47 *CPR, 1381–5*, 405.
48 Fairbanks, 'Last earl of Warenne and Surrey', 211–13, has the details.
49 Ganshof, *Feudalism*.
50 For the statute, see *EHD*, iii, 428. Apparently it was originally intended that the restriction on alienation of entailed land should only last until the fourth generation, whereupon the entail would in effect be converted into fee simple, but in practice entails were regarded as unbreakable; on fourteenth-century landholding customs in general see McFarlane, *Nobility*, 61–82, and J.M.W. Bean, *The Decline of English Feudalism 1215–1540* (1968).
51 On this subject see C.D. Ross, 'Forfeitures for treason in the reign of Richard II', *EHR* (1956). The logic was that since there were always at least two estates in entailed land (the grantee's and the reversioner's), it was unfair to deprive the latter on account of the misdeeds of the former, though as Ross points out this was done in Richard's reign. Enfeoffments to use were also protected from

forfeiture, since at law they were not held by the *cestui-que-use* – he merely enjoyed the profits from them. The first occasion on which land held to uses was forfeited was in 1377, at the trial of Edward III's mistress Alice Perrers, but in passing judgment the lords were careful to point out that it was not their intention that their sentence, 'made for such an odious thing in this special case, should extend to any other person, nor should it in any other case be taken as an example' (*RP*, iii, 14). Among the muniments at Winchester College there is an extensive list of lands of William of Wykeham, bishop of Winchester, entitled 'memoranda de terris et tenementis in quibus W. Episc. Wynton feoffatur . . . et in quibus feoffatur per se . . . et in quibus alii feoffantur ex ordinacoe sua' (Winchester College Muniments, no. 2). It is possible that the list was drawn up at the time of his trial and the subsequent confiscation of his temporalities in October 1376, to distinguish between those of his lands which could be confiscated and those which could not because they were held by others to his use. But despite the sentence on Alice Perrers in 1377, some lands enfeoffed to uses were forfeited by the Appellants in 1397.

52 It is possible that the jointure represents an attempt to restrict the amount of land held by a widow after her husband's death, while at the same time giving her greater security in what land she did hold. Holmes, *Estates*, 43, found that jointures among the higher nobility usually ranged between £100 and £400, which was considerably less than the standard dower third of most comital inheritances. However, his figures were based on a study of marriage contracts and in practice these were sometimes no more than a starting-point, with additional lands being added to the jointure at later stages of life. Yet Wright found that among the fifteenth-century Derbyshire gentry there was an attempt to 'rationalise' provisions for women, with jointures usually in the £10 to £20 range, and 'pressure on a widow to commute her dower rights for a straight cash annuity' ('Gentry Society', 70, 85). Jack, 'Greys of Ruthin', 266, 291–2, noted that Lady Joan Grey's willingness to commute her dower rights for a cash annuity from her son of £150, at a time when the *net* value of the estate was *circa* £1260 a year, helped him greatly.

53 In fact, William never entered the church: see below, pp. 146–7; for the 1345 reorganisation see *CPR, 1345–5*, 251–2, 517–8.

54 *CPR, 1348–50*, 234.

55 Smyth, *Lives of the Berkeleys*, ii, 44f, has the most detailed account of this *cause célèbre*. Although a compromise was reached in 1426, not until a month before his death in 1463 was James reconciled to his cousin Margaret, countess of Shrewsbury, and even then she continued to hound his son until 1467 (GEC, *sub* Berkeley and Lisle).

56 *CPR, 1385–9*, 363–4, lists twenty-five manors and several smaller

properties enfeoffed for the performance of the will, which was probably over a quarter of the whole inheritance. See Holmes, *Estates*, 53, for the will.

57 *CPR*, *1358–61*, 575–6, 580; Holmes, *Estates*, 75–6; Given-Wilson, 'Richard II and his grandfather's will'.

58 Jack, 'Greys of Ruthin', 172–4, 238, 359f.

59 The arrangement made by Pembroke in 1372 is recited in *CCR*, *1374–7*, 286; for the details of the case see R.I. Jack, 'Entail and descent: the Hastings inheritance', *BIHR* (1965).

60 This was by now the younger Reynold, the elder having died in 1388.

61 The conditions under which the Hastings inheritance was to be given to Beauchamp were that he would 'bear the whole arms' of the earl of Pembroke, and that he would 'prevail with the king' to grant him the title of the earldom as well. If he refused to accept these, the same offer was to be made to Sir William Clinton under the same conditions: Clinton was not even a kinsman of John Hastings (*CCR*, *1374–7*, 286). Jack points out ('Greys of Ruthin', 18f) that the two men probably agreed that *at law* Grey would be recognised as the heir (by their collusion they hoped to defeat any other claims to the lands), but that he promptly granted half the inheritance to Beauchamp (though Abergavenny may have been sold, for the knock-down price of 1,000 marks, which in reality was probably just Beauchamp's contribution to Grey's legal costs in defending himself against other claimants). (This evidence is summarised in Jack, 'Entail and Descent', 11.)

62 *CCR*, *1369–74*, 108, 454–5, 468. In his will (quoted by Holmes, *Estates*, 49 n. 3), Earl Thomas stated that William was to be provided with 400 *marks'* worth of land, but the enfeoffed lands included those which had been designed to yield a rent of £373 *per annum* in 1345, and some more besides, and their real value was probably at least £400 *per annum*.

63 It was largely to deal with uses that the equitable jurisdiction of the chancellor developed in the late fourteenth and fifteenth centuries. For discussion of this and other legal problems associated with uses see M.E. Avery, 'The history of the equitable jurisdiction of Chancery before 1460', *BIHR* (1969); J.L. Barton, 'The medieval use', *Law Quarterly Review* (1965); and Given-Wilson, 'Richard II and his grandfather's will'.

64 Archer, 'The Mowbrays', 24; and Archer, 'Rich old ladies', in Pollard (ed.), *Property and Politics*.

65 See above, p. 144.

66 *RP*, ii, 104.

67 *John of Gaunt's Register 1372–1376*, ed. S. Armitage-Smith, ii, 267; McFarlane, *Nobility*, 217–19.

68 Booth, *Financial Administration of Chester*, Astill, 'Medieval Gentry', 69–72. 107–8.

69   Bean, *Decline of English Feudalism*, 126, 180 and *passim*.
70   *CCR, 1374–7*, 286; *CPR, 1381–5*, 313–14.
71   See below, pp. 152–3.
72   Tuck, *Richard II and the English Nobility*, 88–9, 207; *CPR, 1381–5*, 377.
73   The valuation is from Archer, 'The Mowbrays', 28; see McFarlane, *Nobility*, 262–5, for the background, though he suggests a valuation of about £4,000.
74   See above, p. 54.
75   The Wigmore chronicler is quoted in Tuck, *Richard II and the English Nobility*, 88.
76   *RP*, ii, 104, 341.
77   See, for example, Edward III's grant to the earl of Salisbury in 1340 (*CPR, 1340–3*, 57).
78   *Ibid.*, 23.
79   *RP*, ii, 328–9; J.W. Sherborne, 'Indentured retinues and English expeditions to France 1369–1380', *EHR* (1964), 725–7.
80   A. Goodman, 'The military sub-contracts of Sir Hugh Hastings 1380', *EHR* (1980), 114–20.
81   P. Contamine, 'The French nobility and the war', in K. Fowler (ed.), *The Hundred Years War* (1971), 151.
82   Phillips, *Aymer de Valence*, 148–51, 312–15.
83   *CPR, 1348–50*, 145; *CCR, 1349–54*, 556; *CPR, 1348–50*, 104.
84   GEC, *sub* the relevant titles; *CPR, 1348–50*, 223.
85   G.L. Harriss, *King, Parliament and Public Finance in Medieval England to 1369* (1975), 481–7.
86   PRO E403/499, 10 December.
87   PRO E403/554, 2 October, 14 October, 3 November, 1 March.
88   Given-Wilson, *Royal Household*, 130f, 263–4.
89   Archer, 'The Mowbrays', 307–11.
90   *CPR, 1364–7*, 155; John, Lord Nevill, was retained for life by John of Gaunt in 1370, with 50 marks in time of peace and 500 in time of war; some similar examples are revealed by the tax returns of 1436 (see, for example, Pugh, 'Magnates, knights and gentry', in Chrimes *et al.* (eds), *Fifteenth Century England*, 102).
91   McFarlane, *Nobility*, 19f.
92   PRO E403/555, 30 May.
93   Ross, 'Yorkshire Baronage', 439.
94   McFarlane, *Nobility*, 22.
95   Holmes, *Good Parliament*, especially 108–26.
96   Ross, 'Yorkshire Baronage', 74.
97   Salzman, 'Property of the earl of Arundel', 34.
98   PRO C53/145–52; Ormrod, 'Edward III's Government of England', 110–14.
99   *CCR, 1369–74*, 150, and Holmes, *Good Parliament*, 74–7, who discusses his money-lending to the crown over a period of twenty-five years; for a loan of 1,000 marks (or more) to John of Gaunt, see PRO DL 28/3/I, m. 4.

100 CCR, 1354–60, 93 (in fact the marriage never took place); Holmes
     Estates, 43; on marriage-portions generally see McFarlane, Nobility,
     84–7, though he was perhaps inclined to exaggerate the extent to
     which the portion replaced the maritagium in the fourteenth cen-
     tury. Even if the principal element of the dowry was now usually
     in cash, there was quite often a land element included as well.

101 Powell and Wallis, House of Lords, 350.

CONCLUSION

1 The illusion that there was little overlap between peace-time and
   war-time retinues is created partly by the fact that war-time retinues
   were inevitably bigger and therefore included many not retained for
   life by the lord, and partly by the fact that certain members of the
   peace-time retinue had to stay behind to look after the lord's interests while he was away.

2 See, for example, the letter from Edmund Fitzalan, earl of Arundel,
   dated at Arundel 4th June (?) 1321, to the men of his town of
   Shrewsbury, thanking them for their assurances of loyalty and
   commanding them to guard the town carefully because 'nous nen-
   tendons point qe nostre cousin de mortemer qe nous est si pres de
   saunk nous vousist si grant mal surguerre saunz nostre desserte. . . '
   If, through their negligence or connivance, the town is lost or
   ravaged, he threatens to double the debt which they owe him
   (Shrewsbury Record Office, Arundel Deeds 215/1).

3 Booth, Financial Administration of Chester, 123–4.

4 Westminster Chronicle, ed. Harvey and Hector, 396; in 1391 Percy
   exchanged his captaincy of Calais with Mowbray in order to regain
   the wardenship.

5 I. Rowney, 'Resources and retaining in Yorkist England: William
   Lord Hastings and the Honour of Tutbury', in Pollard (ed.), Property and Politics, 145.

6 Bennett, Community, Class and Careerism, 72–3.

7 Given-Wilson, Royal Household, 227–9.

8 See above, pp. 67–8; among the highest echelons of the nobility
   (the earls, for example), the status of the marriage partner was
   probably the overriding consideration, and the chance to acquire
   contiguous estates was thus often passed over.

9 Naughton, 'Bedfordshire gentry', 27; Jack, 'Greys of Ruthin', 164–
   5, 359f.

10 See above, p. 144.

11 As well as a further third or so which his grandmother Margaret de
    Bohun continued to hold in dower until her death in 1391. McFar-
    lane, Nobility, 111, estimated that Edward Courtenay's income circa
    1382 was about £1,350 per annum, rising to about £2,000 after his
    grandmother's death, but Cherry, 'Courtenay earls of Devon', 75
    n. 2, estimated that the whole inheritance (including the dower
    third) was only worth about £1,500 in 1374–5. Details of the

Courtenay estate are to be found in Holmes, *Estates*, 33–6, 48; see also *CPR, 1354–8*, 546; *ibid., 1370–4*, 415; *ibid., 1374–7*, 165; *CIPM*, xiv, 325.

12 The table excludes three more of Hugh and Margaret's sons who predeceased the earl, and their nine daughters.

13 Peter Courtenay became chamberlain of the royal household in 1388; Philip was retained as a king's knight in 1378 and was the king's lieutenant in Ireland in the 1380s (Given-Wilson, *Royal Household*, appendix V; see also *Westminster Chronicle*, ed. Harvey and Hector, 37).

14 *RP*, iii, 302: 'et le dit Mr. Philipp est si grant en ce pais, que null povere homme n'ose envers luy son droit pursuer, ne null povere homme encontre luy verite dire en mesme le Counte.' The petitioner was one Nicholas Potyngdon, who claimed that Courtenay was asserting that he was a bastard and thus could not inherit his father's manor. Philip Courtenay was perhaps a violent character: in the 1402 parliament he was sentenced to imprisonment for dispossessing and imprisoning the Cistercian abbot of Newnham (Devon) and ignoring a summons of the royal council to answer for his conduct (*ibid.*, 488–9).

15 Harvey, 'The Berkeleys in Fourteenth-Century Gloucestershire'.

16 For discussion of this see C.T. Wood, *The French Appanages and the Capetian Monarchy 1224–1328* (1966).

17 Cherry, 'Courtenay earls of Devon', 95–7, and 'The struggle for power in mid-fifteenth-century Devonshire', in R.A. Griffiths (ed.), *Patronage, The Crown and the Provinces in Later Medieval England* (1981).

18 As graphically demonstrated by the maps of the king's houses provided in H.M. Colvin *et al.*, *The History of the King's Works*, i (1963); for the itinerary of the household see Given-Wilson, *Royal Household*, 28–39.

19 Nor was retaining *per se* ever attacked by the fourteenth-century monarchy, though the giving of certain types of livery was at certain times: see the discussion in Given-Wilson, *Royal Household*, 236–43.

20 *Calendar of Charter Rolls*, iv, 400; *CPR, 1350–54*, 60.

21 *List of Sheriffs for England and Wales* (PRO Lists and Indexes, ix, 1963 reprint). Whoever held the castle of Oakham also held the 'county' (including the shrievalty) of Rutland, and from 1348 to 1373 this was the successive de Bohun earls of Northampton. The only two *hereditary* sheriffdoms in fourteenth-century England were those of Worcestershire and Westmorland (held by the Cliffords). In 1385 Henry Percy was made sheriff of Northumberland for life, and John Salisbury, knight of Richard II's chamber, was made sheriff of Wiltshire for life, but his life was ended three years later when he was convicted of treason in the Merciless Parliament.

22 *Victoria County History of Shropshire*, iii, 30–1; Fowler, *King's Lieute-*

nant, 222, 261 n.46; R. Jeffs, 'The Later Medieval Sheriff and the Royal Household', unpublished D.Phil. thesis, University of Oxford (1960), 65, 217, emphasises the military role of the late medieval sheriff.

23 See below, p. 174. Yet it should not be thought that Edward III granted out royal powers indiscriminately. The grant of palatine rights in Lancashire to Henry of Grosmont, for example, specifically excluded the right of exemption from lay and clerical taxation, and pardons of life and limb, and retained for the king (as was usual) 'the supremacy and power of correcting errors done or defaults in the courts of the duke'. Otherwise he was to hold power 'as fully and freely as the earl of Chester holds in the county of Chester' (*CPR,1350–4,*60).

24 R.L. Storey, *The End of the House of Lancaster* (1966), 108–9; see also J.A. Tuck, 'Richard II and the border magnates', *Northern History* (1968).

25 Ross, 'Yorkshire Baronage', 96–121; Given-Wilson, *Royal Household*, 227–9; see also the letter concerning the Percy revolt of 1403–4 in *Royal and Historical Letters during the Reign of Henry IV*, ed. F.C. Hingeston (Rolls Series, 1860), i, 206.

26 Cherry, 'Courtenay earls of Devon', 90–2.

27 Given-Wilson, *Royal Household*, 266, and sources cited there.

28 *RP*, iii, 7, 58–9.

29 Archer, 'The Mowbrays', 16–18; although Gower was officially restored to Richard Beauchamp, earl of Warwick, in 1405, according to Archer the Mowbrays in fact kept it; for Denbigh, see Holmes, *Estates*, 15–16,39.

30 Quoted in Given-Wilson, *Royal Household*, 145, where the case is discussed in more detail; Smith, 'Litigation and politics', in Pollard (ed.), *Property and Politics*, charts the remarkable revival of Sir John Fastolf's fortunes after the death of the duke of Suffolk in 1450.

31 Archer, 'The Mowbrays', 18.

32 See Tuck, *Richard II and the English Nobility*, for some examples of Richard's attitude to property; McFarlane, *Nobility*, 248–67 ('Had Edward I a "policy" towards the Earls?') has described Edward I's unscrupulous property dealings with some of his magnates; for Edward III, see especially J.G. Bellamy, *The Law of Treason in England in the Later Middle Ages* (1970), who argues that the narrow definition adopted in the 1352 Statute of Treasons was to protect lords from the consequences of forfeiture to the crown on the part of their tenants. See also above, pp. 38ff.

33 Walsingham, *Chronicon Angliae*, 353–4, and above, pp. 151–3, and sources cited there.

34 Given-Wilson, 'Richard II and his grandfather's will'; Ross, 'Forfeiture for treason in the reign of Richard II'.

35 The case of the Lancastrian inheritance in 1399 is well known; Richard had also allowed Thomas Mowbray at the time of his exile

in 1398 to give power to his attorneys to receive the profits of the estates of his grandmother Margaret, duchess of Norfolk, should she die before his return, but once again he revoked these when she died (in March 1399): Archer, 'The Mowbrays', 77–8. The ideas expressed in this paragraph are not, of course, intended to imply that Richard was in any general sense 'anti-baronial' – his disregard of the property rights of his subjects was basically for financial reasons.

36 Booth, *Financial Administration of Chester*, 132.

37 For the 'tyrannies' of Edward II and Richard II, see especially Fryde, *Tyranny and Fall of Edward II*; Tuck, *Richard II and the English Nobility*; C. Barron, 'The tyranny of Richard II', *BIHR* (1968). It is worth noting that in the parliament following Richard's deposition in 1399 his chief allies among the lords were specifically prohibited from giving out livery badges again, since, it was claimed, they had committed numerous extortions 'under colour of her Lordeshippes' (*RP*, iii, 452; and Given-Wilson, *Royal Household*, 238–43, for discussion).

38 Astill, 'Medieval Gentry', 161–7; Carpenter, 'Political Society', 46–7, 53.

39 Ross, 'Yorkshire Baronage', 452–4.

40 Powell, 'Arbitration and the law'; Smith, 'Litigation and politics', in Pollard (ed.), *Property and Politics*.

41 C. Richmond, 'After McFarlane', *History* (1983), 57; for the Mowbray affinity in 1405, see above, pp. 82–3.

42 In his introduction to K.B. McFarlane, *England in the Fifteenth Century* (1981), xxvii.

43 For the stability over several decades of the Mowbray and Beauchamp affinities, see Archer, 'The Mowbrays', 271–2, and Carpenter, 'Political Society', 80–1.

44 J.R. Maddicott, 'Parliament and the constituencies, 1272–1377', in R.G. Davies and J.H. Denton (eds), *The English Parliament in the Middle Ages* (1981); and see above, pp. 74ff, and sources cited there.

45 It is interesting to note that when Robert, heir to the lordship of Welles, and his father rebelled against Edward IV in 1469, he styled himself 'Captain of the Commons of Lincolnshire'. His reasons for doing so were no doubt primarily populist and propagandist, but the barons de Welles were closely identified with Lincolnshire politics, and had been established as a family of first rank in the county since the twelfth century. Their lands were closely concentrated around their *caput* at Well Castle on the coast, in the area between Louth and Skegness, where about twenty of their thirty or so manors lay; successive heads of the family were consistently appointed to crown commissions of all sorts in the county, and they had close links with several of the local religious houses (especially Greenfield priory, where most members of the family were buried): GEC and Dugdale, *Baronage*, *sub* Welles.

46 *Cambridge Medieval History*, viii (1936), 382.

47 Carpenter, 'Political Society', 94–8, 110; but Archer, 'The Mowbrays', 297, found no evidence to support Carpenter's view that the Mowbray affinity was used by Beauchamp in Warwickshire politics.

48 S. Armitage-Smith, *John of Gaunt* (1904), 440–6.

49 *RP*, ii, 348; *Victoria County History of Shropshire*, iii, 51, 54, 62, 74.

50 Carpenter, for example, divides Warwickshire roughly into five regions, based partly on magnate 'spheres of influence', and partly on natural groupings of the gentry: 'Political Society', 11, 76–8, and endpaper map. See also Astill, 'Medieval Gentry', 81, 129, 201; Wright, 'Gentry Society', 120.

51 The ten who witnessed twenty or more of the 130 charters issued in the 1360s were Arundel (126), Gaunt (72), Cambridge (62), Oxford (58), Edward, Lord Despenser (58), Guy, Lord Brian (39, but 18 of these were while he was steward of the royal household), Warwick (38), Salisbury (37), Suffolk (24), and Clarence (23). The twelve who witnessed twenty or more between 1372 and 1382 were Cambridge (91), Gaunt (90), Richard, Lord le Scrope (74, but he held high government office for most of this period), Thomas of Woodstock (68, all after 1375, when he was nineteen), Richard, earl of Arundel (32, before his death in January 1376), his son Richard, earl of Arundel (34, all from 1376 onwards), Warwick (39), Sir William Beauchamp (22, almost all while he was chamberlain of the household), William, Lord Latimer (26, while he was chamberlain), John, Lord Nevill (23, while he was steward), the earl of March (28), and the earl of Northumberland (20, almost all in 1377–8, when he was marshal of England): PRO C53/153–9; for the witness lists to the great charters in the years 1348–56, see above, p. 184 n. 12.

52 Quoted in M. Vale, *Charles VII* (1974), 226.

53 Elder, 'The Beauforts and their Estates', 208; Goodman, *The Loyal Conspiracy*, 90–4 (with reference to the duke of Gloucester under Richard II).

54 PRO DL 28/3/I, m. 3; for the general problem of securing payments from the exchequer, see G.L. Harriss, 'Preference at the medieval exchequer', *BIHR* (1957).

55 On this point generally see R.L. Storey, 'Gentleman-Bureaucrats', in C.H. Clough (ed.), *Profession, Vocation and Culture in Late Medieval England: Essays dedicated to the memory of A.R. Myers* (1982), 90–109.

56 This is a theme discussed by Dr Rosemary Horrox in her paper, 'The Political Household of the Yorkist Kings', read to the Cambridge Historical Society in 1985. I am grateful to Dr Horrox for allowing me to see a copy of her paper.

57 J.S. Roskell, 'The problem of the attendance of the lords in medieval English parliaments', *BIHR* (1956).

58 *Historia Anglicana*, i, 299.

59 Richmond, 'After McFarlane', 59.

60 Denholm-Young, *Seignorial Administration*, 76.

61 It is worth noting that the peers were sometimes (if not normally) summoned to special councils just before meetings of parliament, at which presumably much of the real decision-making was done: see for example PRO E403/438, 18 May 1369, messengers sent out by the king to summon all the peers individually to parliament as well as to a council to be held before parliament met, to discuss the king's 'arduous and secret affairs'.

62 G.L. Harriss, 'The formation of parliament, 1272–1377', in Davies and Denton (eds), *The English Parliament*, 29–60.

63 McFarlane, *Nobility*, 120.

64 See above, p. 83, and sources cited there; see also C. Richmond, *John Hopton: A Fifteenth Century Suffolk Gentleman* (1981).

65 G.W. Bernard, *The Power of the Early Tudor Nobility: A Study of the Fourth and Fifth Earls of Shrewsbury* (1985), 180.

66 Richard, earl of Arundel, for example, left 400 marks in his will to buy rents of £20 a year for the poor people of the counties of Shropshire and Sussex (Salzman, 'Property of the earl of Arundel', 35): Richard, Lord le Scrope of Bolton, left in his will £1 to each parish church in Richmondshire (Ross, 'Yorkshire Baronage', 227).

Bibliography

UNPUBLISHED SOURCES

(A) MANUSCRIPTS

Public Record Office: EIOI   Exchequer Accounts Various
                                   C53   Great Charter Rolls
                                   E403   Exchequer Issue Rolls
                                   DL   Duchy of Lancaster Accounts
                                   SCI   Ancient Correspondence
British Library: Harleian MSS 700, 704
Shrewsbury Record Office: Acton of Aldenham MSS.
Arundel Deeds
Winchester College Muniments: MS 2

(B) THESES

Archer, R.E., 'The Mowbrays, Earls of Nottingham and Dukes of Norfolk, to 1432', Oxford D.Phil. (1984).

Astill, G.G., 'The Medieval Gentry: A Study in Leicestershire Society, 1350–1399', Birmingham PhD (1977).

Carpenter, C., 'Political Society in Warwickshire c. 1401–1472', Cambridge PhD (1976).

Elder, A.J., 'A Study of the Beauforts and Their Estates, 1399–1450', Bryn Mawr College PhD (1964).

Gue, E.J., 'The Education and Literary Interests of the English Lay Nobility c. 1150–c.1450', Oxford D.Phil. (1983).

Harvey, B., 'The Berkeleys in Fourteenth-Century Gloucestershire', St Andrews MA Honours dissertation (1983).

Jack, R.I., 'The Greys of Ruthin 1325 to 1490: A Study in the Lesser Baronage', London PhD (1961).

Jeffs, R., 'The Later Medieval Sheriff and the Royal Household', Oxford D.Phil. (1960).

Leland, J.L., 'Richard II and the Counter-Appellants; Royal Patronage and Royalist Politics', Yale PhD (1979).

Mertes, R.G.K.A., 'Secular Noble Households in England 1350–1550', Edinburgh PhD (1981).

Ormrod, W.D., 'Edward III's Government of England c. 1346–1356', Oxford D.Phil. (1984).

Ross, C.D., 'The Yorkshire Baronage, 1399–1435', Oxford D.Phil. (1950).

Smith, L.O.W., 'The Lordships of Chirk and Oswestry 1282–1415', London PhD (1970).

Thurgood, J.M., 'The Diet and Domestic Households of the English Lay Nobility 1265–1531', London M.Phil. (1982).

Wells, R.J., 'Recruitment and Extinction among the English Nobility from 1216 to 1300', St Andrews M.Litt. (1984).

Wright, S., 'A Gentry Society of the Fifteenth Century: Derbyshire *circa* 1430–1509', Birmingham PhD (1978).

PUBLISHED SOURCES

Armitage-Smith, S., *John of Gaunt* (1904).

Armitage-Smith, S., (ed.), *John of Gaunt's Register 1372–1376*, Camden 3rd series, xx–xxi (1911).

Avery, M.E., 'The history of the equitable jurisdiction of Chancery before 1460', *BIHR* (1969).

Barlow, F., *William Rufus* (1983).

Barron, C., 'The tyranny of Richard II', *BIHR* (1968).

Barton, J.L., 'The medieval use', *Law Quarterly Review* (1965).

Bautier, R.H., *The Economic Development of Medieval Europe* (1971).

Bean, J.M.W., *The Decline of English Feudalism 1215–1540* (1968).

Bean, J.M.W., *The Estates of the Percy Family 1416–1537* (1958).

Bellamy, J.G., *The Law of Treason in England in the Later Middle Ages* (1970).

Bennett, M.J., *Community, Class and Careerism: Cheshire and Lancashire Society in the Age of Sir Gawain and the Green Knight* (1983).

Bernard, G.W., *The Power of the Early Tudor Nobility: A Study of the Fourth and Fifth Earls of Shrewsbury* (1985).

Bolton, J.L., *The Medieval English Economy 1150–1500* (1980).

Booth, P.H.W., *The Financial Administration of the Lordship and County of Chester* (Chetham Society, 1981).

Bridbury, A.R., 'Before the Black Death', *Economic History Review* (1977).

Bridbury, A.R., 'The Black Death', *Economic History Review* (1973).

Britnell, R.H., 'Minor landlords in England and medieval agrarian capitalism', *P & P* (1980).

Brown, R. Allen, *English Castles* (2nd edn, 1976).

Calendar of Charter Rolls.

Calendar of Close Rolls.

Calendar of Fine Rolls.

Calendar of Inquisitions Miscellaneous.

Calendar of Inquisitions Post Mortem.

Calendar of Patent Rolls.

Cambridge Medieval History, v and viii.

Carpenter, C., 'The Beauchamp affinity: a study of bastard feudalism at work', *EHR* (1980).

Carpenter, D.A., 'Was there a crisis of the knightly class in the thirteenth century? The Oxfordshire evidence', *EHR* (1980).

Cherry, M., 'The Courtenay earls of Devon: the formation and disintegration of a late medieval aristocratic affinity', *Southern History* (1979).

Chrimes, S.B., Ross, C.D., and Griffiths, R.A., (eds.), *Fifteenth Century England 1399–1509* (1972).

Clanchy, M.T., *From Memory to Written Record: England 1066–1307* (1979).

Clough, C.H., (ed.), *Profession, Vocation and Culture in Late Medieval England: Essays Dedicated to the Memory of A.R. Myers* (1982).

Cockayne, G.E., (ed.), *Complete Peerage*, rev. and ed. V. Gibbs, 12 vols (1910–59).

Colvin, H.M., *et al.*, *History of the King's Works*, i (1963).

Coss, P.R., 'Sir Geoffrey de Langley and the crisis of the knightly class in thirteenth-century England', *P & P* (1975).

Davies, R.G. and Denton, J.H. (eds), *The English Parliament in the Middle Ages* (1981).

Davies, R.R., 'Baronial accounts, income and arrears in the later Middle Ages', *Economic History Review* (1968).

Davies, R.R., *Lordship and Society in the March of Wales 1282–1400* (1978).

Denholm-Young, N., *Collected Papers on Medieval Subjects* (1946).

Denholm-Young, N., *The Country Gentry in the Fourteenth Century* (1969).

Denholm-Young, N., *Seignorial Administration in England* (1937).

Devon, F. (ed), *Issue Roll of the Exchequer Henry III to Henry VI* (1837).

Dobson, R.B., *The Peasants' Revolt of 1381* (1970).

Douch, R., 'The career, lands and family of William Montague, earl of Salisbury', *BIHR* (1951).

Drucker, L. (ed.), *Warwickshire Feet of Fines* (Dugdale Society, 1943).

Dugdale, Sir William, *The Baronage of England*, 2 vols (1675–6).

Dugdale, Sir William, *Warwickshire* (1730 edn).

Dyer, C., 'A redistribution of incomes in fifteenth-century England?', *P & P* (1968).

English Historical Documents, iii and iv.

Fairbanks, E.R., 'The last earl of Warenne and Surrey', *Yorkshire Archaeological Journal* (1907).

Fowler, K. (ed.), *The Hundred Years War* (1971).

Fowler, K., *The King's Lieutenant: Henry of Grosmont, First Duke of Lancaster 1310–1361* (1969).

Froissart, J., *Oeuvres*, ed. Kervyn de Lettenhove, 25 vols (1867–77).

Fryde, N., *The Tyranny and Fall of Edward II 1321–1326* (1979).

Galbraith, V.H., 'A new life of Richard II', *History* (1942).

Ganshof, F.–L., *Feudalism* (3rd edn, 1964).

Girouard, M., *Life in the English Country House* (1978).

Given-Wilson, C., 'Purveyance for the royal household 1362–1413', *BIHR* (1983).

Given-Wilson, C., 'Richard II and his grandfather's will', *EHR* (1978).

Given-Wilson, C., *The Royal Household and the King's Affinity: Service, Politics and Finance in England 1360–1413* (1986).

Goodman, A., *The Loyal Conspiracy* (1971).

Goodman, A., 'The military sub-contracts of Sir Hugh Hastings 1380', *EHR* (1980).

Gray, H.L., 'Incomes from land in England in 1436', *EHR* (1934).

Griffiths, R.A. (ed.), *Patronage, the Crown and the Provinces in Later Medieval England* (1981).

Griffiths, R.A., *The Reign of Henry VI* (1981).

Harriss, G.L. (ed.), *Henry V: The Practice of Kingship* (1985).

Harriss, G.L., *King, Parliament and Public Finance in Medieval England to 1369* (1975).

Harriss, G.L., 'Preference at the medieval exchequer', *BIHR* (1957).

Harvey, B., 'The population trend in England between 1300 and 1348', *TRHS* (1966).

Harvey, B. and Hector, L.C. (eds and trans.), *The Westminster Chronicle 1381–1394* (1982).

Harvey, P.D.A., 'The English inflation of 1180–1220', *P & P* (1970).

Harvey, S., 'The knight and the knight's fee in England', *P & P* (1970).

Hatcher, J., *Plague, Population and the English Economy 1348–1530* (1977).

Hilton, R.H., *Bond Men Made Free* (1972).

Hilton, R.H., *The Decline of Serfdom in Medieval England* (Studies in Economic History, 1969).

Hilton, R.H. and Aston, T.H. (eds.), *The English Rising of 1381* (1984).

Hingeston, F.C. (ed.), *Royal and Historical Letters during the Reign of Henry IV*, 2 vols, Rolls Series (1860).

Holmes, G.A., *The Estates of the Higher Nobility in Fourteenth-Century England* (1957).

Holmes, G.A., *The Good Parliament* (1975).

Holt, J.C., *Magna Carta* (1965).

Holt, J.C. and Gillingham, J. (eds), *War and Government in the Middle Ages* (1984).

Hyams, P.R., *Kings, Lords and Peasants in Medieval England* (1980).

Jack, R.I., 'Entail and descent: the Hastings inheritance 1370 to 1436', *BIHR* (1965).

Johnson, C. (ed.), *Dialogu de Scaccario* (1950).

Johnstone, H., 'Poor-relief in the royal households of thirteenth-century England', *Speculum* (1929).

Kapelle, W., *The Norman Conquest of the North* (1979).

Keen, M.H., *Chivalry* (1984).

Keeney, B.C., *Judgement by Peers* (1949).

Kershaw, I., 'The great famine and the agrarian crisis in England 1315–22', *P & P* (1973).

King, E., *England 1175–1425* (1979).

Kingsford, C.L., 'The Barons de Mauley', *EHR* (1896).

Kosminsky, E.A., *Studies in the Agrarian History of England in the Thirteenth Century* (1956).

Lapsley, G.T., *Crown, Community and Parliament in the Later Middle Ages* (1951).

List of Sheriffs for England and Wales, PRO Lists and Indexes, ix (1963).

Lodge, E.C. and Somerville, R. (eds.), *John of Gaunt's Register 1379–1383* (Camden 3rd series, lvi–lvii, 1937).

Loyn, H.R., *Anglo-Saxon England and the Norman Conquest* (1962).

Lumby, J.R. (ed.), *Chronicon Henrici Knighton*, 2 vols, Rolls Series (1895).

Maddicott, J.R., 'The county community and the making of public opinion in fourteenth-century England', *TRHS* (1978).

Maddicott, J.R., 'The English peasantry and the demands of the crown', *P & P Supplement* (1975).

Maddicott, J.R., 'Law and lordship: royal justices as retainers in thirteenth and fourteenth century England', *P & P Supplement* (1978).

Maddicott, J.R., 'Magna Carta and the local community 1215–1259', *P & P* (1984).

Maddicott, J.R., *Thomas of Lancaster 1307–1322* (1970).

McFarlane, K.B., *England in the Fifteenth Century* (1981).

McFarlane, K.B., 'The investment of Sir John Fastolf's profits of war', *TRHS* (1957).

McFarlane, K.B., *Lancastrian Kings and Lollard Knights* (1972).

McFarlane, K.B., 'Loans to the Lancastrian kings: the problem of inducement', *Cambridge Historical Journal* (1947).

McFarlane, K.B., *The Nobility of Later Medieval England* (1973).

Martin, M.T. (ed.), *The Percy Chartulary* (Surtees Society, 1911).

Medcalf, S. (ed.), *The Context of English Literature: The Later Middle Ages* (1981).

Miller, E. and Hatcher, J., *Medieval England: Rural Society and Economic Change 1086–1348* (1978).

Mingay, G.E., *The Gentry* (1976).

Miskimin, H.A., *The Economy of Early Renaissance Europe* (1969).

Naughton, K., 'The Bedfordshire gentry in the thirteenth and fourteenth centuries', *Leicester University Occasional Publications* (1973).

Nicolas, N.H. (ed.), *Proceedings and Ordinances of the Privy Council of England*, 2 vols, Record Commission (1834).

Orme, N., *From Childhood to Chivalry: The Education of the English Kings and Aristocracy 1066–1530* (1984).

Oschinsky, D. (ed.), *Walter of Henley and Other Treatises on Estate Management and Accounting* (1971).

Painter, S., *Studies in the History of the English Feudal Barony* (1943).

Palmer, J.J.N., 'The parliament of 1385 and the constitutional crisis of 1386', *Speculum* (1971).

Phillips, J.R.S., *Aymer de Valence, Earl of Pembroke, 1307–1324* (1972).

Pollard, A.J. (ed.), *Property and Politics: Essays in Later Medieval English History* (1984).

Postan, M.M., *The Medieval Economy and Society* (1972).

Powell, E., 'Arbitration and the law in England in the late Middle Ages', *TRHS* (1983).

Powell, J.E. and Wallis, K., *The House of Lords in the Middle Ages* (1968).

Powicke, M.R., *Military Obligation in Medieval England* (1962).

Powis, J., *Aristocracy* (1984).

Prestwich, M., *The Three Edwards* (1980).

Prestwich, M., *War, Politics and Finance under Edward I* (1972).

Register of Edward the Black Prince, 4 vols, HMSO (1930–3).

Reports of the Lords Committees Touching the Dignity of a Peer of the Realm, i (1829).

Richmond, C., 'After McFarlane', *History* (1983).

Richmond, C., *John Hopton: A Fifteenth Century Suffolk Gentleman* (1981).

Riley, H.T. (ed.), *Annales Ricardi Secundi et Henrici Quarti*, in J. de Trokelowe et Anon., *Chronica et Annales*, Rolls Series (1866).

Roskell, J.S., *The Commons and their Speakers in English Parliaments 1376–1523* (1965).

Roskell, J.S., *The Impeachment of Michael de la Pole, earl of Suffolk, in 1386* (1984).

Roskell, J.S., 'The problem of the attendance of the lords in medieval English parliaments', *BIHR* (1956).

Ross, C.D., 'The estates and finances of Richard Beauchamp, earl of Warwick', *Dugdale Society Occasional Papers* (1956).

Ross, C.D., 'Forfeitures for treason in the reign of Richard II', *EHR* (1956).

Ross, C.D. (ed.), *Patronage, Pedigree and Power in Later Medieval England* (1979).

Salzman, L.F., 'The property of the earl of Arundel, 1397', *Sussex Archaeological Collections* (1953).

Sanders, I.J. *English Baronies: A Study of Their Origin and Descent 1086–1327* (1960).

Saul, N.E., *Knights and Esquires: The Gloucestershire Gentry in the Fourteenth Century* (1981).

Sherborne, J.W., 'Indentured retinues and English expeditions to France 1369–1380', *EHR* (1964).

Sherborne, J.W. and Scattergood, V.J. (eds.), *English Court Culture in the Later Middle Ages* (1983).

Smyth, J., *Lives of the Berkeleys*, ed. J. Maclean, 3 vols (1883).

Somerville, R., *History of the Duchy of Lancaster*, i (1953).

Steel, A., *Receipt of the Exchequer 1377–1485* (1954).

Storey, R.L., *The End of the House of Lancaster* (1966).

Strachey, J., *et al.* (eds), *Rotuli Parliamentorum*, 6 vols (1783).

Sutherland, D.W., *'Quo Warranto' Proceedings in the Reign of Edward I 1278–94* (1963).

Tuck, A., 'Richard II and the border magnates', *Northern History* (1968).

Tuck, A., *Richard II and the English Nobility* (1973).

Vale, M., *Charles VII* (1974).

Victoria County History.

Walker, S., 'Profit and loss in the Hundred Years War: the subcontracts of Sir John Strother 1374', *BIHR* (1985).

Walsingham, Thomas, *Chronicon Angliae 1328–1388*, ed. E.M. Thompson, Rolls Series (1874).

Walsingham, Thomas, *Historia Anglicana*, ed. H.T. Riley, 2 vols, Rolls Series (1863–4).

Wolffe, B.P., *The Royal Demesne in English History* (1971).

Wood, C.T., *The French Appanages and the Capetian Monarchy 1224–1328* (1966).

Index

N.B. Members of the nobility are indexed under family name (e.g. Beauchamp), rather than under title (e.g. earl of Warwick). Members of the royal family are indexed under their Christian names (e.g. Edward, the Black Prince).